Exposing the "Pretty Woman" Myth

D1571387

Exposing the "Pretty Woman" Myth

A Qualitative Investigation of Street-Level Prostituted Women

Rochelle L. Dalla

LEXINGTON BOOKS

A division of
ROWMAN & LITTLEFIELD PUBLISHERS, INC.
Lanham • Boulder • New York • Toronto • Oxford

LEXINGTON BOOKS

A division of Rowman & Littlefield Publishers, Inc.
A wholly owned subsidiary of The Rowman & Littlefield Publishing Group, Inc.
4501 Forbes Boulevard, Suite 200
Lanham, MD 20706

PO Box 317
Oxford
OX2 9RU, UK

British Library Cataloguing in Publication Information Available

Library of Congress Cataloging-in-Publication Data

Library of Congress Control Number: 2006927367

ISBN: 978-0-7391-2325-6

Printed in the United States of America

♾™ The paper used in this publication meets the minimum requirements of American
National Standard for Information Sciences—Permanence of Paper for Printed Library
Materials, ANSI/NISO Z39.48–1992.

*For my parents, whose physical presence, emotional support,
and unconditional love are guaranteed; that I "belong" is absolute.*

Contents

Figures

Tables

Illustrations

Abbreviations

M (or x̄)   Refers to the mean or average and represents the sum of all items divided by the number of items.

SD   SD refers to standard deviation and is an index of variability used to characterize the dispersion of measures in a given population. It is the square root of the average squared deviation from the mean.

N (or n)   Refers to number, such as number of participants (N = 43) or number of participants with children (*n* = 38).

p   Refers to probability or p value. All results obtained from statistical methods suffer from the disadvantage that they might have been caused by statistical accident. The level of significance is determined by the probability that this has *not* happened. P is an *estimate* of the probability that the result occurred by statistical accident. P is typically reported as: p<.05 or p < .01 indicating a 5 in 100 or 1 in 100 chance that the results obtained occurred by chance alone.

r   Refers to correlation coefficient. This represents the strength of association between two sets of scores. Correlation coefficients range from -1 to 1. The closer to zero, the weaker the association. A positive correlation indicates a relationship in the same direction. A negative correlation indicates a relationship in opposite directions.

ANOVA   ANalysis Of VAriance (ANOVA) is a calculation procedure to allocate the amount of variation in a process and determine if it is significant or is caused by random chance. ANOVA is used to test for significant differences between means.

F   F is a statistical indication of significance when using ANOVA techniques. F is the measurement of distance between individual distributions. As F goes up P goes down (i.e., more confidence in there being a statistical difference between the two means). To calculate: Mean Square of X / Mean Square of Error).

ns   "Not significant"; measure did not reach statistical significance.

FOREWORD

By John DeFrain

This is an extraordinary book. The author, Dr. Rochelle Dalla of the University of Nebraska-Lincoln, introduces you to a world in which – thanks to good fortune and perhaps a roll of life's dice – you will never have to live in.

Dr. Dalla, a developmentalist and family scientist, is a gifted researcher and interviewer. She helps the reader really see, most likely for the first time, the grim, violent, drug-addicted and degrading world of women trapped in the vicious cycle of poverty, despair, and street-level prostitution.

Dalla's gifts include both an empathy leading to intimate emotional connection with the women that makes it possible to see their world from an insider's perspective; and Dalla also has a courageous gift for looking, unflinching, at unending and horrendous tragedy. Dalla does this because she wants to *get it right* in a way that the world of street-level prostitution has not been described before.

Though the rest of the world is likely to turn its back on *prostituted women,* as Dalla encourages us to think about them, the reality is that these women are likely to be both tragic victims of early life trauma in chaotic, violent, and emotionally abusive and disconnected families; and, likewise, these women are remarkable for the strength and survival skills they demonstrate as they grapple with the insanity of an impossible and relentlessly punishing life they live.

If the reader is unfamiliar with the devastation wrought by the crack-cocaine epidemic, it is not likely this unfamiliarity will last for long. Most of us can shelter ourselves with the belief that the drug epidemic is something for television or the movies. But the reality is the epidemic is likely to be much closer than we may hope to believe: down the street, in our office, where your children go to school, perhaps hidden in a bedroom drawer.

There are, indeed, powerful addictive drugs menacing our world, and though we are loathe to admit it in our hearts, bad things do happen to good people. All the time. To underscore the validity of this point, Dalla did not conduct her research in a poverty-stricken big-city ghetto with a stereotypic sample of minority women. Instead, her research has been conducted for many years in Omaha, Nebraska – Anytown, U.S.A., and ground zero for so-called Heartland Middle America. The women she introduces us to – very real, compelling people, indeed – are a diverse group of women: white, black, American Indian, from a spectrum of family backgrounds and social classes, and representing an age span stretching from teens to long into middle age.

Dalla's skill in helping us to see, and more important, to feel some of the things that prostituted women feel is remarkable. Her belief that the prostituted life is part-and-parcel of a society that still degrades women in countless ways – though we are well into the fifth decade of the latest wave of the feminist movement – this belief is hard to challenge and may, just may help move us as a society to a more understanding and compassionate approach toward the tragedy of these women's lives.

One can only hope....

Dr. John DeFrain, Extension Professor of Family and Community Development, University of Nebraska-Lincoln.
Co-author of *Marriages and Families: Intimacy, Diversity, and Strengths* (5th Ed.).

Preface

This book describes results of a long-term research investigation designed to examine the lives and developmental trajectories of women prostituted on the streets. Between 1998 and 1999, I conducted in-depth, personal interviews with 43 street-level prostituted women. Three years later, between 2001 and 2002, I was able to locate and interview 18 of the original 43 women. The follow-up investigation was designed to determine factors which promoted and/or challenged each woman's ability to exit prostitution and remain drug-free. This book describes my journey as a researcher and scientist interested in the extraordinary lives of a unique group of women.

Although my research into the lives of vulnerable female populations began in graduate school (1991), my focus on inquiry into the lives of street-level prostituted women didn't begin until 1997. At that time, I was a new Ph.D., a member of the University of Nebraska-Lincoln faculty, hopeful about my future, and confident in my ability to succeed in the world of academia. I spent my first year as an Assistant Professor adjusting to the responsibilities and demands associated with a tenure-track position at a research institution. I focused my energy on teaching, as I was not yet certain what my scholarly "niche" would be.

I must admit that my curiosity into the lives of others—into how they think, process information, interpret life events, and give meaning to their worlds–is *not* research-specific. This interpersonal inquisitiveness is a central component of my personality. Thus, late one blustery Nebraska-winter afternoon, following an advising appointment with one of my students, I began asking her questions about her personal, non-academic life. I was curious to discover who she was as a person, not just another student. In the process, I learned that she volunteered her time at WellSpring, a program run through the Salvation Army aimed at helping prostituted individuals leave the sex industry. [WellSpring literally means the head or source of a spring, stream, or river; a fountainhead; the source of anything, especially considered inexhaustible[1]]. My interest was instantly piqued. After continued questioning, I further learned that WellSpring was the only program of its kind in the entire state. Needless to say, the path of scientific inquiry that I would pursue for years to come revealed itself on that day.

As I began reading the academic literature about prostitution, and street-level prostitution specifically, I learned several important points that laid the foundation for my own research. First, although "prostitute" is a term often used to refer to someone "who exchanges sexual favors for money, drugs, or other desirable commodities,"[2] all prostitution is not the same. Many *types* of prostitution exist.

And, like divisions within any field or profession, the various forms of prostitution are hierarchically organized. High-class call girls, who often work within a safe environment (e.g., a penthouse), with regular clientele, and for whom prostitution is often an extremely lucrative business, occupy the highest echelon of the hierarchy. Street-level sex work, in contrast, is the least lucrative, least "glamorous" and most dangerous form of prostitution. Women's experiences in the sex-industry vary widely depending on the type of sex work in which they participate.

Second, I became acutely aware that scholarly interest in street-level prostitution had increased dramatically over the previous decade. This attention had largely been spurred in response to governmental funding requests fueled by public health concerns and fear of sexually transmitted diseases, especially HIV and AIDS. Thus, given funding mandates, many investigations into street-level prostitution focused primarily on health-compromising behaviors such as drug use and abuse, needle-sharing, and condom use. Research regarding behavioral "risk" factors that may or may not contribute to the spread of various life-threatening and contagious infections had dominated.

This led to my third realization: that very little was understood about the social worlds or developmental trajectories of prostituted women. Information about them as *individuals* with unique histories and experiences, with parents and siblings, and with partners and children, was visibly absent in the published literature. This oversight was largely a result of the scientific questions being asked (e.g., risky behaviors), and also due to the methodology used to gather the information. Survey methods, or self-report questionnaires, had been used most frequently. Although such methodology has unquestionable scientific merit, one compromise is that rich details and thick descriptions of the phenomena of interest cannot be adequately captured. Participants' *voices* go undetected.

Finally, I began to recognize that stereotypes and misconceptions about this particular population were (and still are) pervasive. A dichotomy exists in the portrayal of women prostituted on the streets. At one extreme are popular images depicted in movies such as *Pretty Woman* (with Julia Roberts), *Leaving Las Vegas* (with Elizabeth Shue), and *Taxi Driver* (with Jodie Foster), of the young, beautiful prostitute who (at least in Julia's case) meets a wealthy, handsome prince who "saves" her. This is *the "Pretty Woman" myth*. Street-work is presented as an employment *choice*, with ample rewards from generous and kind clients. Prostitution is presented as a *temporary* phase until the heroine finds love and happiness and she suffers few physical or emotional scars from her brief stint on the streets. In sharp contrast, are images of women sauntering along dark, deserted streets or soliciting clients on busy thoroughfares. They are dressed in typical prostitute gear: high heels, short skirts, and black fishnet stockings. The image is completed when an abusive, controlling, and perhaps drug-pushing pimp, enters the scene.

Needless to say, I was skeptical. Neither of these portrayals, I believed, accurately represented the *reality* of the lives of street-level prostituted women or the phenomena of street-level sex work. Neither explained *why* or more importantly, *how* the women got to the streets, what kept them there, or how they perceived or made sense of their own private worlds.

Researcher Biases

This research was designed in response to the gaps in the academic literature and the stereotypical images of prostituted women created and maintained throughout society. The purpose of my work was to examine, in depth, the "game"[3] known as streetwalking prostitution and more specifically, the lives of the women who engage in such.

It is important to inform the reader, at the outset, of my own biases and beliefs. Because these biases are a part of me, they necessarily impact the nature of my research. Researcher biases, including values and belief systems, impact the research process in both subtle and obvious ways by influencing the questions that are asked, how those questions are asked, the theoretical lens through which a study is framed and organized, and how the data are interpreted.

I am a developmentalist and a family scientist. I began this work believing that streetwalking prostitution is *not* freely chosen over a vast array of alternative career choices. Instead, I believed (and still do) that women who sell themselves on the streets do so because of lack of (perceived or real) options. I also began this work biased by my beliefs that individual experiences, beginning in the formative years, influence unique interpretations of, and reactions to, future events and experiences. In other words, through individual-specific developmental processes and interpersonal and contextual influences, future *options* are set into motion.

As a family scientist, I strongly believe that personal attributes and characteristics, coupled with cumulative family and interpersonal interactions, exert powerful influence over developmental trajectories. I also believe that human beings are uniquely equipped with the capacity for free will, that we are actors and players in the unfolding of our own lives. We have agency and initiative and thus, we actively participate in personal life-course maneuvering.

Given my personal beliefs and biases, it is only natural that, in my research with street-level prostituted women, I would afford my greatest effort toward documenting and understanding the participants' formative years, their family relationships, their relationships with partners, children, and significant others, and their interpretations and personal reflections of contextual events and life experiences.

The Organization of this Book

Overview of Book

This book is organized into three sections. Section I (*The Journey Begins*) is comprised of three chapters and begins with an in-depth examination of five of the 43 women who participated in this study. This is followed by an overview of the theoretical framework guiding my study (chapter two) and complete methodological details which defined the research (chapter three). The goal of Section I is to orient the reader to the women and to the research processes employed in this investigation. For those readers who are decidedly *uninterested* in the science used to collect and analyze the data, but rather in the women themselves, I suggest that you read chapter one and then skip immediately ahead to chapter four.

Four chapters comprise Section II (*The Larger Perspective: Patterns of Commonality*). It is in this segment of the book that the bulk of information about the lives of the 43 participants is presented. Focus centers on *commonalities and shared experiences* among them. Chapters four through seven are organized developmentally, beginning with the women's childhood and adolescent experiences, followed by their entry into sex work and struggles to exit the street-level sex-industry.

Section III (*Follow-Up and Application*) presents results of a longitudinal investigation (chapter eight) that was initiated three years after the original interviews were conducted. Suggestions for intervention, policy formation, and advocacy efforts on behalf of prostituted women is presented in the chapter nine.

Chapters in Preview

Chapter one provides an in-depth look into the lives of a *sub-sample* of five women, including: Amy, Sam, Marlee, Chancey, and Tami. Although all five were involved in street-level sex work, the contexts of their lives, particularly prior to prostitution entry, differed vastly. Specific nuances, personal experiences, and life events which culminated into street-level prostitution vary between them. Childhood sexual abuse and family dysfunction, for instance, are *not* universal in the lives of prostituted women. And, although chemical dependence is common among women prostituted on the streets, for many (at least for many who participated in this investigation), drug abuse *follows* prostitution entry. Though subtle, such distinctions are critical in order to better understand the cultural milieu surrounding street-level sex work and the women who enter and remain involved.

In chapter two, the importance of conducting theory-guided research is detailed as is the manner by which theory selection is determined. Two theoretical orientations, ecological systems theory and family systems theory, are presented. These theories provided the overall theoretical thrust of the entire investigation. Systems theorists seek to explain the behavior of complex, organized systems; their attention focuses on the interdependence between and across variables of interest (from individuals, to families, to entire societies)[4]. Some scholars contend that general systems theory- of which both ecological systems theory and family systems theory were derived, is not a theory, but is instead a 'world view'[5] which requires *systems thinking*. Both theories provided unique contributions to this study; their relevance for investigating life cycle development among street-level prostituted women, is thus discussed in detail.

Chapter three provides an overview of the research methodology used for data collection, analyses, and interpretation. Recruitment strategies (i.e., how the 43 women were located) and demographic information about each participant is presented. This is followed by description of the types of information that were collected (i.e., specific interview questions) and the procedures used to gather the information (i.e., how, when, where). This chapter further describes data analyses procedures and ends with explanation of the methodological limitations of my work.

Intergenerational patterns of parent-child relationship dynamics are explored in chapter four. I begin the chapter by presenting an overview of the women's relationships with their parents or parental caregivers (i.e., their families of origin) during the formative years. Themes of *symbolic* and *literal abandonment* are revealed and described. The remainder of the chapter focuses on the women's relationships with their own children (i.e., their families of procreation) and ends with discussion of the inter-generational, parent-child relationship similarities; that is, relationship similarities between the prostituted women and their parents, and between them and their own children.

The phenomena of street-level prostitution is stripped of mystery and myth in chapter five. Focus here centers around the *social context* and culture of street-level sex work. I devote attention to describing relationships between the women and the significant men in their lives, including pimps, intimate partners, and clients (e.g., 'johns' or 'dates'). Relationships between the women participants and *other* street-level prostituted women are also explored. Given the pervasive use of illicit drugs by street-level prostituted women, chapter five also explores drug use and abuse among the women who participated in this study. Broader analyses of the economic and social impacts of crack cocaine on the culture of street-level sex work is presented.

The sub-culture of street-level prostitution is notorious for excessive violence and life-threatening danger. Because of its prevalence, an entire chapter (chapter six) is devoted to documentation and exploration of the women's adulthood experiences with sexual, physical and emotional abuse. The brutality of clients, male partners, and pimps is delineated. The second half of the chapter presents results from *quantitative* data (i.e., self-report survey questionnaires) completed by the women. These survey instruments were used to assess various social and personal attributes of the women including coping strategies, impulse control and social support.

Chapter seven describes *why* the women were attempting to exit the "game" of street-level sex work. They describe short- and long-term challenges to exiting prostitution, remaining drug-free, and reestablishing relationships with significant others. The chapter ends with a brief summary of the participants' hopes, dreams, and future aspirations.

Chapter eight describes a follow-up investigation initiated to ascertain factors which promote and challenge women's attempts to exit sex-work. In this chapter, I described interviews with 18 of the original sample of 43 women, that were conducted three years after the initial interviews were completed. Five of the 18 women had *not returned* to prostitution in the three years spanning our first and second interviews. The remaining 13 women had returned to prostitution, drug use, or other illegal activities. Comparisons are made between the five who had successfully avoided the "game" and their 13 peers.

Using an ecological framework, chapter nine provides suggestions for application of the research findings. Implications for intervention at the individual, community, and societal levels are presented. Challenges to systemic and multi-pronged service creation and delivery are also outlined and discussed, as are policy initiatives and advocacy efforts on behalf of prostituted women. The book ends with final thoughts about my work with this very unique population of women, and the phenomena of street-level prostitution.

What This Book is Not About

This book is *not* about sex, nor is it about "prostitution," per se. This book is about prostituted *women*. It is about the lives and relationships and pivotal occurrences in the developmental trajectories of vulnerable females. The women's involvement in street-level prostitution is a central feature of their lives, certainly; but it is but one segment only in an entire spectrum of experiences that define who they are as individuals and as women. This book presents the entire spectrum. In doing so, it is hoped that the stereotypes and myths surrounding street-level prostitution, and the women who engage in such, are tempered with perspective, with insight, and with greater understanding.

Acknowledgments

Meghan Smith, I thank you, once again, for introducing me to WellSpring and the women seeking assistance there. It is because of you that this work began. Susan Ascoli, Director of WellSpring when this project took flight, encouraged my work and accommodated my needs. She allowed me, an outsider, to attend WellSpring's Saturday group meetings for nearly two years. Access to and recruitment of this population of women would have been exceedingly difficult, if not impossible, had it not been for Susan's collaboration and support. Greg Ort and Sheryl Baney (Lockwood) also provided invaluable assistance by allowing access to the women incarcerated at ICCW (the Iowa Correctional Center for Women). In addition, they provided a quiet space within the prison for me to meet privately with 14 women incarcerated within the prison walls. Sheryl, especially, worked double-duty as she assisted in participant recruitment at both the original and follow-up data collection periods.

Wendy Gamble, my very first academic mentor, demonstrated the value of personal integrity and professional ethics when engaged in research with vulnerable populations. Her enthusiasm for my research and monumental guidance and support, have been unwavering. In addition to being a role-model in the professional realm, Wendy also conveyed the following life-affirming values: (1) be patient; we are all works in progress; (2) humor is essential, regardless of the situation; and (3) family, above all, takes precedence.

Doug Abbott, my friend and colleague, provided constructive comments and insightful suggestions throughout the book's preparation. I thank you for your consistent support, encouragement, and excellent advice! The comic strip he gave me, over ten years ago still hangs in my office as a reminder of my priorities. Doug, you are always looking out for me and I cannot tell you how much your presence in my life is appreciated! Brenda Moran, your eye for detail and willingness to assist– at the eleventh hour no less– was invaluable! Jan Quinley, your advocacy, diligence, and hard work have resulted in many successes on behalf of prostituted women. I thank you for your support to the larger cause and willingness to dialogue with me at a moment's notice! I also wish to thank the Society for the Scientific Study of Sexuality (SSSS), the Society for the Psychological Study of Social Issues (SPSSI), and the University of Nebraska-Lincoln Layman Trust Fund. Each contributed financial support to ensure the successful completion of this project.

Finally, my greatest gratitude is to each of the 43 women who participated in this investigation. Intimate details of their lives were laid bare. To a virtual stranger they shared experiences of excruciating pain and unimaginable betrayal. They revealed moments of profound despair and shameful humiliation. They also spoke of renewed hope, of dreams, of belief in humanity, and of visions of solitude. It was an honor.

Notes

1. Webster's Encyclopedic Unabridged Dictionary of the English Language, Deluxe Edition, New and Revised. (New York: Gramercy Books, 1994).

2. Christine Overall, "What's Wrong with Prostitution?: Evaluating Sex Work," *Signs* 17, no. 4 (1992): 705-724.

3. "The game" is a term used by street-level sex workers in describing the culture of streetwalking prostitution in which women attempt to receive goods (e.g., money or drugs) doing as little 'sex-work' as possible, and in which their clients attempt to obtain sexual services as cheaply as possible. Some also use the term to denote that street-walkers "play with" (i.e., risk) their lives. The term was used by participants and adopted by the author.

4. Gail G. Whitechurch and Larry L. Constantine, "Systems Theory," in *Sourcebook of Family Theories and Methods: A Contextual Approach*, ed. Pauline G. Boss, William J. Doherty, Ralph LaRossa, Walter R. Schumm, and Suzanne K. Steinmetz (New York: Plentum), 325-351.

5. Whitechurch and Constantine, "Systems Theory," 325.

Section One

The Journey Begins

Chapter One

Images of Individuality

> We are not human beings on a
> spiritual journey. We are spiritual
> beings on a human journey.
> — Stephen Covey

The term "prostitute" is derived from the Latin verb prostituere which literally means "to set up for sale"[1]. Women involved in street-level prostitution are exploited, abused, stigmatized, and perceived as morally reprehensible[2-3]. Despite their visibility on the streets, they live marginalized lives on the fringe of society. They are rarely recognized as individuals with life histories, parents and siblings, husbands and partners, or children.

This book is devoted to sharing the lives of 43 prostituted women. As an introduction however, I have chosen to begin by devoting an entire chapter to a small group only. In the pages which follow, five unique individuals whose lives have been forever altered by street-level prostitution, are introduced. These brief case-histories are intended to provide the reader with a contextualized and personalized glimpse into the lives of prostituted women. I wanted them to be as real to the reader as they are to me. The women I interviewed as part of this investigation are more than research participants, they are *individuals* with life-histories, families, lived experiences, and vibrant stories to tell– stories that deserve to be told and stories that should be heard if the complex phenomena of street-level sex work is to be better understood.

Although any of the 43 women who participated in this investigation could have been highlighted in this chapter, the five women described below were selected for several reasons. First, and most importantly, we established rapport quickly. Each seemed quite comfortable being interviewed and their honesty and genuineness was evident throughout the interview process. Also, their typical responses to my questions were full of depth and detail. They often provided extensive information that gave their lives color, substance, and dimension. Simply stated, they were verbally engaging, vocal, and openly and without hesitation answered any question

I posed. Their words were authentic and their feelings undisguised.

Additionally important, these five women comprise a diverse group with respect to age, ethnicity, education, drug abuse, relationship patterns with significant others, and experiences in the sex industry. These demographic differences provide context for envisioning numerous developmental paths which culminate into street-level prostitution. Their unique characteristics are representative of the diversity which exists in the larger sample of 43. They are presented in the order in which they were interviewed.

Amy[4]

Amy was a 34-year-old Black woman with a contagious laugh. I met her in the spring of 1998 as she was a regular attendee of WellSpring's (see Preface, page xix) Saturday "group" meetings. When I approached her and described the research, she readily agreed to participate. Amy had a deep voice, a welcoming smile, and was well-respected by the other WellSpring group members because of her willingness to speak truthfully and directly.

Amy was the mother of two boys, ages six and eight. At the time of the interview, her children were in foster care; they had been in the foster care system for nearly a year although Amy had recently completed all state-ordered mandates to regain physical custody. Those mandates required that she be drug-free, legally employed, and have permanent housing. Amy worked full-time as a cashier at Burger King earning minimum wage. She lived in a half-way house run by the Salvation Army.

The interview with Amy, as with the other women, began "in the beginning" so to speak. I asked her to describe her childhood, including where she grew up and the dynamics of her early family-life. Amy was born and raised in Salt Lake City, Utah and was the youngest of eight children, including five girls and three boys. She described her family as "very dysfunctional." When asked to elaborate, she stated,

> Well, alcoholic parents. My dad beat my mother [and] there was no affection. There just wasn't any. I was raised in a lot of shame. I was embarrassed about the way I lived, just ashamed of myself as a person. I've always felt less than. I never felt accepted, not even in my own family, never got love. I don't even remember the last time my parents said they loved me. I don't remember them ever saying it to each other. It was just dysfunctional.

Amy's most significant childhood memory was described as follows:

> I remember my dad beating the shit out of my mom one night and he ripped her shirt open and she had on a white shirt and a white slip. She sat in the kitchen and her lip was bleeding and she had a butcher knife to her chest. And after that I made up my mind that a man would never, ever hit me, because I would kill him.

By age 12, Amy was an orphan. Her mother had died from a brain tumor and her father from cancer. She lived intermittently in various foster homes and then, around age 17, "...basically just went on my own." She described moving from place to place staying with siblings, family friends, boyfriends, and girlfriends. Although she had many older siblings, they were "just around"; most were involved in the legal system for a variety of offenses. With regard to her own drug use, Amy explained, "I started smoking weed and drinking when I was probably 12 or 13, got really heavily into it about 14. There was no structure in my life, I don't know– it was just kind of wild." Somehow, despite lacking structure or stability, Amy managed to graduate from high school.

At age 18, she tried prostitution for the first time. She was picked up by an undercover police officer, arrested, and sentenced to thirty days in the county jail. A friend had introduced her to the streets. Still, prostitution was not a new concept to Amy as her older sister had been prostituting for drug money for years. This sister, noted Amy, also worked for a violent and abusive pimp. In reference to her sister, Amy stated, "I never thought I would become one of her. Not as bad, but I did become one of her." In other words, she never imagined that she, too, would be drug addicted and working the streets.

Despite being arrested on her initial prostitution attempt, Amy's involvement in the sex industry continued. At age 22 she developed an intimate relationship with a former client, named Gerald. Together, they moved from Salt Lake to the Midwest where Amy became a gas station attendant. She, Gerald, and her two sons lived together. Slowly, Amy returned to prostitution. Gerald was aware of this but "He didn't have a problem with that [her involvement in the sex industry], we never discussed it."

The money she made while prostituting was spent on necessity items, such as rent and food, but also on drugs– especially crack cocaine. Amy eventually became a "runner," that is, the middle-person who exchanges drugs and money between the drug buyers and sellers. This afforded her unlimited access to crack because, as part of her "run," she would stash a bit for her personal use. Chemical dependence, she stated, "is a disease, it just progresses." She described her descent into addiction:

> At first I just used Fridays, then just weekends and then slowly it turned into like maybe Wednesdays and Fridays and Saturdays, and then it went to everyday–maybe like three times a day everyday. And then it went to all day everyday.

Her daily use continued for three years. Gerald also became addicted to crack cocaine. He, however, was able to maintain legal employment despite his chemical dependence. Amy was not and during the height of her addiction, she would bring "dates" (i.e., clients or tricks) to her home. She explained, "If I had a date I'd give my kids some money and I'd send them to the store and when the kids got back from the store, whether he [the client] was done or not, he got done."

Amy's relationship with Gerald ended when her youngest son tested positive for crack cocaine. Both children were placed in foster care. Within a few months, Amy entered treatment; Gerald continued to use. At the time of our interview, Amy had not engaged in any type of prostitution for seven months and had been drug-free for nine months. Her initial motive to enter and remain in treatment was to regain custody of her children. With time, a new motive emerged:

> Now, it's [treatment] for me to live a normal life, to be a good mother, to not have to live hustling and struggling. My life is not at risk. I don't have to go out and sell my ass. I don't have to rob and steal and cheat and manipulate people... I like myself now.

Sam

Like Amy, Sam was also a client at WellSpring and had been attending their meetings regularly for about 4 months when I met her. At the time, she was working as a waitress in a 24-hour restaurant and living in a Christian-based homeless shelter. She was Caucasian, with shoulder-length light brown hair. Our interview took place in a small office located in the shelter where she lived. Although somewhat reserved when I first turned the tape-recorded on, Sam quickly opened up and described the process that led to her involvement in the street-level sex industry.

Sam came from a family that was "very well-off, but very disorganized." She had two older brothers and described how, when she was six-months-old, her father kidnaped the children and abandoned her mother. They moved from California to the Midwest. Sam explained, "He [father] told us that she [mother] had left us, that she deserted us." For the next 20 years, Sam believed what her father had said: that her mother did not want her. As an adult, Sam learned that her mother had attempted to contact her many, many times only to be told that Sam and her siblings were doing fine and didn't want to see her. Eventually, Sam's mother stopped attempting contact.

Sam's father was a workaholic and a violent alcoholic. She and her brothers spent much of their early childhoods living with their paternal grandmother and an uncle. The uncle was their full-time babysitter. It was an opportunistic situation for him, as he was a child predator and sexually abused all three children for years. Sam remembered, "It [sexual molestation] was continuously happening. It started as soon as my dad brought us from California." In addition to her uncle, Sam was also sexually molested by one of her brothers. She explained her feelings about the early abuse with the following:

> A lot of women, you know, they say how dirty they feel and how they've been affected by it [sexual abuse]. I'm sure it's affected me, but I don't feel dirty or nothing for it happening. I guess it was just normal. It was something that has always happened to me.

Sam began running away from home at the age of ten and spent the next seven years living with various family members, foster families, and in group homes. She was admitted to a specialized facility for troubled girls on four separate occasions before turning 17.

She also dropped out of high school her senior year and was married by age 19. Her first husband was

> ...real good to me. He was more like security. He was somebody that I knew cared about me, but I didn't really care about him in the same way. When I finally realized that, that I didn't love him, I told him and then I left him.

By age 23 Sam was divorced with two small children and few employable skills. That same year, Sam's other brother, the only person she felt close to, was tragically killed in a motorcycle accident. She described the void as "enormous." Perhaps not surprisingly, Sam was re-married within a year. Unlike her first marriage however, her second was "real rough. My husband was very abusive." The physical violence began within months of the wedding. She described being "beaten quite a bit, on a weekly basis." He wouldn't allow Sam to work and isolated her from family and friends; eventually she couldn't even leave the house. Together, she and her second husband had two children. Despite being terrified of him, Sam explained, "I thought I needed him... even if it was unpleasant, it was a home, with kids, you know? That whole thing."

The abuse continued relentlessly and, although Sam was hospitalized on numerous occasions, she but never pressed charges. She attempted to leave many times, but he always brought her back. However, after four years of marriage and with the help of her husband's parents, Sam finally escaped. Her youngest child was only four-months-old at the time. She moved to Texas, where her father and stepmother lived. "My whole goal was to prove to my dad that I'm not all the rotten things he thought I was. I worked my butt off." She held three different jobs including bartending and janitorial services. Eventually, the stress was too much:

> I couldn't handle it anymore. I was going crazy working too hard. And his wife [stepmother], it was like she was jealous or something. She would call and give me such a bad time and then I'd tell my dad and he'd say, 'You lying little bitch, you whore!' You know? And I just couldn't take it no more, trying to prove how good I am and all's he did is tell me how worthless I was and how I'll never amount to nothing.

When she was 30, Sam and her children left Texas and moved back to the Midwest. She worked in a convenience store and believed "I was getting it together. I was starting to get it together." But raising four children on minimum wage was tough, and soon after, Sam met a wealthy businessman willing to pay well for her companionship. He became her "Sugar Daddy."

> He was the first guy. He just took care of me, you know? He gave me money and helped me out and then he introduced me to a couple other business men. I would just go out to eat and you know– do what ever they wanted. Sometimes it was just going to fuck. You know? But they paid me. They helped with my rent, helped me pay bills and stuff.

She met many other businessmen through this initial contact; all were married. She continued receiving money and spending time with various Sugar Daddies for the next five years, until a house fire forced Sam and her children into the streets. Three of her four children went to live with their fathers, Sam and her 15-year-old daughter moved in with a friend. The friend was a drug addict, "and that's when the drugs started coming into my life." At 37, Sam tried crack cocaine for the first time and was immediately addicted. "It [crack] just got me...When I started doing drugs, I started getting reckless with my life."

Like Amy, Sam developed an "hourly" addiction. It was then that she started working the streets because, she explained, the "Sugar Daddies didn't want nothing to do with me anymore." She tried to hide her addiction, but eventually,

> I just got carried away. I just went crazy, totally crazy. I didn't care about no bills, I didn't care about getting my kids back. Eventually, my daughter got started smoking crack and my daughter started working the streets. I was so far gone into drugs that I took her right with me. And in my drug mind, I was thinking well, it's better to have her with me than her being out there on the streets alone, you know, where she can get hurt.

Sam described herself as "an extremist" and noted "When I do something, I go all the way." Within two years, Sam was arrested for prostitution and possession of a controlled substance. She was sentenced to six months in jail and three years probation. While in jail she learned about WellSpring and began attending Saturday meetings. By the time I interviewed her in 1998, Sam was 39 and had been off the streets and drug-free for eight months. Two of her children were in foster care. Her oldest son was incarcerated and charged with armed robbery. Her oldest daughter was married and, according to Sam, no longer using drugs or involved in prostitution. Reflecting back over her life, Sam commented:

> I love life and I think it's what you make it. I can't blame anybody for the way I live or for what I've been through. I know I had my choices. I know that. I've always known that and I just–I just made the wrong ones.

Marlee

Marlee was a petite, attractive, 36-year-old Black woman whom I met through a referral; she had never attended WellSpring. My interview with Marlee took place in her home. It was a modest one-story, wood-frame house in the central part of the city. Her home well-maintained and nicely furnished with a leather couch and loveseat, and a big-screen television. When I arrived at her home, Marlee greeted me warmly and offered coffee.

Marlee had two siblings and all were raised in a mother-headed, single-parent home. Marlee's father died when she was just six-years-old. She recalled:

As a child, I was never deprived of anything. My mother was not on welfare. She had me when she was 15½, but she was a strong, independent woman. My mother wasn't the type to run the streets. She never smoked cigarettes, drank alcohol, used drugs, or nothing. All she did was worked and took care of me and my brother.

Marlee was adamant in her belief that her involvement in prostitution occurred *despite* having positive role models in her life. Although she acknowledged that parents played a significant role in their children's development, Marlee also believed that:

...you can't always fault the parent. When I realized what I was doing [prostitution] and what it was doing to her [mother], I wrote her a letter. I told her, 'I don't fault you at all.' I couldn't ask for a better parent. I couldn't. I think maybe she sheltered me *too much.*

Marlee had a large extended family. Her mother was the eldest of eleven children and Marlee was close to many them, including her maternal grandmother. At age 17, Marlee had sex for the first time with a man she had been dating. That same year she also dropped out of high school. At age 18, she met Martin at a dance club.

He started following me around and talking to me and I started sneaking off with him. That's when I got put out of the house [kicked out by her mother]. He was trying to tell me about the streets and he was like 'Just give it [prostitution] a try— give it a try.' And I went out there one night and I've been trying it ever since!

She was not afraid of the streets and remarked: "I had to *learn* how to get scared. I think I was too naïve at the time." Her involvement in the sex industry happened quickly, Marlee explained: "Yeah, I had a pimp. It was not drugs that took me to the street, it was a man that tripped me on the streets." When asked what, if anything, she liked about working the streets, Marlee said, "It must have been the excitement because I wasn't keeping the money to myself— so I must have been likin' it!"

Her relationship with Martin, the man who "tripped her on the streets," lasted for four years. It ended "because he's the type of person that don't want nothing out of life and I didn't come from nothing. We was living in hotels and stuff. And he done wanted to turn me on cocaine." She continued:

I was just dumb to where I had never even seen a rock [crack cocaine] before. I went down with him to Tucson and he and some friends was just in there [hotel room] smokin' that stuff and when I went to bed I started crying. The girl asked me why I was crying and I said, 'Is this what he's doing with my money?' I said, 'We don't even have a car!' I said 'I do not have to live like this.'

That night, she "...was forced to smoke crack the very first time I did. I was forced to. I had a choice to either hit the pipe or get beat up. That was to make me so I wouldn't complain about the money." When they returned to Omaha, the first person Marlee called was her mother.

> My mom came to the hotel where we was and she was like 'I have had enough of this!' She walked in there and said [to Martin], 'When you took my daughter she was *not* wearing plain label shoes' because my mom always dressed me up– and I was wearing tennis shoes from Payless! And she said, 'It would be a different story if my daughter was being taken care of the way I took care of her. You don't mean her no good and I am not taking it no more.' She said to me, 'You get your shit and you're going with me today or else I'm killing you and this son of a bitch right up here and now.' And she pulled a .357 Magnum out of her purse. She grabbed my clothes and she went out the door!

Needless to say, she followed her mother and Martin did not try to stop her.

Within weeks of the incident, Marlee was sent to Florida to live with an aunt. She was gone six months and, when she returned home, she went out one night and, "then I ran into this other guy and then I ended up going back on the streets again." According to Marlee, the man had "the gift of gab." She moved in with him and he became her pimp.

Marlee's first two pimps were violent and both expected that she earn a minimum amount of money each night. If she didn't, she would be "put out" without a place to stay. I asked Marlee if she *wanted* to stay with these men, to which she replied: "It was not by force." She was with the second pimp for only six month because his violence was uncontrollable. She explained an incident in which he brutally beat her. She commented, "And that's one time I thought I was dead." He was arrested and she left him for good.

Marlee began working the streets for herself but, within a year met Westin, a man eleven years her senior. Westin was the man she would eventually marry. They were still together after 12 years. Westin also became Marlee's pimp, although she explained that he was "... more like a hustler. It didn't matter if I got the money or not. It wasn't like I *had* to make it. He had way more money than I did." She continued, "He speaks like seven different languages. He knows books and everything. He plays the saxophone. He's very intelligent."

Although Westin had used drugs, he was clean by the time Marlee met him. In fact, according to Marlee, it was Westin that convinced her to *stop* using drugs.

> He wouldn't get mad at me when I was doing it [crack] he would just leave me and I had to make a choice. It was gonna be him or the crack. So I said, 'Well, you know, I think I like him more than this drug.' And I just stopped.

Together, Marlee and Westin "hustled" the streets for more than a decade. They traveled to various cities working the streets in Washington D.C., New York, Denver, Los Angeles, and Las Vegas. Frequently, Westin had several women working for him at once. Their "business" became quite lucrative.

Although Marlee actually liked the excitement of the streets, she admitted that they held a darker side. Her life had been in danger on multiple occasions, and, she noted: "I've got the marks to show it." She described one night in particular:

> There was this time I was in the car with this guy and I was getting ready and he starts to cry– he reaches over the visor, pulls out a gun and says, 'You're gonna give me a blow job without the money. I'm not paying you nothing.'

Marlee complied. "On the streets," she noted, "once you hit dirt ground you ain't promised to come back home."

Marlee always carried condoms when she prostituted, in fact, she "never did nothing without them. I wouldn't do nothing without a condom." She continued, "Lots of people think that prostitutes are just dirty. I think they're cleaner than regular women, because you're going to the bathroom constantly to keep yourself checked."

Although Marlee could not have children, one of the main reasons she and Westin exited the sex industry was because his daughter from a previous marriage moved in with them. Marlee refused to expose her stepdaughter to the type of life she and Westin had been living. Additionally, she indicated that the streets had changed over the years, largely due to the presence of crack cocaine. The streets, she believed, had become exceptionally violent and dangerous. In addition, the prevalence of crack use had another impact on the street-level sex industry as well–an economic impact. The tricks were too cheap. Crack cocaine had, in effect, lowered the "going rate" for sexual services and prostitution was no longer worth her time. When interviewed, Marlee had been out of the "game" of street-level prostitution for more than six years.

Tami

Tami was located while serving time in Iowa's maximum-security correctional facility. Our interview took place in the prison's library. She began to cry as soon as she sat down, and, although I suggested that we cancel the interview, e responded, "No, no I want to stay."

Tami was 31-years-old, but could have easily passed for much younger. She grew up in Indiana and was raised by her mother and stepfather. Her biological father had abandoned her and her mother when she was only two-years-old. Tami had six siblings, three brothers and three sisters, although her family was far from the Brady Bunch. In her family, she recalled, "There was a lot of alcohol and fighting." She was also sexually molested by her stepfather. The sexual abuse began early, when she was about three-years-old, and continued until she was seven.

Tami ran away from home when she was only 12. I asked her to provide additional information, to which she replied, "I got in a truck with a truck driver and just left. I wound up in Florida. Later, I called my mom and she flew me home." At age 14, Tami's mother died unexpectedly from a heart attack. The day her mother died was the very last day Tami attended school; she dropped out in the eighth grade.

Within six months of her mother's death, Tami's stepfather remarried. She and her stepmother were not close because, as she explained,

> My other sisters had put my mom through a lot with running away and their involvement in drugs. It's like she just automatically assumed that I was going to end up like that.

Like Sam and Amy, Tami also spent much of her early adolescent years in various foster homes due to "incorrigibility." Over the span of one year, Tami had lived in two different foster homes and a group home. She ran away from all. I asked if there was trouble in the foster homes and she explained, "No, it wasn't their fault. It was mine because I was rebellious. They were really nice but it wasn't my family, you know?" She continued, "then they emancipated me at 14, which gave me the right to live on my own." She had been on her own ever since.

Although she had exchanged sexual services for "favors" such as transportation during her runs beginning at age 12, Tami felt that she didn't engaged in "prostitution," per se, until she was 14. She explained,

> I ran around with truck drivers most of my life, carnivals, you know, state to state, things like that. But this guy offered me $100 to spend the night with him, and that's how I got started [in prostitution].

Tami also became pregnant and had a child when she was only 15. She kept her daughter for seven months before giving her up for adoption. In retrospect, Tami believed the pregnancy was purposeful, "to fill a void. But I was too young.." Tami later commented, "I didn't give up my daughter because I didn't want her. I gave her up because I wanted her to have a life, you know?"

Tami spent the majority of her adolescence as a homeless teen, living on the streets, in abandoned houses, and under bridges. Money made from prostitution was usually spent on drugs and hotel rooms. She noted, "There's a lot of people from the streets that I miss." Tami had spent most of her life traveling cross-country. She never stayed in any one city too long and had lived in California, New York, New Jersey, Tennessee, Rhode Island, and Florida. She noted:

> Truck drivers will pay your way wherever you want to go. A lot of them just want you to ride with them because they're lonely. It's how I would get my clothes, how I'd get a little bit of money, then I'd find a town where I would think 'hmmmm' and something would tell me just get out of the truck and go.

She would go straight to the streets, meet people, pick up clients, make some fast cash, and then buy drugs. She tried crack for the first time when she was 16. Tami noted that she had been addicted to "almost everything–alcohol, crack, heroin and pot." For Tami, prostitution provided a means for basic necessities (e.g., food, clothes, shelter) but it primarily supported her drug addictions. Her experiences in the sex industry were extensive:

> I have danced, worked at escort services, I've even made a couple of movies that I'm not proud of– and I think I did it because you've got the control over the situation to where you're basically the one that they want. And you get it in your head that you're accepted, you know?

Like Marlee, Tami also described dangers associated with street-level prostitution. Tami's view was different from Marlee's however, because "Every time I got in the car I knew my life was in danger. But I didn't care." Tami had been raped on four separate occasions; she had also been beaten to the point of unconsciousness. Still, she didn't harbor anger against her rapists. Instead, she explained, "I don't blame them anymore. I know somewhere down their line something had to have happened traumatic to them–but I forgive them for it. It's just something I'll never forget."

Tami had an extensive history prostituting on the streets. She had been involved in the "game" for almost 16 years and, as part of our interview, discussion turned toward her clients. Tami had kept several "Regulars" in various cities where she had lived. Most of them were married. In retrospect, this fact had a chilling effect on her.

> What hurts me now is that I know there are a lot of families out there that don't even realize it's going on in their families, that their husbands or dads are doing it [picking up prostitutes], and there are a lot of them who are. And it's the ones that you really don't think would be doing it that would shock me. I had doctors and lawyers, I had everyday businessmen that would pay me $100, $500 for my time. And then, now that I think about it, where's the money for their children and stuff going, you know? At that time I didn't care.

Her comment led to a brief conversation about "love" and what it meant to her to love others and be loved in return, to which Tami explained, "To me, it's not just a four-letter word like a lot of people throw it around. To me, it's unconditional, you know? Some people say you can't trust love, but sometimes love is the only thing that you can trust."

At the time of our interview, Tami was serving a two-year sentence. She was nonchalant about the time she had spent behind bars noting, "This two years I'm doing is for all the things that I didn't get caught for. That's how I have put it in my mind." Tami was due for release in about six months. While serving her sentence, she had attended classes and was working toward her General Equivalency Degree (GED). She hoped to one day receive a degree in psychology and work with troubled teens. She also wanted to "settle down" and develop a more stable existence. She was considering the possibility of deviating from her former transitory lifestyle and setting up roots somewhere. But she would not be contacting her family. She had neither seen nor spoken to any of her biological relatives. "Basically," she explained:

> ...you go through life, you might have brothers and sisters, but you find out a lot. Just because you're blood doesn't mean that they're always going to be there for you. And they can be your worst enemies, they really can. And you've got to learn to detach from a lot of that in order to save yourself.

She continued, "If I keep holding on to the belief that my family is going to be 'okay' one day- then *I'll* stay sick. You know? I'll stay using [drugs]."

Chancey

At 56, Chancey was the oldest woman who participated in the investigation. She was extremely articulate and intelligent, and had completed two years of college. She was raised in a small, rural community where her parents were Lutheran, very religious, very strict, and considered "pillars of the community." Her family was also quite wealthy.

She described her father as a "good provider" and a "workaholic" who owned his own business and "was gone a lot and working all the time." Chancey's mother was never employed outside the home.

> My mother– she had a lot of mental problems. She was very neurotic. Very neurotic. She took a lot of sleeping pills and tranquilizers and things like that to keep the lid on her anxiety and panic attacks. But she had a lot of anxiety and was always doctored. She spent a lot of time resting and laying down. She had a lot of outside help– people that came in to do laundry and clean the house.

Chancey also had two older siblings and a sister 15 months her junior. She described her mother's inability to parent as follows:

> My mother should have only had two children. I probably should have never been born. She [mother] probably could have handled two children, but she couldn't handle three and she certainly couldn't handle four. She basically 'shooed' me away most of my life. That was my feeling anyway– that she didn't want to be bothered with me.

Chancey emphasized that all of her mother's attention was "focused on my younger sister, the baby. And since she couldn't handle both of us I basically got turned over to whoever." Chancey was raised primarily by her older sister, although when her father wasn't working, he too spent a good deal of time with her. Her father, she explained, was verbally abusive to all the children and physically abusive to her older brother. During her childhood, there were multiple times when she actually thought her father "was going to kill my brother" from beating him so severely.

Chancey's introduction to prostitution began when she was only five-years-old.

She was given money by the chief of police in the small town where she lived, in exchange for oral sex. Those exchanges continued for approximately five years. "He told me not to tell anyone and I thought he was going to put me in jail." The molestation ended when Chancey and her family moved.

In addition to the police chief, Chancey had been sexually abused by several others throughout her childhood, including her father. "I tried to tell my mother that my dad was hurting me, but it was like she didn't want to be bothered with it... I just gave up." Her father also sexually abused her older sister.

By the time she was eight-years-old, Chancey was stealing her mother's prescription pills. "I didn't know one pill from another but I knew they were supposed to make me feel better." By ten, Chancey had come to the attention of school officials. She was required to see a psychologist and recalled: "The psychologist asked all kinds of questions about my home life and how I was treated by my parents, was there any abuse, everything like that...of course, I gave all the right answers." Chancey described the "no-win" situation in which she had been placed by the psychologist. On the one hand, if she told the truth about her home life she was afraid she would be accused of lying and would not be believed. After all, her family was regarded highly within the community. On the other hand, if she were believed, she was afraid of being taken away from her family. She reasoned, "So either way, I couldn't tell him [psychologist] because he'd either believe me or he wouldn't."

At age 15, Chancey was sent to Kansas to live with an aunt and uncle because "My mother couldn't deal with me anymore." The couple owned a truck stop and Chancey worked as a waitress in their restaurant. It was there that she began "prostituting with truck drivers. They were coming through with drugs." Although her stay in Kansas was brief, she nonetheless "learned a lot about sex from the truck drivers and you know–about drugs."

Chancey spent the next two years at a Lutheran boarding school. It

> ...was supposed to straighten me out. [But] I wasn't a very good student. I was using drugs and drinking most of the time and running around with an Air Force guy. My dad was a good contributor to the school, though, and that's the only way I ever graduated. I'm sure.

Following graduation at age 17, Chancey met a man who became her pimp. "At that time," she explained, "was when I really more or less started working the streets." She was arrested for prostitution and her father bailed her out. By 18, she had met and married her first husband, who was a physically abusive alcoholic. They were married for 10 years during which time her involvement in the sex industry continued. Thus, despite having three children while married, she was uncertain as to the biological father(s) of her children and all three were born addicted to heroin. The state intervened and all were also removed from the home and spent a total of seven years in foster care.

Eventually, Chancey and her husband divorced. The divorce included an extensive custody battle. "He could prove, of course, that I was a criminal and prostitute and all I could accuse him of was being a bad father and an abusive husband." Neither of them were granted custody and the children remained in foster care.

A year later Chancey sought treatment for her heroin addiction. It was in treatment that she met her second husband, a recovering alcoholic. They were married for seven years; He was the first and last man that Chancey ever really "loved." Not long after the second marriage, Chancey regained custody of her children. She and her second husband had two additional children.

Throughout her adulthood, Chancey worked intermittently in the labor force and had obtained highly employable skills. In fact, she had been the executive director of a health agency at one point. Still, her evenings were often consumed with prostitution. She was "addicted to the danger [of prostitution], to the risk, the excitement." As her involvement in sex work continued, Chancey became quite savvy about the industry.

> I got to know what brought in money and what didn't. I got into mostly high-risk sex, kinky stuff, S and M [sado-masochism] stuff. It got to where I preferred that. That was my preference. It was my preference because of the danger, because of the risk. And the money was much better. I got to where I would try to talk people into going into the more high-risk sex.

Not unexpectedly, Chancey noted that her five children "had horrible teenage years. Just awful. Drugs and alcohol and legal problems." When asked how her children were doing now, as adults ranging in age from 27-37, Chancey indicated that none were doing well. Their adult lives had, for the most part, been consumed with substance addictions and failed relationships. Her daughter had recently relapsed into alcohol abuse and was "living with this pimp and a criminal who's basically been running escort services." She maintained little contact with her children.

At the time of our interview, Chancey was trying to pull her own life together. Work in the sex industry had been a defining feature of her life for over 40 years. In fact, there were only 12 years, out of her entire 56-years of life, that Chancey had not been involved in street-level sex work or any other type of prostitution. She had tried to exit the sex industry on numerous occasions, but she always returned. Prostitution appealed to Chancey for many reasons: the danger, the risk, and her sense of being "in control" of men.

Importantly also, Chancey described herself as a "sex addict." This, more than anything she believed, significantly influenced her inability to permanently exit the sex industry. Prostitution provided a self-destructive means of meeting her compulsive needs. Still, when interviewed, Chancey was again seeking assistance and attempting to exit; she was a client at WellSpring and had been off the streets for more than a year.

Summary

The five women described here shared many similarities. Noteworthy though, are also the significant differences in their personalities, childhood memories, relationships with caregivers and with intimate partners and children, and in their general, overall life experiences. They are, certainly, more than "prostitutes." They are women with histories and with futures who are embedded within textured physical, emotional, and social contexts. Their case histories provide a starting point, a "frame of reference," so to speak for further examination of the reality of the lives of women who become embroiled within the "game" of street-level prostitution.

Although the next two chapters focus on research methodology, the remainder of the book examines the women's lives in depth. Beginning in chapter four, patterns of commonality in the life histories of the entire group of 43 are shared in an attempt to de-mystify the phenomena of street-level prostitution and those who become entangled within the "game."

Notes

1. Susan V. Carr, "The Health of Women Working in the Sex Industry: A Moral and Ethical Perspective," *Sexual and Marital Therapy 10*, (1995): 201-213.

2. Christine Overall, "What's Wrong with Prostitution?: Evaluating Sex Work," *Signs* 17, no. 4 (1992): 705-724.

3. Gail Pheterson,"The Category 'Prostitute' in Scientific Inquiry." *The Journal of Sex Research* 27, no. 3 (1990): 397-407.

4. Names of all participants, including their significant others, family members, and children, presented in this chapter and those which follow, are fictitious.

Chapter Two

Theoretical Overview

> The aim of science is not to open the door
> to infinite wisdom, but to set a limit to
> infinite error.
> – Bertolt Brecht

For knowledge to be scientific, scholars must explain the empirical facts (data) through the use of ideas or theory[1]. Theory, writes Miller[2], makes two significant contributions to scientific inquiry. First, theory organizes and gives meaning to facts. Second, theory informs further research. Importantly, theory also guides practical intervention and the formation of social policy.

Graduate school was, for me, my first formal training in conducting theory-guided research. For novices like myself, an analogy may be useful for explaining the application of theory and theoretical formulations to the study of social phenomena. One might compare *theory* to a pair of sunglasses. Sunglasses, just like theories, provide a *lens* through which the world is filtered. Examining data from a particular theoretical perspective does not change the data; instead, what is altered is the manner in which we approach, organize, and make sense of the data. (Just like examining the environment while wearing sunglasses does not change the environment, but it does influence our perception of the environment). This chapter describes the lens through which I approached, organized, and made sense of the data that were collected as part of this investigation.

Theory Selection: Discipline-Specific

The sunglasses analogy can be expanded further to include theory selection. That is, why *particular* theoretical formulations are chosen to examine certain phenomena and not others. Think for a moment about purchasing a pair of sunglasses. Several key variables impact the ultimate choice made, including: availability, activities for which the sunglasses will be used (e.g., snow-boarding or riding a motorcycle versus daily wear), personal style, and comfort– or how well they fit.

Theory selection, to some extent, parallels sunglass selection. Theoretical formulations from which one might base an investigation depend on one's field or discipline (i.e.,"availability"). A family scientist examining intra-familial communication patterns, for instance, would not formulate her investigation based on a theory of macro-economics or cosmic evolution. Theories, in other words, are largely discipline-specific[3]. It is unlikely that a physicist and a family scientist would ever use the same explanatory devices or theoretical formulations because the objects of their inquiry are so remarkably different.

Theory Selection: Research Goals

Further, sunglasses are selected based on the activities for which they will be used. One would not purchase a high-tech pair of ski goggles for daily wear. Similarly, theories differ in *abstraction* and *scope of content*, and are based on the phenomena of inquiry and the amount of *explanatory power* necessary to address specific research questions.

Theories differ considerably with regard to their explicitness (or abstraction), on the one hand, and their breadth (or scope of content), on the other. *Formal propositional theories* are sets of abstract statements designed to explain a particular phenomena (e.g., "The greater the marital quality, the greater the marital stability")[4], which could be tested in a particular study. *Middle-range* theories usually involve elaborate theoretical writing about a particular *domain* which can be tested through a variety of studies (i.e., not a single study) using a variety of methods. Whereas *metatheories* deal with the philosophy of science itself and the study of one's field of knowledge, rather than the study of a particular topic within the field[5]. One would not select a metatheory, for example, for guiding an investigation of conflict between teenagers and their parents. Theory selection is thus based on the *research questions* being asked, within a particular domain (e.g., psychology, family studies, sociology, physics, electrical engineering).

Theory Selection: Personal Philosophy, Beliefs and Values

And finally, we ultimately purchase sunglasses based on our unique tastes, sense of style, and "fit." Similarly, researchers choose theories that reflect their personal philosophical values and belief systems, in other words, their unique tastes and style. I am a contextual developmentalist and a family scientist. My research is fundamentally driven by theories of human development which emphasize person-environment interaction, with particular focus on the family (e.g., influence of family dynamics, family relationships, and patterns of interaction for individual development). Two theories, ecological systems theory (EST) and family systems theory (FST), guided my exploratory research with prostituted women. These theories were selected because they are cornerstones in the family science and developmental fields, because they emphasize human development as influenced by personal characteristics and environmental influences, and because they reflect my personal philosophical beliefs and values.

Ecological Systems Theory

According to EST, individuals are embedded within multifaceted and multilayered social systems which mold and shape personal life experiences, thus setting developmental processes in motion. The primary interpersonal social system of which most of us are embedded is the *family unit*. However, systems beyond the family unit also influence developmental trajectories. Ecological systems theory[6], developed by Urie Bronfenbrenner, purports that development results from the interaction between the person, including all of her personal characteristics (e.g., physical features, temperament, personality) and her environment (including all people in that environment and their personal characteristics), through time. Development is a life-long process. Bronfenbrenner, whose writings on human development are largely influenced by Vygotsky[7-8] and Lewin[9], reports:

> The ecology of human development is the scientific study of the progressive, mutual accommodation, *throughout the life course*, between the active, growing human being, and the changing properties of the immediate settings in which the developing person lives, as this process is affected by the relations between these settings, and by the larger contexts in which the settings are embedded.

EST presents human development as a reciprocal and life-long process of interaction between person and environment. The theory incorporates four unique 'systems' (*micro-, meso-, exo-, and macro-systems*). These can be visualized as hierarchically organized to encompass the developing person, with more proximal systems (i.e., micro- and meso-) having the most direct influence and more distal contexts (i.e., exo- and macro-) influencing development indirectly (see figure 2.1 below).

The *micro-system* is defined as a "pattern of activities roles, and interpersonal relationships experienced by the developing person in a given face-to-face setting... containing other persons with distinctive characteristics of temperament, personality, and systems of belief"[10]. Such settings typically include the family, peer, work, and church or religious groups. It is the people within these groupings, not the physical settings per se, whose *patterns* of interactions with and expectations for, the developing person exert the greatest influence on her developmental outcomes. The micro-systems of a street-level prostituted woman (e.g., social group on the streets such as other street-level prostituted women and tricks and johns, treatment facility, jail), would, one might imagine, be exceptionally different, from the micro-systems of a non-prostitution-involved woman living in the same city (e.g., work, family, church).

The *meso-system,* according to Bronfenbrenner, comprises the linkages and processes taking place between two or more settings containing the developing person– or between two or more micro-systems, such as the interactions between work and home, home and school, or school and church group. The meso-system is a "system of microsystems"[11] and was created in recognition of the overlapping

Figure 2.1: Ecological Systems Theory

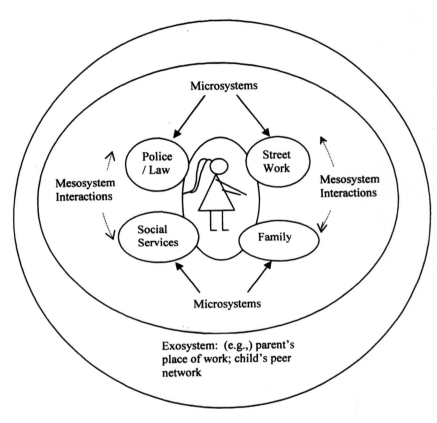

influences between micro-systems. Prostituted women, for instance, often report having experienced childhood sexual abuse. Although the sexual abuse occurred in a single micro-system (e.g., family), the implications of the abuse may reach far beyond the walls of the family home. To illustrate, child sexual abuse may impact a child's self-concept so that she becomes depressed, frightened, confused, and self-conscious; she may develop a damaged or contorted self-image. How she feels about herself, will necessarily be reflected in her actions and behaviors and thus, may strongly influence how she acts and interacts in other micro-systems, such as at school or with peers. She may avoid peers or behave inappropriately toward them (e.g., sexual acting-out). She may become withdrawn and have difficulty concentrating on school work. In turn, she may be labeled as "learning disabled" or have difficulty making friends– thus contributing further to her lowered self image. The connections between the two micro-systems (interactions between the girl's family environment and her school work and relationships with her peer group) represents *meso-system* influences.

The *exo-system* encompasses the linkages and processes taking place between two or more settings, at least one of which does *not contain* the developing person, but where events occur that influence processes within the immediate setting that does contain that person[12]. To simplify a very complex and lengthy definition, the exo-system embodies patterns in a particular environment of which the developing person is *not a member* (e.g., parent's place of work) that nonetheless influence the person. For instance, a parent's place of work influences the parent, the parent, in turn, influences the child. Although the child is not a part of the parent's work place, she is impacted by the work environment, albeit indirectly. In this investigation, prostituted women were asked to describe how *their prostitution involvement* impacted their children. Even though the children were not themselves involved in the "game" of street-level prostitution, they were *necessarily* impacted by it due to it's influence on their mothers. In this example, the "game" represents an exo-system to the children of the prostituted women. .

Finally, the *macro-system* consists of the overarching pattern of micro-, meso-, and exo-systems; the macro-system is a *societal blueprint* for a particular culture, subculture, or other broad social context[13]. In this investigation, the sub-culture of street-level prostitution (including violence, pimps, johns, and the street-level drug trade), economic structures in the larger society (e.g., poverty and indigence), and societal stigma against prostituted women comprise components of the macro-system that are theorized to influence their development. Individuals are impacted by broad, societal patterns even if such influences are not consciously recognized by the developing person.

Significant Features of EST

EST emphasizes the dimension of *time* in affecting developmental trajectories. Change *and* constancy through time influence individuals and the environments within which they are embedded[14]. Time is significant on two accounts: (1) future developmental alternatives and outcomes are partially determined by present situations, and (2) present situations reflect the unfolding of historical events and experiences. In other words, present circumstances (i.e., a woman prostituting on the streets) cannot be fully understood without careful observation of the entire ecological context within which she is embedded, including historical events and situations (e.g., early childhood developmental experiences), social relationships (e.g., support received from others), and environmental factors (e.g., poverty, indigence). In turn, these factors will also influence, in large part, her future options, such as legal employment possibilities and other alternatives for "exiting" the sex industry.

It is important to note that, within EST, *individual characteristics* are given credibility and validation; between-person variability is expected. Two people living in similar neighborhoods, having similar family dynamics, sharing similar ethnic or racial backgrounds, with similar economic challenges and opportunities, are nonetheless *individuals*, with person-specific attitudes, beliefs, and behaviors that will influence their reaction to and interaction with the various micro-, meso-, exo-, and macro-systems. Personal attributes evoke reactions from others and involve an active orientation toward and interaction with the environment[15]. Bronfenbrenner refers to these as *developmentally instigative characteristics*. Developmentally instigative characteristics include, for instance: social-seeking behavior (the tendency to seek out and sustain human relationships), intellectual curiosity, adaptability , and conception of self as an *active* agent in a responsive world[16]. Such characteristics are theorized to impact the developing person's interaction with her environment, and by extension, the environment's reaction toward her. EST provides a particularly useful approach for examining the developmental trajectories of street-level prostituted women, in context and through time.

Family System Theory

According to family systems theory, interpersonal relationships, particularly those involving members of the family system, are vitally important for shaping developmental trajectories. This is not to say that family dynamics *determine* development– but that family-level dynamics and structure provide a *framework* which molds development by impacting the human psyche, including one's social and emotional functioning, personal goals, dreams, values and ambitions. According to EST, the family system is an interpersonal network comprised of key players (e.g., parents or parental figures, siblings, and extended kin). Furthermore, the relational dynamics and patterns of interaction between those individuals, the family's belief system and values (e.g., children should be seen, not heard; physical violence is appropriate for obtaining compliance), and the manner through which those belief systems and values are transmitted to each family member (e.g., such as modeling and direct instruction) exert powerful influences on human development[17-18].

FST emerged in the 1970s[19-20] and was firmly established within the discipline of family studies within a few years[21-22]. Several core assumptions are critical for understanding family systems theory. First, central to systems' thinking is the concept of *holism*. Holism implies that individual development cannot be understood without examination of the larger family context within which individuals develop. Individuals are embedded within family *systems*, and thus, their development should be examined contextually.

Second, within FST the concept of *interconnectedness* is critical. *Interconnectedness* refers to the notion that change in one part of the system, or within one family member, influences other parts of the system[23]. A nice analogy for explaining this concept is a baby mobile. Think for a moment of the baby mobile hanging above an infant's crib. Visualize each individual character hanging from that mobile (e.g., lion, tiger, bear) as a particular family member (e.g., mom, dad, brother). If one were to touch the lion, for instance, the other characters would simultaneously also sway or move. Such is the case in families. According to the concept of interconnectedness, an individual does not necessarily have to be the recipient of a particular action, for instance, (e.g., physical brutality or other forms of abuse) to be emotionally and behaviorally affected by that action. In my investigation with prostituted women, participants routinely described the impact of *witnessing* physical violence and brutality within their homes. Thus, even though some women were not the target of the violence, they nonetheless described being deeply impacted by it.

Third, *intergenerational transmission*[24-25] asserts that patterns created in one generation are, characteristically and often unconsciously, re-created in future generations. In essence, individuals often transmit patterns, rules, values and belief systems learned in the family of origin, to the next generation– or one's family of procreation. This occurs regardless of whether those patterns, rules, values and belief systems foster positive or damaging personal or relational effects. This is *not to say* that human behavior is predetermined based solely on familial experiences; it is to say, however, that family system dynamics provide a powerful and direct influence on developmental trajectories, with such influences beginning as early as birth.

Finally, family systems theorists recognize and acknowledge the family unit as embedded within larger systems, referred to as *supra-systems*[26]. (The supra-system correspond to the *macro-system* described in ecological systems theory). The supra-system includes extended kin, neighborhoods, racial and ethnic subcultures, and societal variables like political systems and economic structures. Individuals, in other words, are embedded within families, which are embedded within larger, social and cultural systems.

Family systems theory and ecological systems theory complement each other well. FST emphasizes family-level dynamics and relationships, while EST emphasizes multiple-contextual and environmental systems; both provide insight for examination of human development.

Social Bonds: Support Network Influences

Ecological systems theory and family systems theory both emphasize *social interactions* and the connections between and among people as influential in developmental outcomes. I began this research believing that interpersonal patterns of interaction play a critical role in the culmination of events that result in a women's participation in street-level prostitution. Likewise, I further assumed that interpersonal patterns play an equally crucial role in determining how, when, or even if a woman will (or will be able to) leave the streets. Thus, it is important here to provide additional information related to social support and social network influences.

Rook[27] contends that social bonds are essential for healthy functioning. Isolated people, or those lacking social bonds, are presumed vulnerable to emotional and physical problems because of diminished social interactions. A lack of social attachment, or relationships characterized primarily by tension and conflict, may challenge optimal adjustment and diminish one's ability to cope constructively with personal crises.

Noteworthy also is that social systems exert both positive (i.e., enhancing) and potentially negative (e.g., destructive) influences on individual development. According to Thoits[28], there are three specific mechanisms through which social support enhances well-being. First, role relationships provide a set of *identities* by answering questions such as "Who am I?" and "Where do I belong?". Thus, social network members afford purpose and meaning to individuals, and quite possibly, feelings of security. Additionally, through social support, role relationships *prevent or reduce* anxiety and despair, particularly during periods of tension and stress. Those experiencing personal crises (e.g., incest, physical abuse) will benefit from the sense of security attained through having strong networks of social support. Finally, role relationships also provide a context for positive *self-evaluation*, or reflected self-esteem. Support network members who give aid, advice, and display emotional concern contribute to positive self-evaluations. Alternatively, network stresses such as disapproval from primary others may instigate feelings of "...shame, guilt, anxiety, frustration and despair"[29]. Rook[30] argues that social network *stressors* are stronger negative influences of mental health status than supportive features are positive influences. In other words, negative, conflictual and dysfunctional support networks jeopardize well-being to a greater extent than positive networks enhance well-being.

Summary of Theoretical Orientation

This investigation was conceptualized, and the data interpreted, from the juxtaposition of two mutually reinforcing and equally prominent theoretical frameworks: ecological systems theory and family systems theory. Embedded within each are explicit principles and implicit assumptions regarding the critical role of *other people* and social networks in shaping human development. The primary theoretical thrust of my research with prostituted women may thus be summarized as follows: (1) individuals develop within unique historical and environmental contexts; (2) the family unit comprises a particularly influential system within those environmental contexts; (3) developmental trajectories are guided and shaped by the *mutually reinforcing* interaction between person and environment; (4) person/environmental patterns of interaction are often repeated through time (i.e., cross-generationally) within families and across generations; and (5) supportive, positive social networks are essential for healthy functioning and optimal mental, physical, and emotional health.

Notes

1. David M. Klein and James M. White, *Family Theories: An Introduction* (Thousand Oaks: Sage, 1996), 3.
2. Patricia H. Miller, *Theories of Developmental Psychology*, 3rd ed. (New York: W. H. Freeman and Co., 1993), 8.
3. When adequate theoretical models do not exist, in which theory *development* or *modification* will occur.
4. William J. Doherty, Pauline G. Boss, Ralph LaRossa, Walter R. Schumm, and Suzanne K. Steinmetz, "Family Theories and Methods: A Conceptual Approach," in *Sourcebook of Family Theories and Methods: A Contextual Approach*, ed. Pauline G. Boss, William J. Doherty, Ralph LaRossa, Walter R. Schumm, and Suzanne K. Steinmetz (New York: Plenum, 1993), 21.
5. William J. Doherty and others, "Family Theories and Methods: A Conceptual Approach," 3-30.
6. Urie Bronfenbrenner, "Ecological Systems Theory." in *Six Theories of Child Development: Revised Formulations and Current Issues*, edited by Ross Vasta. (Philadelphia: Jessica Kingsley Publishers, 1989), 187-249.
7. Lev S. Vygotsky, *Mind in Society* (Cambridge, MA: Harvard U. Press, 1978).
8. Lev S. Vygotsky, "The Problem of the Cultural Development of the Child," *Journal of Genetic Psychology* 36 (1929): 415-34.
9. Kurt Lewin, *Field Theory in Social Science* (New York: Harper & Brothers, 1951).
10. Bronfenbrenner, "Ecological Systems Theory," 226.
11. Bronfenbrenner, "Ecological Systems Theory," 227.
12. Bronfenbrenner, "Ecological Systems Theory," 227.
13. Bronfenbrenner, "Ecological Systems Theory," 228.
14. Bronfenbrenner, "Ecological Systems Theory," 187-249.
15. Urie Bronfenbrenner and Ann C. Crouter, "The Evolution of Environmental Models in Developmental Research," in *Handbook of Child Psychology: Vol. I. History, Theory, and Methods*, ed. Paul H. Mussen (New York: Wiley, 1983), 357-414.
16. Urie Bronfenbrenner, "Ecological Systems Theory," 187-249.
17. David H. Olson, "Family Systems: Understanding Your Roots," in *Research and Theory in Family Science*, ed. Randal Day, K. Gilbert, B. Settles, & Wesley Burr (Pacific Grove, CA: Books/Cole), 131-53.
18. John Scanzoni, Karen Polonko, Jay Teachman, and Linda Thompson, *The Sexual Bond: Rethinking Families and Close Relationships* (Newbury Park, CA: Sage, 1989).
19. Reuben Hill, "Modern Systems Theory and the Family: A Confrontation," *Social Science Information* 10 (1972): 7-26.

20. Carlfred Broderick and Jeremy Smith, "The General Systems Approach to the Family," in *Contemporary Theories About the Family: Vol. II. General Theories/Theoretical Orientations*, ed. by Wesley R. Burr, Reuben Hill, Ivan Nye, and Ira L. Reiss (New York: Free Press, 1979), 112-29.

21. Wesley R. Burr, Reuben Hill, Ivan Nye, and Ira L. Reiss, eds., *Contemporary Theories About the Family: Vol. II. General Theories/Theoretical Orientations* (New York: Free Press, 1979).

22.Gail G. Whitechurch and Larry L. Constantine, "Systems Theory," in *Sourcebook of Family Theories and Methods: A Contextual Approach*, ed. Pauline G. Boss, William J. Doherty, Ralph LaRossa, Walter R. Schumm, and Suzanne K. Steinmetz (New York: Plentum), 325-51.

23. David Reiss, *The Family's Construction of Reality* (Cambridge, MA: Harvard University Press, 1981).

24. Klein and White, *Family Theories*, 149-77.

25. Carlfred Broderick, *Understanding Family Processes: Basic of Family Systems Theory* (Thousand Oaks, CA: Sage, 1993).

26. Whitechurch and Constantine, "Systems Theory," 325-51.

27. Karen S. Rook, "The Functions of Social Bonds: Perspectives from Research on Social Support, Loneliness and Social Isolation," in *Social Support: Theory, Research and Applications*, ed. Irwin G. Sarason and Barbara R. Sarason (Boston: Dordrecht, 1983): 253-67.

28. Peggy A. Thoits, "Social Support and Psychological Well-Being: Theoretical Possibilities," in *Social Support: Theory, Research and Applications*, ed. Irwin G. Sarason and Barbara R. Sarason (Boston: Dordrecht, 1983): 59.

29. Thoits, "Social Support and Psychological Well-Being," 61.

30. Rook, "The Functions," 253-67.

Chapter Three

Research Methodology

> There is one thing even more vital to science than
> intelligent methods; and that is the sincere desire
> to find out the truth, whatever it may be.
> – Charles Sanders Pierce

In this chapter, I provide an overview of the research methodology used to recruit participants, and to collect and analyze the data. The methodology used as part of this investigation is presented to allow the reader an accurate context from which to interpret the results of this study. I alone initiated, designed, and managed this research and thus, any and all methodological inadequacies or oversights are my sole responsibility.

This chapter is divided into several sections. The first provides detailed demographic information about the women who participated. In the second section, the procedures that were used to identify and recruit the participants are documented and the type of information collected is also presented. The third section outlines the data analyses procedures. Issues surrounding *trustworthiness* are considered in the fourth section and the chapter ends with discussion of the study's methodological limitations.

The Women Who Participated

Between 1998 and 1999, 43 women involved (or formerly involved) in street-level prostitution were located and invited to participate in this exploratory research investigation. To be included in the study, participants had to meet several requirements, including that they be female, either currently or formerly involved in *street-level* prostitution, and at least eighteen years of age. All participants lived in Nebraska or were incarcerated in Iowa's maximum-security correctional facility for women.

Demographic Variables

As evident in Table 3.1 (see below), participants ranged in age from 19 to 56 (average age = 33.4 years). The majority of the women identified themselves as Caucasian (n = 20) or Black (n = 18); five were American Indian. In terms of marital status, half (n = 22) were single and had never been married. Ten were married, nine were divorced, and two were legally separated from their spouses. The majority of the women lived in shelters (n = 16) or were incarcerated (n = 14). Years of formal education ranged from 7 to college experience (average number of years of education was 9.3). Fourteen of the women who had not completed high school had received a General Education Degree (GED).

Most of the women (n = 38) had children. The number of children of each ranged from 1 to 7 (mean = 2.4). Of 105 total children born to these women, only 10 remained in residence with their biological mothers. Most children lived with their biological fathers, with extended family (e.g., grandparents, aunts), or were in foster care.

On average, these women first entered the sex industry at 19.4 years of age[1], although the age range varied considerably; one prostituted for the first time at age 11 and another was 31 when she first participated in any type of prostitution. At the time they were interviewed, most of the women (n = 40) reported that they were no longer involved in the sex industry, although length of time since the last incident of prostitution varied dramatically, from less than 6 months (n = 17), to 6-12 months (n = 13), to one or more years (n = 10). Total time spent in the sex industry was also quite varied, from 6 months to 44 years (average number of years involved in the sex industry was 11.5).

Only two of the forty-three women indicated that they *had never* been chemically addicted. Drugs of choice included crack cocaine, methamphetamine, heroin and alcohol. Sixteen reported that they were addicted to illegal drugs *before they entered* the sex industry. By far, the majority (n = 25) indicated that their addictions *coincided with or followed* their entry into world of prostitution.

Participant Recruitment

Participants were recruited in several manners: (1) through WellSpring, (2) while imprisoned, and (3) through word-of-mouth. None were recruited directly from the streets; this decision was based on several factors. First, street-level prostituted women are an elusive population and largely suspicious of "outsiders." It is unlikely that anyone would have agreed to participate in research, had I approached people on the streets. It is also highly unlikely that, had any agreed to participate, they would have allowed the interview to be tape-recorded. Because I wanted to capture the essence of their stories, in their own words, tape-recording the interviews was deemed critical to the research.

Table 3.1. Participant Demographic Data

Variable	Total Sample ($n = 43$)
Age	
Mean	33.4
Mode	37.0
Range	19 - 56
Race/ethnicity(n)	
White / Black	20 / 18
American Indian	5
Marital status(n)	
Never married	22
Married	10
Divorced / Separated	9 / 2
Residence(n)	
Shelter	16
Prison	14
Partner/husband	6
Alone/with children	4
Friends	3
Education	
Mean	9.3 years
Range	7th grade - 2 yr. college
GED(n)	14
Mothers(n)	38
Number of children(total)	105[a]
Mean	2.4
Range	1 - 7
Child(ren)'s Residence(n)	
Mother / Father	10 / 19
Extended Family	26
On Own	14
Foster Care / Adopted	22 / 8
Other[b]	6

Continued on next page

Table 3.1. Participant Demographic Data (Continued)

Variables	Total Sample ($n = 43$)
Prostitution	
Age at entry	
Mean	19.4
Mode	18
Range	11 - 31
Time in sex industry[c]	
Mean	11.5 yrs.
Range	6 mos. - 44 yrs.
Drug Abuse (n)	41
Pre-prostitution entry	16
Concurrent with entry	8
Post-prostitution entry	17

[a]Does not include total number of pregnancies (e.g., miscarriages, abortions).

[b] "Other" includes those living on their own, in mental health facilities, and who were incarcerated.

[c]Multiple modes exist and includes prostitution in a variety of venues, including: streetwalking, escort services, strip-club work, and involvement with Sugar Daddies.

Second, the majority of prostituted women working the streets use drugs. I did not want to compromise the credibility of the results by interviewing women under the influence of mind-altering substances. It is also important to note that the sub-culture of street-level prostitution is very dangerous. I was not willing to risk personal injury by recruiting women actively working the streets.

WellSpring

The majority of participants ($n = 26$) were recruited through a non-profit intervention program, called WellSpring. WellSpring is specifically designed to assist prostituted women (and men) in leaving the sex industry. The program offers a variety of services, including individual and group counseling, and referrals for housing assistance, drug treatment, and employment. Ninety percent of WellSpring clientele are voluntary participants; approximately 10% attend as a requirement of probation[2]. WellSpring clients typically learn about the program through word-of-mouth (e.g., on the streets, in jail). Due to the voluntary nature of the program, group attendees are transitional. In other words, their involvement in the program is often sporadic, with clients attending the program for several weeks and then disappearing for weeks or months at a time only to resume program attendance at a later date[3].

With support from the WellSpring Program Director, and approval of WellSpring members, I attended weekly group-counseling sessions, every Saturday, for seventeen months. It was unknown prior to each group session which Well-Spring clients would show up; some weeks new faces arrived, but on many occasions the same core group of women were the only members present. Every week during introductions, I explained who I was, why I was attending the group meeting, and the purpose and goals of my investigation. If a woman was interested in participating, she and I spoke further and arranged an interview time and place. To obtain a *diversified* sample, including women not involved in a formal intervention program, two additional recruitment strategies were used.

Incarcerated Sample

Fourteen women were interviewed while serving time in prison. The first step in recruiting these participants involved contacting the prison warden. The details and all methodological procedures (e.g., tape-recorded interviews) were explained. All documentation, including the survey instruments and interview questions, were then sent to the warden who in turn obtained formal approval for the study from his superior.

Prior to my arrival at the prison, the warden created a list of all incarcerated women with prostitution charges on their records. When I arrived, I was searched and then escorted to the prison library where women with a history of prostitution were individually escorted to me by a prison guard. I explained to each potential participant who I was and the reason for my visit. I also described the purpose of the study and data collection procedures. These women were then asked if they would be willing to participate. Only one women, out of 15 who were eventually escorted to the library, was not interested in participating. I made eight separate trips to the prison.

Snowball Sampling

Finally, three additional participants were located through referrals or word-of-mouth. Following my interviews with the WellSpring participants, they were asked if they knew anyone else, who was currently or had ever been involved in street-level prostitution, and if that person might be interested in participating in the research. None of the three women who I contact through referral procedures had ever been involved in formal intervention (e.g., counseling, therapy) services.

Compensation

All women recruited through WellSpring and by referral were compensated $20.00 for their time. Due to prison regulations, the incarcerated women were not allowed to receive compensation of any type.

Data Collection

Qualitative and quantitative data were collected. *Qualitative* data refers to information obtained *without* the use of numbers. Qualitative methods, such as case studies, interviews, or diary analyses, allow a researcher to examine phenomena in depth and from the participant's point of view. These methodological strategies are typically used: (1) when little is understood or known about a particular phenomena, (2) when the researcher seeks *subjective* information, and/or (3) for theory creation or development.

Quantitative methods (e.g., survey instruments, experiments) are techniques which focus on obtaining numbers and frequencies, rather than on meaning and experience, and are often used for the purpose of drawing statistical inference. Both techniques provide unique types of information, and both have strengths and weaknesses. In this investigation, each participant engaged in an in-depth, tape-recorded interview and also completed a series of survey instruments.

In-Depth Interview / Qualitative Data

When I began this investigation, very little was known or understood about the developmental histories or social networks of street-level prostituted women. Because of this, I sought subjective information; I wanted the participants' voices to be heard. Thus, the majority of information was obtained through the use of in-depth personal, tape-recorded interviews guided by a series of open-ended questions[4].

The interviews were *semi-structured*, that is, a core set of questions was predetermined based on my personal interest and the available literature about prostituted women (see Appendix 1 for interview questions)[5]. The length of time spent discussing each question, the ordering of questions, and follow-up or spontaneous questions that were asked varied considerably from one interview to another depending on each woman's personal life experiences and verbosity. To illustrate, one key question centered around childhood sexual abuse. If a woman indicated she had not been sexually victimized as a child, questioning about this topic ceased. However, if she had been sexually abused, the questions which followed focused on the sexual abuse itself, including her age when the abuse began and ended, her relationship with the perpetrator (e.g., father, uncle), and whether or not she revealed the molestation to anyone.

The *semi-structured* interview technique allows for in-depth discussion of a variety of issues in an informal, non-threatening manner. Each interview lasted an average of 90 minutes (range = 50 to 180 minutes) and all of the women were interviewed in private locations including their residences, rooms in shelters, parks, or the prison library.

Survey (Quantitative) Data

In addition to engaging in an in-depth, open-ended interview, participants also provided demographic information and completed a series of six self-report survey instruments[6]. These are described below.

Life Events

To assess life events, or potential stressors in the women's lives, a revised version of the Family Inventory of Life Events (FILE)[7] was used. This instrument asks individuals to indicate whether or not they have experienced any of 26 different events (e.g., divorce, violence, legal trouble, substance use) in the previous year. Scoring the FILE involves a simple calculation of frequency of items. Higher scores indicate a greater number of potentially stressful events. An average of 13.3 events was reported by each respondent (range = 4 - 21 events).

Depression

Depression was assessed as an indicator of emotional well-being. Participants were asked to indicate the extent to which they had experienced each of seven different feelings over the previous two months. Items included, for instance: "I have had little energy and not felt like doing anything" and "I have felt depressed." A 4-point scale was used for recording answers: 1 = rarely, 2 = sometimes, 3 = often, and 4 = most of the time. Scores were summed and then an average depression score was calculated. Higher scores indicated greater feelings of depression. The scale mean was 2.5 (range = 1.3 - 4.0). The instrument demonstrated high reliability (.83) using Cronbach's alpha.

Locus of Control

Locus of control (LC) refers to the extent to which individuals see themselves as in control of and responsible for events that occur in their lives. An *internal* locus of control indicates self-perceptions of personal agency and responsibility, and often results in feelings of empowerment and competence in modifying or changing unpleasant or unwanted life circumstances or events. A person with an internal LC may study hard for an exam, for example, feeling that if she masters the material she will receive a high score. This person recognizes her ability to impact the situation.

Individuals with an *external* LC often believe they are powerless in impacting the outcome of events, and often believe that their destiny is controlled by external forces, such as fate or luck. An external locus of control often results in feelings of helplessness. Using the example above, an individual with an external locus of control may not study for an upcoming exam, believing that she will fail regardless of her efforts because the tests are unfair or she is not smart enough to pass.

LC was assessed using a seven item instrument that included statements such as: "I have little control over the things that happen to me" and "I often feel helpless in dealing with problems in life." Participants responded to each using a 4-point scale ranging from 1(not true) to 4 (always true). Item scores were summed and an average LC score was computed. Higher scores indicated a greater *external* LC. The scale mean was 1.6 (range = 1.0 - 3.3) and it demonstrated high reliability (Cronbach's alpha = .65).

Impulse Control

Impulse control (IC) refers to the ability to delay gratification. Those *lacking* impulse control will frequently act on the spur of the moment without thinking about potentially negative consequences of their actions. IC was measured using a 20-item instrument. Participants indicated the extent to which each item applied to, or was characteristic of, themselves. Sample items included: "I often act on the spur of the moment without stopping to think" and "I like to test myself every now and then by doing something a little risky." Response choices ranged from 1 (strongly disagree) to 5 (strongly agree). Items were summed and an average impulse control score was computed. Higher scores indicate *limited* (or little) impulse control. The average scale score was 3.0 (range = 1.0 - 3.29) and demonstrated high reliability (.70) based on Cronbach's Alpha.

Social Support

Because of the vital role of social support in influencing emotional and physical well-being, the Norbeck Social Support Questionnaire (NSSQ)[8-9] was administered. This survey consisted of two parts. In part one, participants are asked to name up to ten "significant" people in their lives. This allows for exploration of support network composition. Part two involves assessing the *type* (e.g., emotional support, practical support) and *amount* of support provided by each network member.

Emotional support was assessed with four questions, including for example: "How much does this person make you feel liked or loved?" (Sub-scale mean = 2.9; range = 1.10 = 4.35). *Practical support*, the giving of symbolic or material aid, was assessed by asking two questions, one of which was: "If you needed to borrow some money, get a ride to the doctor, or some other form of immediate help, how much could this person help you?" (Sub-scale mean = 2.64; range = 1.12 - 4.53). Participants answered each *question* for *each person* on their network list using a five-point response scale with choices ranging from 1 (not at all) to 5 (a great deal). The total scale demonstrated a mean of 2.6 (SD = 1.3).

Coping

Finally, to assess participants' strategies for managing stress, the Coping Resources Inventory- Form D[10] was used. This instrument was designed to measure five types of coping: *social* (e.g., talking to someone), *escapism* (e.g., eating, using drugs), *externalizing* (e.g., hitting someone or something), *internalizing* (e.g., keep feelings to self), and *active* (e.g., do something about the situation). Participants were asked to think about their typical reactions when in conflict with other people. Next, they were asked to indicate the extent to which they would react in any of 26 different ways (e.g., "avoid the other person and not speak to him or her," "hit or kick someone or something," "yell or scream at the other person," and "forget about it by not thinking about it"). Response choices ranged from 1 (would not do) to 4 (would always do). Total scores were computed for each *type* of coping strategy (i.e., social, escapism, externalizing, internalizing, and active). Average scores for each sub-scale are as follows: social ($\bar{x}$ = 2.3), escapism ($\bar{x}$ = 2.4), externalizing ($\bar{x}$ = 2.4), internalizing ($\bar{x}$ = 2.5), and active ($\bar{x}$ = 2.3). Each subscale demonstrated high reliability: (social = .77), (escapism = .72), (internalize = .71), (externalize = .77), and (active = .78).

Data Analyses

Analyses of Interview Data

The tape-recorded interviews were transcribed (i.e., type into a computer file) by trained research assistants and then analyzed using Thematic Analysis[11-12], a technique for analyzing text-based information. The process begins by thoroughly reading all protocols (i.e., interviews) and documenting *patterns of experience*. As I read each interview, I took extensive notes documenting the primary issues discussed (e.g., childhood abuse, running away, drug use, violence on the streets). Participants' descriptions of each of these issues represented a "pattern of experience." Patterns of experience were then pulled from the text and labeled with descriptive, identifying terms (e.g., childhood sexual abuse).

The next step involved identifying all information related to an already classified pattern of experience. The purpose of this step is to capture all information about a particular experience. (Frequently, individuals will elaborate on or provide additional details about a particular topic at various places throughout an interview). These steps were then repeated for each of the 43 interviews.

The third step involves cross-person analyses and requires cataloging and combining patterns of experience across the participants' interviews. Cross-person analyses allows for *differences and similarities* among participants to be revealed. The result is the creation of themes. Themes, notes Aronson[13], are "...pieced together to form a comprehensive picture of participants' collective experiences". The process requires interpretation based on rigorous identification and compilation of related ideas, thoughts, and experiences, into meaningful concepts when examined together. As an example, in analyzing the women's descriptions of their relationships with the primary caregivers during childhood, a theme emerged characterized by *relationship fissure*. That is, many of the women described an interruption in their emotional and/or physical connection with adult caregivers, often as a result of abuse or neglect.

Typically, as themes are examined in detail through case analyses, slight differences in patterns of experience emerge and sub-themes are often revealed. The result is greater clarity and understanding about the larger theme. To illustrate this concept, comparison of all participants' experiences with *relationship fissure* revealed two unique sub-themes. These were subsequently labeled as *literal abandonment* and *symbolic abandonment*. Thus, although the majority of women experienced relationship fissure with adult caregivers, the manifestation of this occurred differently for different women: some experienced fissure through *literal* abandonment (i.e., physical separation) and some through *symbolic* abandonment (i.e., emotional, rather than physical, disconnect). A much deeper, richer understanding of *relationship fissure* was thus exposed.

As one might imagine, conducting qualitative research often requires intense time commitment and rigorous attention to individual and group experiences. However, the information that results is rich, detailed, and process-oriented; information that is difficult to capture using quantitative (e.g., survey) means only.

Analyses of Survey Data

All survey data were coded, entered into a computer file and analyzed using SPSS 11.5 (Statistical Package for the Social Sciences, version 11.5). Analyses of the survey data involved the use of simple descriptive statistics, such as means/averages, ranges, and frequency tables. More elaborate techniques involving correlation and multiple regression analyses were also used. Although the sample size ($n = 43$) provided a massive amount of interview data, complex statistical techniques typically require a much larger participant group. Still, given the exploratory nature of this investigation, descriptive statistics were adequate for answering the questions of interest. Survey data were used to supplement the interview data, results of which are presented in chapter six.

Trustworthiness

One of the greatest challenges of conducting qualitative research, in the words of Lincoln and Guba[14], is "persuading [one's] audiences that the findings of an inquiry are worth paying attention to, worth taking account of...". Answering this question, for any social scientist, is largely an issue of establishing *trustworthiness*.

Trustworthiness is determined through evaluation of internal and external validity, reliability, and objectivity. However, these constructs are inappropriate for qualitative, or naturalistic, studies. Instead, *credibility, transferability, dependability,* and *confirmability* provide a means for determining the trustworthiness of qualitative research methods. Table 3.2 (see below) provides a simple comparison between the naturalistic and conventional terms used to determine a study's trustworthiness.

Table 3.2. Conventional and Naturalistic Determinations of Trustworthiness

Construct	Conventional or Quantitative Term	Naturalistic or Qualitative Term
Truth Value	Internal Validity	Credibility
Applicabiltiy	External Validity	Transferability
Consistency	Reliability	Dependability
Neutrality	Objectivity	Confirmability

Credibility

Credibility refers to demonstration that the inquiry was conducted in such a manner as to ensure that the phenomena was accurately identified and described[15]. Lincoln and Guba[16] recommend the use of *triangulation* and *member checking* as strategies to increase credibility.

Triangulation
Triangulation refers to the "act of bringing more than one source of data to bear on a single point"[17]. Triangulation may take several forms including the triangulation of sources, methods, and/or theories. In the present study, triangulation of *method* was achieved through the mixed method approach (i.e., qualitative and quantitative data collection) which allowed for two complementary types of information to be examined. Oftentimes, a woman's response on one of the survey indices was "double-checked" during the interview process. To illustrate, the demographic survey required that participants provide information regarding number of children, children's residence, and age of entry into prostitution. I examined surveys prior to beginning the tape-recorded interview. Then, during the course of the interview, if a participant provided information that appeared contradictory to what was indicated on the demographic survey, I mentioned the discrepancy and clarification was obtained. Similarly, during the course of the interviews, participants were asked to describe relationships with their primary social support network members. I would "cross-check" their descriptions with information provided on the Norbeck Social Support Survey. If they failed to mention a particular person in the interview that was noted on the survey, I would ask about the person to obtain better understanding and to clarify my understanding of information provided.

Moreover, as described in chapter one, two primary theories guided this investigation. In effect, various perspectives were incorporated to reduce bias and *increase* clarity.

Member Checking

Member checking is another common technique for establishing credibility. In the member check, participants evaluate the researcher's understanding of information. This technique allows for the original participants to indicate whether or not the researcher's interpretation of the information "fits" or "make sense"to them. In this study, the member check was utilized during the course of each interview whereby I interpreted or reiterated statements made by the participants, and requested clarification and/or confirmation about *my understanding* of the phenomena they described. If my interpretation was incorrect, participants provided additional information. If my interpretation was accurate, participants confirmed my understanding and the interview proceeded.

Second, member checking was utilized in a continuous fashion across the participants throughout data collection. In other words, statements made or issues raised in a particular interview were often discussed in subsequent interviews. This allowed for multiple perspectives on particular areas of interest to be obtained. To use a specific example, in one of the first interviews that I conducted, the term *strawberry* was mentioned. The participant described this term as referring to prostituted women who provide sexual services in direct exchange for crack cocaine. She also noted that this was the "lowest" form of street-level prostitution and that strawberries had a bad reputation and were not respected by other prostituted women. In subsequent interviews, I asked participants to explain the term "strawberry" to me in order to confirm or disconfirm the original definition provided.

Finally, member checking may also involve returning to several participants to obtain validation of the study results. I also used this strategy. After analyzing the data and writing up preliminary findings, I returned to several participants who provided feedback on my interpretations and on the conclusions I had drawn.

Transferability

Transferability refers to the *generalizability of results,* or the ability of the information to be generalized to a larger group beyond the sample from which the data were collected. To get at transferability, one might ask: to what extent can the results of this investigation be generalized to all street-level prostituted women? Qualitative research, by design, involves obtaining large amounts of rich, detailed, descriptive information from a small number of participants; a primary strength of this approach lies in the *depth* of information obtained. However, because the number of participants in qualitative studies tends to be small, such samples are, by extension, necessarily *less* representative of the larger population from which the sample was selected. Due to sample size and potential biases, I attempted to diversify the sample to increase transferability. To do this, I recruited 17 women who had no involvement in WellSpring or any other formal agency designed specifically for those wanting to exit the sex industry.

Guba and Lincoln explain[18], "The original inquirer cannot know the sites to which transferability might be sought, but the appliers can and do... the responsibility of the original investigator ends in providing sufficient descriptive data to make such similarity judgments feasible". To the extent possible, extensive descriptive information about my study is provided, especially with regard to: the participants, the methodological strategies used to collect and analyze the data, the theoretical orientations which guided the study, and my personal biases and assumptions. Given such information, the reader must determine the extent to which these data are transferable to other street-level prostituted women (see Limitations section below for additional information).

Dependability

Dependability, referred to as reliability in quantitative investigations, refers to *consistency* and is typically demonstrated through replication. If "two or more repetitions of essentially similar inquiry processes under essentially similar conditions yield essentially similar findings, the reliability of the inquiry is indisputably established"[19]. In qualitative studies, replicability is nearly impossible.

In research utilizing interview methods, a host of factors impact and influence the interview process and therefore, the replicability of results. Pareek and Rao[20] and others[21] identify these influential factors as: the characteristics of the researcher, the questions asked and how they are asked (e.g., tone of voice, facial expressions and non-verbal communication), the characteristics of the respondents, the timing of the interview (e.g., morning, afternoon, evening) and its setting (i.e., location), the questions as understood by the respondent (e.g., did s/he understand the question as it was intended?), the respondent's motivation to answer, the answer given by the respondent, and finally, the answer as understood by the interviewer (e.g., did s/he understand the response as it was intended?).

Despite these potential influencing factors, several strategies were utilized to help establish the *dependability* of information obtained. First, throughout the course of the interviews, similar questions were often asked in multiple ways. This allowed me to assess the consistency of participants responses; if inconsistencies were revealed, these were discussed and clarification was obtained.

Importantly also, I was able to assess dependability of the participants' information, to a large extent, during the longitudinal phase of this research. The original interviews were conducted in 1998 and 1999. Three years later (2001 and 2002) I interviewed 18 of the original 43 women. Prior to the second interviews, I returned to the original interviews and carefully re-read each. Then, during the course of the second interview, I frequently asked questions about information provided during the first; some of these questions were *very specific*, such as the clothing worn during their first experience prostituting on the streets, or the motivation for the break-up of a particular relationship. Invariably, the same information was provided at both the original and follow-up interviews.

Confirmability

Finally, confirmability captures the traditional concept of objectivity. In naturalistic inquiries, Lincoln and Guba[22] argue that the issue of neutrality or objectivity lies, not in the characteristics of the researcher, but rather in the characteristics of the data themselves. They discuss several techniques for assessing confirmability, including the use of member checks and triangulation.

Limitations

Four primary limitations have been identified: transferability (i.e., generalization of the data), the use of retrospective accounts, the incorporation and analyses of cross-generational data, and the geographic location in which the data were collected.

Transferability
    The women who participated in this investigation represent a *unique population* of prostituted women.
    Street-Level Prostitution. All of the participants were involved, at some point in time, in street-level prostitution. The experiences of these women, therefore, should not be assumed to reflect the experiences of women involved in other types of sex-work (e.g., those working for escort services or in brothels).
    Women Attempting to Exit Prostitution. Moreover, the majority of the women who participated (40 of 43 or 93%) were not *actively* involved in prostitution when they were interviewed. Some were voluntarily attempting to exit prostitution while others had been *in*voluntary removed from the sex industry due to imprisonment. Women actively involved in street-level prostitution may perceive events and describe experiences quite differently from those not actively engaged in sex-work.
    Involvement in Formal Intervention. Relatedly, more than half of the sample (61%) had participated in a formal intervention program specifically targeting prostituted populations. Although this sampling bias was partially remedied by including others with little or no formal intervention experiences, this limitation is worth noting.
    Taken together, the representativeness of this population of prostituted women is limited; results should not be interpreted to apply to all prostituted women, nor to women *actively* involved in the "game" of street-level sex work.

Retrospective Accounts

Another limitation involves the use of retrospective information. Specifically, one of the goals of this investigation was to document developmental trajectories of the women– experiences spanning their entire lives, beginning in childhood. By necessity, early-life events were described *retrospectively*. Despite the clarity with which childhood phenomena (e.g., such as exposure to violence and victimization) were reported, memories of the formative years were nonetheless filtered and interpreted through an "adult" lens.

Intergenerational Accounts

Third, one aspect of this investigation involved documenting intergenerational patterns of parenting and parent-child relationships (i.e., between the participants and their parents, and between the participants and their own children). Thus, a great deal of time was spent discussing relationships with parents/parental caregivers, early family environments (e.g., domestic violence, presence of drugs/alcohol), and abuse (e.g., neglect, childhood sexual abuse), in addition to the women's perceptions of their relationships with their own children, the family environment their children had been exposed to, and victimization experienced by their children. The methodological limitation is that all information was obtained from the *women* only. The view points of their parents (or parental caregivers) and children were not sought and thus, not included.

Geographic Location

Finally, all women recruited through WellSpring and word-of-mouth lived in a *mid-sized Midwestern* city (500,000 population). The prison where the incarcerated women were held was located in an adjacent state. It is quite possible that geographic location (e.g., east and west coast states vs Midwest states) or city size (e.g., a mid-sized city vs a sprawling urban metropolis) exert unique influences on the street-level prostitution phenomena that are not captured in the data. To illustrate, "pimp-controlled" prostitution is reported as exceedingly more common in larger metropolitan areas, such as Chicago[23-24], than was reported by the participants of this investigation. Thus, the possibility of geographic distinctions and idiosyncracies should be kept in mind while reading and interpreting the results.

Preface to Remainder of the Book

The remainder of this book is dedicated to sharing results of the data that were obtained through intensive interviews and survey reports. Themes and patterns which emerged during data analyses are described in detail. The reader is afforded a unique opportunity to explore the developmental characteristics and environmental contexts that propel women into the "game" of street-level prostitution. To the extent possible, the women's own words are incorporated into the text. They, after all, are the experts of their own lives. They are uniquely equipped to share their worlds and the sub-culture of street-level prostitution. My intent in documenting their experiences was to maintain fidelity to the content, tone, and intent of their words.

Notes

1. The women were asked how old they were the first time they traded sexual services for money, drugs, or other desirable commodities (e.g., housing, food, shelter). Thus, age of entry into the sex industry is a broad concept and is *not* necessarily the age when they first engaged in *street-level* prostitution.

2. Of the twenty-six study participants recruited from WellSpring, it is not known which were volunteers and which were court-ordered to attend. This information was confidentially maintained by the WellSpring Director so that all program clientele were *assumed* to be voluntarily participating in order to reduce potential biases.

3. Although WellSpring provides a greatly needed service to prostituted men and women, the organizational structure (i.e., voluntary attendance) clearly creates significant difficulties for program evaluation.

4. Prior to being interviewed, all participants completed an Informed Consent Form (required by the Institutional Review Board or IRB) which outlines the goals and procedures of the investigation and provides sample questions. Each participant was informed that she did not have to answer any question that she was uncomfortable with and that she could end the interview at any time, without loss of compensation. Also, each participant was provided a list of names, addresses, and phone numbers of local shelters and counseling services. Participants were informed that any information provided would be strictly confidential; that access to data would be limited to myself and my research assistants, and that none of the information obtained would be accessible by WellSpring staff, any social service agency, or any judicial body (e.g., courts, probation/parole office).

5. Given the exploratory nature of the investigation, interview questions were written based on: (1) gaps in the existing literature (i.e., family dynamics, social support), (2) ecological systems theory, (3) family systems theory, and (4) my personal academic training and background (i.e., human development, family science).

6. Prior to completing the instruments, all participants were asked if they would prefer to answer the survey instruments on their own, or if they would rather that I read each question, including all response choices to them. Approximately two-thirds of the women preferred that I read each question to them.

7. David H. Olson, Hamilton I. McCubbin, Howard Barnes, Andrea Larsen, Marla L. Muxen, and Marc Wilson. *Family Inventories: Inventories Used in a National Survey of Families Across the Life Cycle*, 1982. (Available from 290 McNeal Hall, University of Minnesota, St. Paul, MN, 55108).

8. Jane S. Norbeck, Ana M. Lindsey, and Virginia L. Carrieri, "The Development of an Instrument to Measure Social Support," *Nursing Research* 30 (1981): 264-69.

9. Jane S. Norbeck, Ana M. Lindsey, and Virginia L. Carrieri, "Further Development of the Norbeck Social Support Questionnaire: Normative Data and Validity Testing," *Nursing Research* 32 (1982): 4-9.

10. Allen L. Hammer and Susan M. Marting, *Coping Resources Inventory-Form D* (Palo Alto, CA: Consulting Psychologists Press, 1987).

11. Jodi Aronson "A Pragmatic View of Thematic Analysis." *The Qualitative Report* 2, no. 1 (1994): 1-3.

12. Steven J. Taylor and Robert C. Bogdan, *Introduction to Qualitative Research: The Search for Meaning*, 3rd ed. (New York: John Wiley & Sons, 1998).

13. Aronson, "A Pragmatic View," 2.

14. Yvonna S. Lincoln and Egon G. Guba, *Naturalistic Inquiry* (Beverly Hills: Sage Publications, 1985), 290.

15. Catherine Marshall and Gretchen B. Rossman, *Designing Qualitative Research*, rev. ed. (Thousand Oaks, CA: Sage, 1995).

16. Lincoln and Guba, *Naturalistic Inquiry*, 298-311.

17. Marshall and Rossman, *Designing*, 146.

18. Lincoln and Guba, *Naturalistic Inquiry*, 298.

19. Lincoln and Guba, *Naturalistic Inquiry*, 299.

20. Udai Pareek and Venkateswara T. Rao, "Cross-Cultural Surveys and Interviewing," in *Handbook of Cross-Cultural Psychology*, vol. 2, ed. Harry C. Triandis and John W. Berry (Boston, MA: Allyn and Bacon, Inc., 1980), 127-79.

21. Steinar Kvale, *Interviews: An Introduction to Qualitative Research Interviewing* (Thousand Oaks, CA: Sage, 1996).

22. Lincoln and Guba, *Naturalistic Inquiry*, 298-311.

23. Celia Williamson and Terry Cluse-Tolar, "Pimp-Controlled Prostitution: Still an Integral Part of Street Life," *Violence Against Women* 8 (2002): 1074-92.

24. Jody Raphael and Deborah L. Shapiro, *Sisters Speak Out: The Lives and Needs of Prostituted Women in Chicago.* (Center for Impact Research, August 2002), 1-35.

Section Two

The Larger Perspective:
Patterns of Commonality

Chapter Four

Families of Origin and Procreation

> Life must be understood backward,
> but it must be lived forward.
> – Søren Kierkegaard

Previous studies involving street-level prostituted women have identified developmental experiences including childhood sexual and physical abuse, and patterns of run-away behavior as common precursors to prostitution entry. Early family environments of prostituted women have been further characterized as chaotic and disorganized. Documentation of specific events and experiences in the formative years, and their associations with adulthood prostitution, provides valuable information for better understanding developmental processes that may influence a woman's prostitution entry. This information is additionally valuable for designing effective prevention and intervention services.

What is largely missing in the academic literature, however, is information documenting female sex-workers' *perceptions and interpretations* of early childhood experiences, and particularly perceptions of early family contexts and relationships with adult caregivers. In other words, knowing that certain childhood events and experiences commonly occur among women who eventually the sex trade provides part of the story; with much left to be learned.

Alfred Adler, considered by many to be one of the very first humanists[1], believed early childhood experiences greatly affected personality development. Importantly also is that Adler believed it was not necessarily *what* happened in a person's past that exerted the most influence on developmental outcomes, but rather, on one's *memory* and *interpretation* of what happened[2]. I hold similar beliefs.

Thus, one of the primary goals of my investigation was to obtain information from the participants about their early childhood experiences, certainly, but also to ascertain the women's perceptions and feelings about those experiences. Guided by family systems theory, a secondary goal was to investigate inter-generational patterns of family dynamics. I wanted to explore the possibility that similar parent-child relationships patterns had been transmitted from the women's families of origin (i.e., how they were parented) and their families of procreation (i.e., how they parented their own children).

The first section of this chapter presents an overview of previous studies examining the early developmental experiences of prostitution-involved women. This information sets the stage for understanding my participants' reports of their own childhoods and early family environments. In the second section, information from the participants about their families of procreation, including their perceptions of relationships between themselves and their own children, is presented.

Overview:
Early Developmental Experiences of Prostituted Women

Childhood sexual abuse is frequently associated with adulthood prostitution involvement. The percentages of street-level prostituted women who have experienced early sexual abuse vary considerably, from 10% to more than 70%[3-5]. However, unclear and open for further exploration are the causal pathways linking childhood sexual abuse with later life prostitution. Two models have been proposed.

Some believe a *direct* connection exists between childhood molestation and prostitution entry. James and Meyerding[6] report that childhood sexual abuse results in the separation of emotion from sexual activity. The sexually abused victim begins to view herself as debased, a process referred to as "mortification of self" by some[7]. Self-depreciating labels become internalized, thus facilitating self-identification as a "prostitute." The transition into prostitution activity is a behavioral reaction, a consequence of a person's already debased sense of self. Simply stated, prostitution activity corresponds with a an individual's self-prescribed label. One "becomes" what one has labeled herself. Miller[8] similarly argues that emotional distancing, a direct result of childhood sexual victimization, is reenacted during sexual activities with clients, thus allowing a person to more easily engage in sex-work.

In contrast, others[9-10] argue that the link between childhood sexual abuse and later prostitution is *indirect* and largely mediated by run-away behavior. To investigate the "runaway" link, Nandon, Koverola, and Schludermann[11] compared teenagers who were actively involved in prostitution with another group of youth who had been sexually abused but who *had not* worked in the sex industry. The two groups reported similar experiences with childhood sexual abuse. However, those involved in prostitution were *more likely* to be or to have been runaways. Similarly, in a study comparing sex workers with a comparable control group, Potter and colleagues[12] reported that the sex workers were significantly more likely to have left home earlier or to have run-away. Thus, several studies offer support for the "mediating" link between early childhood sexual abuse and later prostitution involvement.

Importantly however, not all prostitution-involved women have experienced childhood sexual abuse. And certainly not all sexually abused women have entered, or even considered entering, the sex industry. Other developmental processes must also exist and play a pivotal role in a woman's decision to enter and remain involved in sex-work. In attempting to decipher probable linkages between early developmental experiences and later prostitution, psychological and contextual factors have also been examined.

Susceptibility vs. Exposure

Potterat and colleagues [13] introduced two concepts, susceptibility and exposure, for expanding our understanding about the causal pathways leading to prostitution entry. The *susceptibility* model contends that psychological characteristics, such as alienation and feelings of worthlessness, in conjunction with traumatic events (e.g., incest), predispose some women to the lure of prostitution. (The susceptibility model is similar to the work presented earlier by James and Meyerding, and Miller). *Exposure*, on the other hand, refers to interpersonal contacts with individuals familiar with prostitution and its unique subculture. According to the exposure model, prostitution entry is believed to involve both "receptiveness to the influences of a significant other engaged in prostitution and an effective inducement from that other person" [14].

To test these models, Potterat and colleagues compared prostitution-involved women with a carefully selected control group with regard to: patterns of early socialization, adolescent experiences, and exposure to significant others involved in prostitution. Arrest records and reports of delinquency were similar in the two groups, as were experiences with childhood sexual abuse and running away from home. Many in the control group had been exposed to others involved in prostitution, but had chosen paths that did not include sex work. In fact, few differences at all emerged between the two groups of women. In other words, neither model was strongly supported.

Nandon and colleagues [15] succinctly summarize the bulk of research on developmental antecedents to sex-work by stating, "when an appropriate comparison group is used, known precursors of prostitution *fail* to discriminate between the prostitution and nonprostitution groups" [italics added]. Bullough and Bullough [16] concur: "When all is said and done, no single factor stands out as causal in a woman becoming a prostitute". [Factors other than early family contexts have also been examined in relation to women's prostitution entry including economic need and deprivation in addition to chemical dependence. These are explored in chapter five].

Summary

Attempts to definitively understand developmental experiences leading to street-level prostitution entry have been elusive, despite persistent attempts. Looking for a single causal path is misleading, as undoubtedly, entry and continued involvement in the sex industry results from the cumulation of multiple interdependent personal and contextual factors; none of which may exist in the same form or to the same degree for all women. Although strong correlations exist between prostitution and various life experiences, such as early sexual abuse and running away from home, many women are exposed to similar childhood traumas or events, a large majority of whom *never engage* in prostitution-related activities[17]. Simply stated, similar experiences do not necessarily lead to parallel developmental trajectories.

Clearly, more information regarding the contexts of individual development among female street-level prostituted women is warranted. The family context, and the parent-child relationship specifically, constitutes the earliest and most influential factors that set developmental trajectories in motion[18]. Building on the work of others, this investigation attempted to expand the literature by examining the early childhood experiences of 43 prostitution-involved women. An important consideration was the women's *interpretations* of their childhood experiences.

Results: The Formative Years

Participants were asked to describe their early developmental experiences, with particular emphasis on their relationships with parents, or other adult caregivers. As expected given previous studies of prostituted women, the participants commonly reported being the victims of sexual victimization, emotional abuse, domestic violence and neglect. Further analyses of their interpretations of these experiences revealed a prevalent theme centering around relationship fissure (i.e., feelings of being "abandoned"). An additional theme, running away, also emerged. Running away was interpreted as a behavioral response to feelings of abandonment.

Abandonment

Ninety-five percent of the women who participated in this investigation ($n = 41$) reported perceptions of *relationship fissure.* Relationship fissure, defined as severance of ties with adult caregivers, resulted from feelings of abandonment. Specifically, participants commonly spoke of being *abandoned* or *left behind* by parents or parental figures during the formative years–during childhood or early adolescence. Extensive analyses of relationship fissure revealed two sub-themes: *literal abandonment* and *symbolic abandonment.* Thus, although the majority of participants described feeling abandoned by adult caregivers in their early lives, not all *experienced* abandonment in the same manner. Some were physically abandoned, while for others, abandonment was not physical, per se, but emotional and psychological.

Literal Abandonment

Literal abandonment was defined as the cessation of physical contact between parent (or parental caregiver) and child. Literal abandonment resulted from a variety of events, but was most frequently associated with: children being removed from their families of origin (either voluntarily or involuntarily), being literally left behind or abandoned, or with parental death. It is important to point out that only five of the 43 women (or 12%) had remained in the physical care and custody of their biological parents throughout childhood and adolescence.

Removal from Family

Physical separation between the women and their adult caregivers frequently resulted from out-of-home placement. Removal from the biological home typically occurred in one of two ways. Some of the women were informally removed. That is, they were voluntarily placed by their parent(s) in the care of extended family. The second common pattern involved formal intervention in which the women were involuntary taken from their biological homes due to state or legal intervention. Regardless of whether out-of-home placement was voluntary or not, it typically was a consequence of severe family dysfunction involving domestic violence, parental incompetence, and/or chemical addiction.

Extended Family/Informal Removal. Fourteen participants lived intermittently with relatives (e.g., grandparents, aunts, or older siblings) during their childhoods. Unfortunately, the new living situations were often similar to those from which the women had been removed and typically involved domestic violence and various forms of addiction. To illustrate, one of my participants, Alli, noted that she had been born to a 15-year-old mother and a 16-year-old father. She was subsequently placed in the care of an alcoholic grandmother and a verbally abusive grandfather. She explained, "I wasn't too close with them [grandparents] 'cuz I always felt like I was a burden to them, you know?" By 13, she "just started pushing myself away from my family." She began smoking marijuana that year, and by age 18 she was smoking crack cocaine.

Of the fourteen who spent part or all of their formative years with extended family, only one, Sam, recalled that her new living situation was an improvement. At age 10 Sam was sent to live with an aunt in a "real good environment." She explained, however, that she "was already too lost by then." Sam recognized how, by age 10, even a "good environment" (one offering some semblance of stability) could not eradicate or atone for the damage that had been previously inflicted from years of sexual abuse.

Foster Care/Formal Removal. In contrast to parents voluntarily placing their children in the care of extended kin, twelve other participants had been involuntarily removed from their families of origin due to state or legal intervention. These individuals spent most of their childhoods living with foster families or in state operated youth facilities. Unfortunately, their new living situations were far from optimal. Most offered a continuation of the abuse and victimization the women had suffered in their families of origin.

Jenna, for instance, described her biological mother as an intravenous heroin addict and her father as an alcoholic. One of her earliest memories was of her mother "shooting up and passing out... She fell flat on her stomach. She was pregnant with my little sister at the time." Child Protective Services removed Jenna and her three sisters. They were each placed in a different foster home and Jenna was eventually adopted by an older couple. Jenna's foster mother was "verbally abusive– she always told me I would end up like my birth mom– never amount to shit." At 15, Jenna had a daughter and at age 16, when her daughter was still an infant, Jenna's adoptive mother pulled a gun on her and kicked them both out.

Kendra's situation was equally disturbing. She was raised without knowledge of her father and spent five years in foster care, beginning at age 12. At age 14, she was molested by her foster mother's son and became pregnant. Consequently, she was removed and placed in a succession of other foster homes and eventually in a female detention center. At 19 she "aged-out" of the system. Out-of-home placement was not much better for Tonya; she had lived in 27 different foster before she turned 18. Family stability, or the development of meaningful relationships with an adult caregiver was completely foreign to her. Eleven of the women who participated in this investigation had been raised, from childhood onward, in state-sponsored detention centers and four had been admitted to mental-health facilities prior to adolescence due to patterns of emotional or behavioral disturbance.

Being Left Behind

In contrast to those who were removed from their families of origin, three participants reported simply being "left behind" by their parents. Autumn is a case in point. She and her two siblings were left in the care of family friends "temporarily." But her parents never returned. Autumn was only five-years-old at the time. She was sexually abused in the home and, within a month, all three children were placed in foster care. The siblings were separated and Autumn spent the next 10 years living with a variety of foster families. At the time that she was interviewed, Autumn had not seen her father in 20 years and had only recently been reunited with her mother after 16 years. Similarly, due to alcoholism and domestic violence, Barb's parents divorced when she was 12. Barb felt abandoned by her mother because:

> She [her mother] promised she would take us [Barb and her three sisters] with her. She didn't do that. I have a lot of resentment toward my mother... I thought I was always really close to my mother until that promise got broke. For me, that's what it was, when I was 12.

Barb explained her relationship with her mother further by saying, "I cannot trust her. She causes chaos, just out of meanness. I don't participate in anything that has to do with her and I don't know if I ever will." Finally, Jewel described how she was "given away" to an aunt. "My mom had four other children that were older and she really didn't want a girl I guess. When I was born she called up my aunt and said, 'come to the hospital and get her'." Jewel never lived with her biological mother or siblings and her aunt turned out to be an extremely violent woman.

Parental Death

Participants also described feeling abandoned due to parental death. Eight participants experienced the death of one or both parents during early childhood. Some parent(s) died from natural causes, others committed suicide. Parental suicide, one might think, would leave a child with greater feelings of abandonment than a child whose parent(s) died of natural causes. This was not necessarily the case, as described by Amy. Both of her parents died of natural causes before she turned 12. She recalled:

> I always felt really weird having parents that were alcoholics, but then after they died, I really felt weird because most people had parents. When my parents died I felt cheated, I felt abandoned.

Others reported similar feelings of loss and abandonment. At age 13, for example, Sharia became the care-taker of her mother who was dying of cancer. Within 18 months, her mother was gone. Four months after her mother's death, Sharia's father remarried and Sharia felt abandoned by her mother and rejected by her father. She ran away from home the same year and never returned.

Likewise, when she was only eight years old, Michelle's mother committed suicide. When asked what happened next she explained, "We [siblings] stayed with my Dad. Two days later he moved the woman in that he had been fuckin' when my mom killed herself." By age nine, Michelle was being sexually molested by her father. She described anger at her mother for "bailing" on the family and "hatred" toward her father for "causing" her mother's suicide and inflicting additional trauma through sexual abuse. She then stated,

> I love my mom to death, but I think she's a fucking coward. People say to give it time, that you will come to terms, but it has been 18 fuckin' years and I ain't come to terms yet. I think she was a coward.

Jackie also experience parental death; her father died from a drug overdose: "They found him in the bathtub with a needle in his arm." She was only six. Her mother remarried that same year and, when Jackie was asked about her initial reactions to her stepfather she responded, "I thought he was all right, you know. Like we finally got a dad." However, her stepfather was not what he appeared and sexually molested Jackie for the next eight years.

Granted, parent-child separation due to parental death is unique. The loss is forever, the possibility that the parent(s) may someday return to reclaim their children does not exist, and reunification is impossible. Abandonment due to parental death is clearly different from that due to parental incompetence. Nonetheless, such distinctions are irrelevant in a child's mind. Separation is still separation, loss is still loss, and feelings of *abandonment* still resulted.

Summary
     To briefly summarize, literal abandonment, a term adopted by the author, was described by participants as a physical severance of ties between themselves and their parents. Literal abandonment resulted from children being physically removed from their families of origin, from parents leaving their children and never returning for them, or from parental death (see Figure 4.1). Early family contexts were described as chaotic; family relationships were tainted by multiple forms of abuse and children's out-of-home placement, whether with family members or foster families, rarely resulted in improved circumstances. Out-of-home placement for these women provided a change in geography only. New living situations which could have *potentially* provided the opportunity for emotional support, protection, and the development of trust, did not materialize. In the majority of cases, participants were often subjected to continued abuse, neglect, and instability.

Figure 4.1: Manifestations of Literal Abandonment

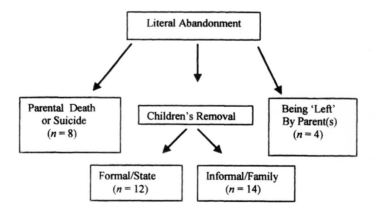

Symbolic Abandonment

     Unlike literal abandonment, symbolic abandonment refers to situations in which adult caregivers were *physically* present, but emotionally absent and rejecting of their children. In situations involving symbolic abandonment, parents were either unwilling or unable to provide for their children's basic physical and emotional needs. Frequent manifestations of symbolic abandonment included: parental failure to protect against childhood sexual abuse, and parental unavailability due to drug addiction and/or mental illness.

Symbolic Abandonment: Failure to Protect

Sexual Victimization. Thirty-two participants (74%) reported that they were the victims of childhood sexual abuse. Sexual molestation, in and of itself, does not necessarily result in damaging long-term consequences or feelings of abandonment. Contextual factors surrounding sexual abuse largely influence short- and long-term repercussions. Sauzier and colleagues,[19] note that the perpetrators' relationship with the victim, the longevity of abuse, the child's age when the abuse began, the severity of abuse (e.g., fondling versus penetration) and whether or not someone intervened on behalf of the victim as significant in determining the potential impact of childhood sexual victimization. Psycho-social damage is greatest when the perpetrator is a trusted adult, especially if the perpetrator is a member of the child's nuclear family, when the abuse is sustained over a long period of time, and when the acts involve penetration[20-21]. Based on this knowledge, participants who had been sexually molested during childhood were asked to described the contextual features surrounding their experiences as victims of sexual abuse.

Perpetrators, Age, Duration, and Severity. Sexual perpetrators, in the order most commonly implicated by the participants, included: biological fathers, step-fathers, family friends, brothers and uncles. Other perpetrators, including grandfathers, adopted fathers, foster fathers or foster brothers, neighbors, and mothers' boyfriends were also mentioned. One woman was sexually molested by her biological mother and another by an older sister. Eight participants (25%) had been victimized by more than one individual. Five participants reported that, in addition to themselves, their siblings were also victims of sexual abuse.

Although several participants were unable to report how long the molestation continued, others were quite cognizant of this information. Longevity of the sexual victimization, among those who remembered, ranged from 2 years or less ($n = 5$), to 3 to 5 years ($n = 4$), to 6 to 8 years ($n = 4$), to 10 or more years ($n = 6$). Molestation began for eight (25%) of the women during infancy or toddlerhood (age three or earlier).

With regard to severity of abuse, participants described a variety of acts including penetration, fellatio, and fondling. Three of the women had been impregnated by their abusers: one at age 11 by her older brother, another at age 13 by her biological father, and the third at age 14 while in foster care.

Intervention. Participants were asked to describe whether or not they informed anyone about the abuse, and if so, to explain the individual's reactions. Ten of the 32 women who had been sexually victimized reported that they *had reported* the sexual abuse to another adult. Unfortunately, reporting the victimization did not result in the molestation ceasing. Seven of the ten were not believed by the individuals they turned to for support; instead, they were accused of lying. Adrian, for example, told her mother that her stepfather was sexually molesting her. Her mother beat Adrian for lying and then threatened to commit suicide. Not surprisingly, the molestation continued.

Although the three remaining women who exposed their perpetrators to other adults were not accused of lying, reactions from the people they turned to for assistance were just as disturbing. For example, Char told her mother that she and her siblings were being molested by their stepfather. Char explained her mother's reaction with the following: "My mother was real mean when I told her. She said, 'that's between you and him [stepfather], not me'." In a similar vein, Cammie told her mother that she and her sister were being sexually molested by an uncle. Her mother responded by saying, "Sometimes things happen and you just have to let them go." Cammie continued, "I was basically told to forget about it... I have a lot of resentment toward her [mother] now." Likewise, Sam and her three siblings were sexually molested by their uncle. Sam reported the abuse to her father; he did nothing. Sam explained, "Back in them days, we didn't talk about it [sexual abuse]. But that wasn't even my problem. My problem was that my dad allowed us to still stay there after it was going on–which is the reason I don't talk to my dad today. I don't have nothing to do with him."

Even after being exposed, the sexual perpetrators were not removed from the home, denied access to their victims, or punished for their transgressions. The victims, however, were further admonished when they sought help; they were accused of lying, told to "forget it," or physically beaten. Simply stated, they turned to others for protection, but protection was not forthcoming. In this sense then, they were symbolically abandoned and forced to fend for themselves.

Six other victims of childhood sexual abuse reported that they didn't reveal the molestation to anyone because others, including their mothers, did not *need to be told*–they were already aware of the abuse and simply in denial. When she was 14, for example, Jackie informed her grandmother that her stepfather was sexually molesting her. The grandmother then confronted Jackie's mother who responded, "No, it's not him, he's not doing that to my girls. It's them girls. They walk around here and they try to be all pretty. They lead him on." Regarding her mother, Jackie stated, "She was in denial. She was really in denial."

Angel described a particularly horrific situation. She was sexually abused by her biological father for nearly seven years; it began when she was only 6. At age 13 she was impregnated by him. During the third trimester of her pregnancy, was forced to have an abortion. However, in the state where she lived third-trimester abortions were illegal. Thus, Angel was taken, by her father, on a weekend trip to an adjacent state in order to legally terminate the pregnancy. When asked if her mother was aware of the sexual abuse, the pregnancy, or the abortion, Angel replied,

I find it hard to believe that she didn't know. I believe she didn't want to see it, but I think she knew. There were too many signs. My sister and I were scared to death to be alone with him [father]. She should have known something was wrong.

Later in the interview, Angel remarked:

It was easy for me to turn a trick because I could just take myself out– like with my dad. It was like I took myself out of the situation and just focused on something else and it was like I wasn't even there.

Whether or not other adults were aware of the childhood sexual molestation experienced by these women is irrelevant. What does matter is that the women themselves *believed* that others were aware but did *nothing* to intervene or offer protection. Importantly also is that sometimes the actions that followed once the sexual abuse was discovered implied that the girls themselves had been at fault. To illustrate, Bryn was sexually abused by a brother eight years her senior. It began when she was only nine and continued until she became impregnated by him at age 11. She explained,

I was young. I didn't know what was going on. He'd get drunk and then come and molest me... It got to the point where I didn't say nothing. But then when I got pregnant that's when everybody found out.

She explained her mother's reaction: "At first, she didn't believe me. But then the doctors and everything– they took him [brother] to jail and took me out of the home and put me in foster care, in a group home." She was also forced to have an abortion.

Finally, sixteen of the 32 women who had experienced childhood sexual abuse reported keeping the victimization to themselves; they didn't tell anyone and didn't think anyone knew it was occurring. Several of the sixteen reported that their silence was a strategy used to protect others. Two of the women were threatened by their perpetrators that if they disclosed the molestation, their younger sisters would be "next in line." Two others remained silent because they wanted *to protect their mothers*. Marti, for instance, was sexually molested for nearly five years by a family friend but ever told a soul because, "I knew my adopted mother would have killed the guy and I didn't want her in jail." And Kristina, who was sexually molested by her step father, also viewed her silence as a form of protection. "I remember thinking to myself that, if I told her [mother], I knew she would kill me, and I knew if she killed me she would go to prison. I didn't want to tell because I wanted to avoid that." As an adult, Kristina did tell her mother about the childhood sexual abuse and commented, "She [mother] was hurt, really hurt. I think in a way she was angry at me for telling her [about the sexual abuse]."

Regardless of whether or not the women reported their sexual victimization and were beaten, or whether they did not report it because there was "no one to tell," the results were the same: they were *symbolically* abandoned and forced to cope with the victimization on their own (see Figure 4.2). For some, like Char, the results were devastating. At the end of my interview with her, I asked Char to describe her feelings about her life experiences to which she responded:

> I'm not talking about my feelings deep down in my heart. I can tell people about this [the sexual abuse] and it doesn't hurt me anymore. It's like, a long time ago if I was to talk about it I would be crying and stuff. I don't even cry about it anymore...Feelings? I don't know— I don't even have them anymore.

Char learned to emotionally "shut-down" early in life; her statement demonstrates the tragic consequences of *mortification of self* described earlier[22-23].

Figure 4.2: Symbolic Abandonment: *Failure to Protect*

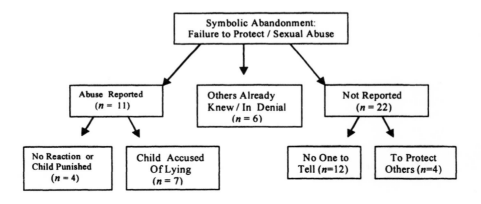

Symbolic Abandonment: Parental Unavailability

Addiction, Domestic Violence, and Mental Illness. Other participants described feeling abandoned because their early home environments were plagued by substance abuse and domestic violence; parental mental illness was also not uncommon. Chaotic family environment often resulted, with parents unable or unwilling to provide for their children's needs.

Roxanne, for one, explained that her mother was addicted to prescription drugs; she also spent a good deal of time in-and-out of jail for check forgery. Emotional expression, in her home, was dealt with in a unique way. Roxanne explained:

> If you had emotions that were nervous or anxious [mom would say] 'you need a pill, you needed a Valium... you needed another.' She started me on prescription pills at nine years old. She started me writing checks [forging] at fourteen.

Lacking adult guidance and supervision, Roxanne reported "running wild" much of the time. Out of sheer necessity, she developed self-reliance early in life.

Cammie's childhood was equally chaotic and she too was forced into self-care early-on. Cammie's mother was an intravenous drug addict and her father was an alcoholic. Cammie began using drugs at age 12, and continuously ran away from various foster families. She began trading sexual services for food, clothing, and shelter before her thirteenth birthday. She summarized: "My childhood was chaos. I raised myself." These examples are illustrative of the early family environments described by the women who participated in this investigation. Unfortunately, homes tainted with the presence of alcoholism and drug addiction were typically also the sites of domestic violence.

Six participants reported being physically abused in childhood by their parents or parental figures and nine witnessed severe and sustained physical violence within their homes. Shan's home environment was characterized by violence and brutality. She frequently witnessed her father beating her mother and explained that, although her mother was *physically* present, she was emotionally absent: "My mother? Well, she just fed us. She was just there. You know?" Landis was raised in a similarly violent home. She was often beaten by both her mother and an older brother. Her brother was " very violent toward me. I got pregnant and he was still beating me and my mom allowed it, it was like she didn't even care." Michelle's home was no different."My mom and dad were alcoholics and my dad liked to beat the fuck out of my mom all the time. And she liked to beat us [the children]." Jewel, who was raised by her aunt, likewise reported:

> Yeah, my auntie was nuts. She was hell on wheels. My auntie was like this: she was very religious, but she was also the type of person that was strong about putting that belt down on you. I got whooped and whooped and she'd be whooping me and saying 'I love you' and then 'Bam!' another whooping. I'd say: 'if you love me, stop hitting me'!

Finally, verbal degradation and emotional abuse also characterized relationships between participants and their parental caregivers. To illustrate, Rachel's older sister was accidently killed two weeks prior to Rachel's birth. Rachel explained how, when angry, her mother would ridicule her by saying, "'I wish you were the *one who died and your sister lived!*'" Rachel's experiences provide but one example of the cruelty inherent in many of the verbal assaults endured by these women during their early years of life. Participants often reported being told they were "no good for anything" or that they were worthless and "would never amount to shit." Figure 4.3 illustrates the various ways in which parental unavailability resulted in feelings of abandonment.

Figure 4.3: Symbolic Abandonment: *Parental Unavailability*

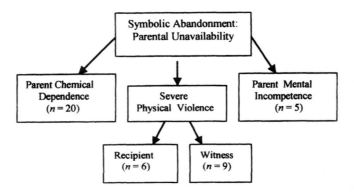

Runaway Behavior

Given the early family contexts described by participants, it was not surprising to learn that many ($n = 21$) had run away from home. They ran away from their biological homes, from their foster homes, and from detention centers. Importantly, they did not describe running *to anything*. Instead, they were attempting to escape and sought an end to the destructive environments in which they were embedded.

Michelle's situation is illustrative. Her mother committed suicide when she was eight; she began running away at the age of nine to escape her father's sexual advances. She ran because "there was no reason to stay." Similarly, Barb explained, "I hated my dad until I was 14. I had no use for a father. He used to hit my mom and stuff, then, at 13, I left home and basically have not been home since then." Barb spent the majority of her adolescent years on the streets or in various foster homes and detention facilities; she was legally emancipated at age 15. Kiley was also a runaway. She was sent to live with her paternal grandparents who were alcoholics when she was 11 and reported: "There was emotional abuse from my grandma because I resembled my mother so much and she despised my mom. So I began running away when I was 13."

Importantly, many of the women noted that their siblings were also exposed to various forms of abuse and brutality. Consequently, it was not unusual for the women to indicate that, during the formative years, their siblings were also in-and-out of foster placements, living with various relatives, or runaways. Monica, who was adopted at the age of three into a very strict, religious, rural family, clearly articulated how such dynamics operated in her foster home:

> He [adoptive father] had adopted six children and I was one of those six. There was me and another daughter. And she kept running away from home and he'd bring her back and she kept running away and he'd bring her back and she kept running away. And he would be especially good to her, so no one really knew why she kept running away, but she did. And after that I realized–I knew what was going on. I was next in line. Something was happening. I was given fair warning, long in advance and I didn't even know it.

Monica was sexually molested by her adoptive father for approximately three years, beginning when she was 12. Like her adoptive sister, she ran away from home many times and was always brought back.

Interestingly, although most participants remained in the same cities as their biological or foster families when they ran, five participants reported hitch-hiking cross-country with truck drivers. Landis left home for the first time at age15; she hitch-hiked from Texas to California because "I thought it [leaving] was the only answer to get away from the abuse." Another participant hitch-hiked from Montana to Houston at age 16 to be with a man she had only known for two weeks. And Tami, as noted in chapter one, left home at age 14 and never returned. Tami reported being "closest to the people I am *not* related to" [emphasis included].

Finally, it would be misleading not to present the unique situations of several other women who also were runaways. Their circumstances are different from the others because they ran away from foster families that were *not abusive*, and according to both, the families they ran from could have had *positive influences* in their lives. Autumn spent ten years in the foster care system due to abandonment and sexual abuse. Despite the early trauma, she described one of her foster mothers as "a very sweet, Christian lady–that's when I first learned who Jesus was. She taught me self respect, how to say 'thank you' and 'please' and learn manners as a child." She continued, "I thought I was robbed of my childhood– but just to a certain extent." At age 11, Autumn ran away from this foster home and when asked to explain why, she stated:

> I don't know. I seen other people runnin' away and I was like 'I want to run away too.' It was a secure, loving family. There was discipline, there was chores. I think that if I would have stayed in there, today I wouldn't be in the situation that I am in because that family was a strong family.

At least three individuals including Autumn, Cheyenne, and Sam, reported sabotaging potentially beneficial placements–those that provided positive role models, structure, discipline, and affection. One can only surmise that they were no longer able to trust the good intentions of others, given that the first decade of their lives had been marred by abuse and various forms of victimization. It is obviously impossible to determine how, or even if, their lives would have turned out differently had they stayed in those homes permanently. Optimism leads me to believe that intervention, as late as middle or late adolescence, can make a significant difference in the lives of even the most damaged souls.

Summary

Family environments poisoned by addiction and abuse often left scars, both physical and emotional, on the young girls raised therein. The physical presence of an adult caregiver accounted for little in the lives of these women if those caregivers failed, or refused, to adopt a protective and nurturing parental role. Symbolic abandonment was frequently described and feelings of insecurity, worthlessness, and self-loathing commonly resulted. Important also is that literal and symbolic abandonment are not mutually exclusive; experiencing one does not negate or alleviate the possibility of also experiencing the other. Some participants, including Sam, experienced both. Recall that she was told by her father that she and her siblings had been abandoned by their mother; they were informed that their own mother did not want them. Although the statement was untrue, Sam believed her father. She believed she had been *literally* abandoned by her mother. Furthermore, Sam was sexually abused during childhood by an uncle. Although her father was aware of the molestation, he failed to intervene to protect her. She was thus *symbolically* abandoned as well. She was not the only one who endured multiple forms of abandonment by parental caregivers.

Intergenerational Legacy of Abuse and Abandonment

What a child does not receive, [s]he can seldom later give.
                                                        – P.D. James

Family relationships often comprise our earliest and most enduring social connections. It is within the family that most of us learn how interpersonal relationships are "supposed" to function and how individuals are "supposed" to treat others, particularly loved ones. Given warmth and support, the development of interpersonal trust and feelings of belongingness and self-worth are set in motion; the mold is set for the formation of rewarding adult intimate relationships. If characterized by distrust, dishonesty, disrespect and abuse, however, healthy social and emotional development is severely challenged. What is learned in the family realm, for better or worse, often becomes a legacy transmitted to future generations.

It is important to note that research on the relationships between prostituted women and their own children is virtually non-existent. In fact, prostitution-involved women are rarely recognized as maternal figures or as even having children. Thus, when I began this study, many questions about the mother-child relationship remained. Some of my questions were *structural* in nature, focusing on timing of birth in relation to prostitution and on children's residence patterns, such as: Were the children conceived prior to or following their mothers' sex industry involvement? Do the children of female street-workers live with their mothers, and if so, are they exposed to or sheltered from the sex industry? Are they aware of their mother's prostitution involvement? Are clients brought to the home and, if so, are the children exposed to these individuals?

Other questions of mine were *process-oriented*. That is, I was also curious about the relationship patterns between the prostituted women and their children. Some of my questions involved the following: Were patterns of abuse and neglect passed from one generation to another? How did the women feel about being parents? Did they feel close to their children? Had they wanted children? Thus, as part of this investigation, I not only wanted to understand more about the developmental experiences of the prostituted women themselves, but also about the legacy of parenting and caregiving within this population.

In the remainder of this chapter, a cross-generational account of parent-child relationship patterns is presented. Understanding inter-generational family processes is critical because behaviors learned in one generation are characteristically, and often unconsciously, transmitted to future generations. Understanding such patterns may provide a means to access, and intervene on behalf of, vulnerable children and youth.

Childbearing in Relation to Sex-Work

As noted in chapter three, most ($n = 38$; 88%) of the women who participated in this investigation were mothers. The number of children of each varied from one to seven (with an average of 2.4 each). Thirteen participants (34%) reported having their first child at or before age seventeen[24]. To the extent possible, participants provided information about their families of procreation and their relationships with their children.

Twenty-two participants (58%) were involved in prostitution *before* they had children. Five participants reported becoming pregnant from clients (i.e., "johns"/ "tricks"), five others from men described as "pimps." For these women, pregnancy itself presented minimal disruption to their sex-work. They continued working the streets, picking up dates, and feeding their addictions to drugs and alcohol during their pregnancies. Ill effects of prenatal alcohol exposure and drug use are difficult to document. Many participants had not seen their children in years.

Sixteen others (42%) entered the sex industry *after* their children were born. Regarding her children and her prostitution involvement, Sam commented, "It [prostitution] was so much against my morals years ago. I wanted my kids raised so perfectly and then I just turned, it's like I gave up." Seven women reported that their children were aware of their prostitution activities, some had entertained clients in their homes while their children were present. Tori described how her oldest daughter knew about her prostitution; Tori would put her daughter in her room when she brought tricks home. She said, "Yeah, she [daughter] was around when I was hooking. She was only five or six, but old enough to know there were too many guys, too many strangers."

Five participants reported that their oldest daughters had followed in their footsteps and also become involved in street-level prostitution. Ironically, Georgette and Candace were both interviewed as part of this investigation while serving time in prison; Candace was Georgette's 26 year old daughter. Candace, like her mother, entered the sex industry when she was only 18. She felt "very close" to her mother and was asked how she felt watching her mother use drugs and engage in prostitution. Candace responded,

> It hurt me at first, it did. This is before I started using. You know, I used to be like 'mommy is queen.' She would be like 'Well, I'm addicted and I can't help it.' I understand where she was coming from, cuz' when I started using I was the same way.

When asked how her mother reacted upon learning that she was also using crack, Candace said, "She was hurt, but she was like, 'Well, I'm not going to knock you because I'm doing the same thing'." Later, when Georgette was interviewed and asked about her relationship with her daughter, she stated:

> We have a good relationship. She's a little messed up right now because she's off into crack too. She's been through five different treatments and completed 'em. But I guess she gets out and goes back to the old playground and her old type of friends and she's right back out there again [prostituting on the streets].

Likewise, Sam's daughter was also involved in prostitution. In fact, they worked the streets together. Sam commented on their relationship by saying: "I know there's a lot of resentment in her, she's just not letting it out." Aside from this obvious pattern of inter-generational prostitution involvement, data analyses revealed additional patterns of repeated cross-generational family dynamics.

Physical Separation

Of 105 total children born to these women, very few remained in the physical care of their mothers. In fact, when the women were interviewed, only six of them were living with their children. Two other women were pregnant at the time of the interviews and hoped to retain custody of their babies. Among the women who still lived with their children, it was unclear whether they would be able to retain custody of them or not. Two of the six reported continued prostitution involvement and drug abuse. And Barb, who had seven children, retained custody of the youngest child only, the other six lived with their biological fathers or had been adopted by non-family members. Children's removal typically resulted from their mother's voluntarily placing them in the care of relatives, or from relatives intervening and removing the children, rather than from state intervention. At the time of the interviews, 45 children were residing with their fathers or extended family members, compared to 30 others who had been legally removed and placed in foster homes. Six children were living in mental health or detention facilities and several others were incarcerated. Patti's 21-year-old son, for instance, was serving a prison sentence for second degree sexual abuse and arson.

Whether legal services were involved or not, the factors preceding child removal typically involved maternal alcoholism or chemical dependence, imprisonment, or unsafe living conditions due to domestic violence. These are the same factors which most often preceded the women's own out-of-home placement when they were children. It can only be hoped that the children's experiences in out-of-home care is exceedingly different from that of their mothers a generation earlier. Still, a comment by Chancey casts suspicion on such a notion. She reported "...continued failed placements with the children and their foster families. My boys were in some awful foster homes. That was really, really hard."

Alcoholism and Chemical Dependence
Seventeen of the 22 women who were involved in prostitution *before* the births of their children reported using drugs or drinking alcohol while pregnant–some during more than one pregnancy. Seven respondents had given birth to children with obvious symptoms of Fetal Alcohol Syndrome or who had been born addicted to crack cocaine. Alli, as one example, used crack cocaine during all four of her pregnancies; her second child was born three months premature. All four of her children had been legally removed from her care. When asked to describe her reactions to her children's removal, Alli stated, "I don't know if I felt anything. I was just blank. I had never been away from them. I was real fucked up–still am." She coped by sinking deeper into her addiction. "After they [the state] took them, I was doing it [crack] every day, all day. That was the only way to escape from the pain." Ellen's children were also placed in foster care due to her chemical dependence. She described falling into a deep depression and recalled,

> I could not cope with that. I could not deal with that. That's when I came into the drugs. That's when I started doing the downers and drinking and through all of that is when I lost my children. I couldn't deal with life, period. My children were taken from me and my parental rights were taken. I allowed my parental rights to be taken. I felt like I could not raise them properly so I allowed my parental rights to be taken.

Unlike Ellen, Trina voluntarily placed her children in the care of extended family due to her drug addiction and prostitution. She explained: "I love my kids and I never stopped thinking about my kids and I never stopped loving them. But I didn't know how to love me, so I couldn't show them the love they needed. And that wasn't fair to them."

Domestic Violence and Neglect

The majority of participants characterized their adult relationships with male partners and pimps as severely abusive. Subsequently, prior to their removal from their maternal homes, participants' children were frequently exposed to interpersonal violence and brutality. Sometimes, the children were the direct recipients of physical abuse, other times they were completed ignored and neglected. Char described her relationship with her second son, a "trick baby," with the following: "He wasn't [conceived from] no love. I whooped him the same way that my mama [would] whoop us. And that's wrong. I didn't know how to love him." Instead of beating her children, Marti simply left them. She " would rather be running the streets than taking care of them." She continued, "I don't like kids. My daughter cried too much and got on my nerves." And, regarding her second child, Marti noted: "I didn't hold him. I didn't want to touch him." Both children were put up for adoption.

Similarly, Angel was also involved in prostitution prior to the births of her two children. She admitted, "I just didn't want to be pregnant. Period. The whole thing was like an inconvenience to me." She continued: " I know that sounds really terrible." Finally, Sharia relayed a particularly chilling incident in which her four-year-old daughter was shot in the head by the baby's father who had been aiming the gun at Sharia. The girl spent 54 days in a hospital and was "just like a newborn baby all over again."

Sexual Victimization

In addition to the repeated patterns of physical abuse, neglect, and parental addiction, sexual victimization was also passed from families of origin to those of procreation. Seven of the women reported knowing that their children had been the victims of sexual molestation. Not only was Sharia's daughter sexually abused by her grandfather, but her grandson had also been sexually molested while in foster care. Likewise, Monica's daughter had been raped when she was only seven years old by a family friend. Another participant's daughter had been sexually molested by a client that this woman had brought to her home to entertained while her children were present.

It is important to note further that, due to her own incarceration, Angel's two children were living with her parents. Although Angel believed her children were safe, their well-being was arguably at risk. Recall that Angel was impregnated by her own father at age 13 and that the sexual molestation had gone unnoticed by her mother. These were the people with whom Angel had entrusted her children.

The actual number of children exposed to sexual molestation is likely much greater that what is reported here for two reasons. First, most participants had been separated from their children, some for years, and thus, had little information about them or the types of traumas that they had been exposed. Second, participants were *not* directly asked about their children's sexual victimization. Information presented about sexual victimization against their children was voluntarily introduced by the participants.

Attempts to Disrupt the Cycle

The *generational transmission principle,* a concept from family systems theory, holds that families tend to transmit their style of life to each new generation. Family life-styles are transmitted as we pass on to new generations ways of behaving, feeling, defining reality, and coping with intimacy and distance[25-26]. Most who participated in this investigation were well-aware that their activities had ultimately transferred a legacy of abuse and abandonment to their own children. Autumn is a perfect example. She knew her five-year-old daughter's childhood paralleled her own. Still, she remarked:

> I know I don't want her raised like I was. I don't want her going through what I have been through and I'm already putting her through it, leaving her, abandoning her, not giving her love. I just keep coming back [to prostitution] because of money.

Despite her not "wanting" her daughter raised as she had been, Autumn was doing little to disrupt the cycle. When asked to describe her future plans, for instance, she reported that, upon her release from prison, she would be moving to Las Vegas with her partner. She was going to leave her daughter with her mother (the daughter's grandmother). At first glance, this appears a potentially promising situation in that Autumn had little motivation to parent her child. Recall however, that Autumn had herself been abandoned at age five by her parents and had only recently been reunited with her mother after a 16 year separation. Understanding the generational transmission principle, as Autumn demonstrated in her statement above, is clearly not enough to disrupt the cycle.

Still, other participants were not only aware of the negative influences of their behavior on their children, they were actively attempting to make positive changes. Lettie was one of those women; she was unique in that she was married and her children had never been removed from her care. Yet, she recognized that she had not been *emotionally* available to her children and that they had suffered because of her prostitution and drug addiction. When asked how she had managed to maintain custody of her children, despite a long history of drug addiction and sex work, Lettie described how she had learned from her own mother to never leave her children.

My father was a stone alcoholic. My father beat my mother when I was like three-
years-old and we ran from him. We did not see him again until I was 13. When we
ran, she [mother] took every last one of us [seven children] and that is why, to this
day no matter where I go, I take my kids.

Lettie's refusal to leave her children based on her own mother's actions, in another
example of inter-generational transmission.

Amy was also attempting to break the cycle of family dysfunction. As noted in
chapter one, Amy was awaiting the return of her children who had spent the
previous year in foster care. In order for her parental rights to be fully re-instated,
she was required to make drastic changes in her life. Due to state-ordered mandates,
Amy entered and completed drug rehabilitation, left the streets, and obtained full-
time employment and stable housing. Her children were scheduled home within two
weeks of our interview. Interestingly, both Lettie and Amy believed God's power
and guidance was key to their progress.

Intergenerational Patterns and Family Legacies:
Final Thoughts and Theoretical Insights

Guiding this investigation was the assumption that few, if any, street-level
prostituted women intentionally or purposely organize their lives to work in the sex
industry. It was further assumed that critical life-events, and more importantly,
interpretation of those events, shape and mold individual experiences in such a way
as to allow for the option of sex-work to become a reality for some. Data were thus
examined from a developmental and subjective point of view, emphasizing family
dynamics and interpersonal relationships.

Abandonment, including physical and emotional absence, was the overarching
theme characterizing participants' early family lives. This theme was mirrored in
the lives of their children. As evidenced here, family legacies can be riddled with
sexual abuse, exploitation, domestic violence, and emotional terrorism. Often, and
without intention, those behaviors are transmitted to future generations. Thus,
children become the victims of long-standing intergenerational dysfunction. It is
important to note that such cycles may continue indefinitely.

Parental absence presents a risk factor to optimal development and well-being.
However, developing a strong emotional bond, with even one significant adult
caregiver, may significantly buffer the potentially damaging impacts of family
dysfunction[27]. Unfortunately, the overwhelming majority of participants were
shuffled from one abusive environment to another. Many were forced into self-care
within the first decade of life. Similar patterns were being repeated in the next
generation.

Generational processes, according to Burr and colleagues "have enormous
influence [in how] we think, feel, relate to others. They influence our aspirations,

our values, our struggles, and our resourcefulness"[28]. The family context provides the foundation and cornerstone for individual well-being, which directly and indirectly influence the well-being of future generations. When family relationship patterns are destructive, future generations are challenged to overcome enormous obstacles if they are to achieve optimal developmental outcomes.

Malevolent parenting is often viewed as an indication of *individual pathology*, rather than a consequence of oppressive environmental contexts[29-30] or intergenerational family malaise. However, we learn how to treat others, and thus, such behavior can be unlearned. To change embedded family patterns, one must make a conscious and concerted effort to change one's behaviors. One must become, in essence, a transitional character. Family systems theory describes transitional characters as those individuals who liberate future generations from destructive family patterns (e.g., abandonment)[31-32]. People who refuse to transmit dysfunctional patterns (e.g., abuse, alcoholism, drug addiction) to future generations, even though they themselves were exposed to such influences, are transitional characters.

Becoming a transitional character requires not only a desire to do so, but also the ability to develop new family patterns and ways of relating. This is not easily accomplished. Without a sense of personal insight, self-efficacy, and knowledge of and access to appropriate support resources, the process is not only difficult, but very likely impossible. Parental abandonment represents, simultaneously, a *cause* and a *consequence* of deeply ingrained family dysfunction. The majority of participants described wanting to change their lives, to leave the streets, and to live within conventional societal boundaries. They described wanting, in other words, to become transitional characters. Unfortunately, they had few, if any, role models to emulate.

Notes

1. Gerald Corey, *Theory and Practice of Counseling and Psychotherapy,"* 6th ed. (Pacific Grove, CA: Brooks/Cole, 2000).

2. Alfred Adler, *"The Progress of Mankind,"* in *Essays in individual psychology,* ed. Kurt A. Adler and Danica Deutsch (New York: Grove Press, 1959), 3-8.

3. Diane E. H. Russell, "The Incidence and Prevalence of Intrafamilial and Extrafamilial Sexual Abuse on Female Children," In *Handbook on Sexual Abuse of Children,* ed. Lenore E. Auerbach Walker (New York: Springer, 1988), 19-36.

4. Mimi H. Silbert and Ayala M. Pines, "Early Sexual Exploitation as an Influence in Prostitution," *Social Work* 28 (1983): 285-89.

5. Chris Bagley and Loretta Young, "Juvenile Prostitution and Child Sexual Abuse: A Controlled Study," *Canadian Journal of Community Mental Health* 6 (1987): 5-26.

6. Jennifer James and Jane Meyerding, "Early Sexual Experience and Prostitution," *American Journal of Psychiatry* 134 (1977): 1381-85.

7. Eloise Dunlap, Andrew Golub, Bruce D. Johnson, and Damaris Wesley, "Intergenerational Transmission of Conduct Norms for Drugs, Sexual Exploitation and Violence: A Case Study," *British Journal of Criminology* 42, (2002): 1-20.

8. Eleanor M. Miller, *Street Women* (Philadelphia: Temple University Press, 1986).

9. Magnus J. Seng, "Child Sexual Abuse and Adolescent Prostitution: A Comparative Analysis," *Adolescence* 24 (1989): 665-75.

10. Ronald L. Simons and Les B. Whitbeck, "Sexual Abuse as a Precursor to Prostitution and Victimization," *Journal of Family Issues* 12 (1991): 361-79.

11. Susan M. Nandon, Catherine Koverola, and Eduard H. Schludermann, "Antecedents To Prostitution: Childhood Victimization,"*Journal of Interpersonal Violence* 13 (1998): 206-21.

12. Kathleen Potter, Judy Martin, and Sarah Romans, "Early Developmental Experiences of Female Sex Workers," *Australian & New Zealand Journal of Psychiatry* 33 (1999): 935-40.

13. John J. Potterat, Lynanne Phillips, Richard B. Rothenberg, and William W. Darrow, "On Becoming a Prostitute: An Exploratory Case-Comparison Study," *Journal of Sex Research* 20, (1985): 329-336.

14. Potterat and others, "On Becoming a Prostitute," 329.

15. Nandon and others, "Antecedents," 207.

16. Bonnie Bullough and Vern L. Bullough, "Female Prostitution: Current Research and Changing Interpretations," *Annual Review of Sex Research* 7 (1996): 158-80.

17. Eugene R. Oetting, and Joseph Donnermeyer, "Primary Socialization Theory: The Etiology of Drug Use and Deviance," *Substance Use Misuse* 33 (1998): 995-1026.

18. Bullough and Bullough, "Female Prostitution," 158-80.

19. Maria Sauzier, Patricia Salt, and Roberta Calhoun, "The Effects of Child Sexual Abuse," in *Child Sexual Abuse: The Initial Effects*, eds. Beverly Gomez-Schwartz, Jonathon M. Horowitz, and Albert P. Cardarelli (Newbury Park, CA: Sage, 1990), 75-108.

20. David Finkelhor, "The Trauma of Child Sexual Abuse: Two Models," *Journal of Interpersonal Violence* 2 (1987): 348-66.

21. A. Nicholas Groth, "Guidelines for the Assessment and Management of the Offender," in *Sexual Assault of Children and Adolescents*, eds. Ann W. Burgess, A. Nicholas Groth, Lynda L. Holmstrom, and Suzanne M. Sgroi (Lexington, MA: Lexington, 1978), 64-98.

22. James and Meyerding,"Early Sexual Experience," 1381-1385.

23. Miller, *"Street Women,"* 1986.

24. Participants were not asked if they (or their siblings) were products of teenage pregnancies, thus, familial patterns of teenage childbearing is not known.

25. Wesley R. Burr, Randal D. Day, and Kathleen S. Bahr, *Family Science* (Pacific Grove, CA: Brooks/Cole Publishing Company, 1993).

26. Gail G. Whitchurch and Larry L. Constantine, "Systems Theory," in *Sourcebook of Family Theories and Methods: A Contextual Approach*, eds. Pauline G. Boss, William J. Doherty, Ralph LaRossa, Walter R. Schumm, and Suzanne K. Steinmetz (New York: Plenum Press, 1993), 325-352.

27. Michael Rutter, "Protective Factors in Children's Responses to Stress and Disadvantage," in *Primary Prevention of Psychopathology*, eds. Martha W. Kent and Jon E. Rolf (Hanover, NH: University Press of New England, 1979), 49-74.

28. Burr and others, *Family Science*, 64.

29. Sharon Hays, *The Cultural Contradictions of Motherhood* (New Haven, CT: Yale University Press, 1996).

30. Evelyn N. Glenn, "Social Constructions of Mothering: A Thematic Overview," in *Mothering: Ideology, Experience, and Agency*, ed. Evelyn N. Glenn, Grace Chang, and Linda R. Forcey (New York: Routledge, 1994), 1-29.

31. Carlfred B. Broderick, *Understanding Family Process* (Newbury Park, CA: Sage, 1993).

32. Carlfred B. Broderick, "Family Process Theory," In *Fashioning Family Theory*, ed. Jetse Sprey (Newbury Park, CA: Sage, 1990), 171-206.

Chapter Five

Life in the "Game"

Never bear more than one kind of trouble at a time.
Some people bear three: all they have ever had,
all they have now, and all they expect to have.
                                    – Edward Everett Hale

Rich, detailed information about the "game," as experienced and perceived by those intimately familiar with the streets, remains largely undocumented. Recognizing prostitution-involved women as embedded within unique social and environmental contexts is vital for developing programmatic intervention for effectively meeting their needs through service delivery. Greater understanding may also help to diminish deeply entrenched stereotypes about prostituted women and to help debunk the "pretty woman" myth.

According to ecological systems theory, to understand developmental trajectories, one must examine not only the person, but the entire ecological context in which she exists. The sub-culture of the street-level sex industry is comprised of unique people, including pimps, clients, and other sex workers, and a variant economic structure fragmented together through illicit drug use, chemical dependence, and street hustlers. Violence is a pervasive by-product. Prostituted women must learn how to play the "game" of the streets if they are to survive; strategies for doing so provide clues into how these women traverse the idiosyncratic landscape of the street-level sex trade.

Two issues central to understanding the complex dynamics of street-level prostitution are discussed in this chapter. These include: (1) economic need and chemical dependence, and (2) the interpersonal relationships between street-level prostituted women and the primary "players" comprising their social worlds. This information provides a framework for understanding the unique sub-culture of street-level prostitution and a reference point for deciphering factors which motivate entry into and continued involvement within the "game."

Review of Current Literature

Although a great deal has been written about economic need and chemical
dependence, surprisingly little attention has been devoted to studying the social
milieu of street-level prostitution. Information on the clientele of female street-
workers, for instance, is visibly absent in the published literature. As noted by
Bullough and Bullough[1], "Missing from almost all of the reported studies of
prostitution is an examination of the patrons." This statement could have easily been
said about pimps too, as this population remains largely a mystery. Finally,
information documenting the nature of relationships between prostituted women is
similarly nonexistent. One could speculate that relationships between prostituted
women relationships are, on the one hand, highly competitive and destructive, as
each attempts to procure more and better paying clientele. However, it is equally
plausible that these relationships are characterized by comradery and kinship, given
that they share a common culture and physical space. Importantly, if supportive
relationships exist among these women, they may provide protection and a buffer
against physical and psychological harm. Thus, in addition to examination of
economic structures and drug abuse as central components of the sex industry, my
research sought to also uncover the hidden social networks and support systems of
women prostituted on the streets.

Economic Deprivation and Chemical Dependence

Economic vulnerability, some argue, forces women into the streets. Hardman[2]
reports, "Because of their restricted access to financial and material resources, some
women may resort to prostitution as a resistance or response to poverty."
Prostitution, in other words, may represent an active coping strategy in the face of
privation. Hardman is not alone in her beliefs. Delacoste and Alexander[3] contend
that, lacking viable alternatives, female sex work remains consistently available.

The demand for prostituted women is staggering. However, economic
deprivation, in and of itself, is an inadequate explanation for prostitution entry
because it fails to distinguish between impoverished women who choose prostitution as a source of income, from those who do not. Simply stated, indigence touches
the lives of countless women, the majority of whom never engage in any form of sex
work. Moreover, although some prostitution venues offer the potential for economic
abundance (e.g., high-class call girls), such is not the case with *street-level* sex
work. A growing body of evidence suggests that street-level sex work is not a viable
pursuit if economic gain is the ultimate goal[4].

By far, the greatest amount of theorizing, studying, and writing on the subject
of street-level prostitution has centered around issues of drug use and chemical
dependence. The connection between street-level prostitution and drug use is
unquestionable. Drug addiction has been examined as not only a precursor to

prostitution entry, but also as a primary factor motivating continued involvement. It is estimated that anywhere from one-fifth to one-half of female prostitutes use drugs regularly, although higher percentages have also been reported[5-6]. Crack cocaine, specifically, and its use by street-level prostitutes, has garnered much recent attention.

Feucht[7] examined the complex interplay between illicit drug use and street-level prostitution. He concluded that, for many streetwalkers, prostitution constitutes a means only of securing funds necessary to feed an established drug addiction. Feucht further notes that prostitutes are often couriers for drug buyers and sellers. As partial or full payment for their courier services, sex workers may be given (or take) a portion of the dope for personal use. Finally, crack dealers and prostitutes often have overlapping markets and therefore, common interests necessitate frequent interaction. Thus, it would difficult, if not impossible, to *not* have a connection (either directly or indirectly) to the illicit drug sub-culture if one engaged in street-level prostitution. However, recognition of a powerful association between chemical use and street-level prostitution does not imply causality.

Drug Use in Relation to Prostitution Entry

Understanding the *timing* of drug use and subsequent abuse, in relation to prostitution entry, may provide significant avenues for creating effective and intervention on behalf of vulnerable female populations. For instance, if chemical dependence typically *precedes* prostitution entry, then services aimed at preventing a downward spiral from drug use→to drug abuse→to street work could be targeted to "at risk" female populations. Conversely, if chemical dependence is a *response* to sex industry involvement, interventions should focus on reducing the violence in prostitution and the stigma women face that leads one to self-medicate and become addicted post-entry.

In a recent investigation, Potterat and colleagues[8] examined the sequence and timing of prostitution entry in relation to drug abuse among prostitution-involved women and a comparable control group. Three primary conclusions were drawn. First, they found that drug use was more common among the prostitution-involved women. Second, drug use preceded sexual activity in both groups,. And third, injecting drug use preceded prostitution. Moreover, the majority (66%) of the prostitution-involved women reported using drugs *prior* to entering the sex industry. An equal number of women reported that drug use and prostitution were initiated concurrently and that drug use followed prostitution entry.

Yet, contradictory evidence also exists. Graham and Wish[9] examined female drug use in relation to deviant behavior, including prostitution, among 164 female arrestees. Sixty percent tested positive for cocaine and 50 percent had a history of prostitution. Interestingly however, these researchers found that drug use/abuse did not always precede prostitution involvement. They contend, instead, that drug use may evolve among street-level prostituted women as a coping strategy and way of reducing inhibitions.

Drug Abuse and Economic Fall-Out

Regardless of whether prostitution entry is addiction motivated or not, the entire culture of street-level sex work has been dramatically altered due to the inundation of crack cocaine. The pervasive presence of crack cocaine on the streets has been directly and indirectly related to the diminishing price of street-level sexual services[10]. Maher[11] reports that women involved in prostitution *prior* to using crack cocaine are less likely to accept crack as payment for sexual services. Yet the "new girls," whose street-level prostitution entry is typically addiction-motivated, are increasingly willing to provide cheaper and more degrading, sexual services in exchange for the drug.

As a consequently of these economic changes, women whose prostitution involvement is financially (not chemically) motivated are, by implication, also impacted. This is not a new phenomenon. Heroin "bag brides" engaged in similar behavior[12]; the difference rests in the sheer magnitude with which the sexual services in direct exchange for drugs has expanded among female crack addicts[13]. Maher[14] argues that, because of the inundation of crack cocaine, the entire culture and context of street-level prostitution has been altered, impacting even those women whose prostitution involvement is not addiction-motivated. Not only have the tricks become cheaper and the violence more pronounced, but street-workers are increasingly viewed as carriers of HIV and as morally contaminated[15].

Crack Cocaine

Heroin is a narcotic. It is a pain killer that produces feelings of warmth, satisfaction, and contentment. In the United States, heroin was illicitly used more than any other drug, except for marijuana, until about 20 years ago[16]. Its popularity was rapidly replaced by cocaine. Crack or "rock" is a special type of freebased cocaine. Freebasing is a method of reducing impurities in cocaine and preparing it for smoking. Freebasing produces a drug that is more powerful than the typical powder-form cocaine[17].

Crack first appeared on the streets in massive quantity between 1985 and 1986[18]. Unlike heroin, crack is a stimulant that is often smoked. When the fumes are absorbed into the lungs, they act rapidly, reaching the brain in about eight to ten seconds. Immediately after inhalation, the nervous system is stimulated by the release of dopamine. The result is an intense rush or high, which usually lasts about three to five minutes[19]. The high is followed by a powerful state of depression which may persist anywhere from ten to 40 minutes–sometimes longer.

Because of the abrupt and intense release of dopamine, the risk of addiction to smoked crack is tremendous[20]; smoked crack is considered by users to be more enjoyable than injected cocaine[21]. Importantly, the marketing of crack and powder-form cocaine is typically also associated with criminal activity. In fact, a report from 1995 indicated than nearly one in three homicide victims in New York City had cocaine, or a derivative of it, in their systems[22].

Summary

Culture is defined as the shared values, beliefs, expectations, world-views, symbols, and appropriate behaviors of a group that provide its members with norms or morés, and rules for social living[23]. The entire milieu of street-level prostitution comprises a sub-culture, or a microcosm of the encompassing society, which is unique unto itself. Within this sub-culture, there are certainly shared values and beliefs with common expectations of appropriate behavior for social living. It is surprising then, with the recent interest in street-level prostitution, that more is not known about this sub-culture. The majority of knowledge that does exist centers around drug use and abuse, but this is only one component of the ecological context comprising street-level sex work. This chapter describes the sub-culture of street-level prostitution as lived and understood by the women involved in this study. Because of my theoretical orientation and personal belief in the significance of interpersonal relations, social relationships take center stage.

The Sub-Culture of Street-Level Sex Work

Each of the 43 women who participated in this investigation were, at one point or another, engaged in street-level prostitution. For some, their only familiarity with the sex industry came from street work. Others however, reported a range of experiences and had worked in a variety of prostitution-related venues. In addition to working the streets, six women had prostituted at truck stops, seven had worked for escort services, two others ran their own escort services, four participated in prostitution as part of their work in massage parlors, and four had engaged in prostitution as an extension of their nude or semi-nude exotic dancing. One additional participant worked in a residence that specialized in sado-masochistic (S & M) sexual services and two had made pornographic videos.

Interestingly, the *type* of prostitution in which the women engaged appears largely based on chemical use and dependence. Stated differently, the women described traveling a variety of routes which culminated in their prostituting themselves on the streets; use and abuse of drugs played a pivotal role in those developmental trajectories.

Women whose initial entry into prostitution was motivated by drug addiction often described a pattern of behavior that began with drug use, and which was quickly followed by drug dependence. To support their ever oppressive addictions, they typically reported selling all of their possessions, engaging in illegal activity (e.g., theft, forgery) and then, as a last resort, turning to the streets. Moreover, as their addictions surged, so did their willingness to accept less money or drugs in exchange for sexual services performed. Figure 5.1, below, illustrates the *developmental trajectories* which culminated in street prostitution among women motived to enter due to drug-addiction.

Figure 5.1. Addiction-Motivated Prostitution

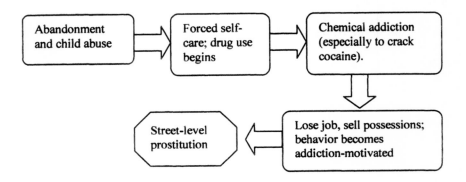

However, another path to street-level prostitution was also described—one not initially motivated by drug addition. Specifically, a large number of participants reported that their initial entry into prostitution was *financially* motivated and thus, not driven by drug dependence. Sex work among these women typically began through involvement with Sugar Daddies, performing in strip clubs, or working through escort services. Money earned from sex work had a functional, survival purpose: paying rent, buying food, and/or supporting dependents. Some reported being "addicted" to the money they earned through such activities. Given extended time and prolonged exposure to the sex industry, however, a pattern emerged in which drug use began or became more severe. The longer these women engaged in sex work, the more self-critical they became. Eventually, self-identification as a "prostitute" ensued, thus allowing these women to psychologically accept the label, resulting in more daring, and admittedly lower status, forms of prostitution (i.e., street-level). In effect, those who initially turned to prostitution out of financial need described a slow, downward spiral, culminating in the lowest form of prostitution. Figure 5.2 illustrates this developmental process. It is important to point out that, although drug use and abuse played a central role in women's street-level sex work, the original factors which motivated prostitution *entry* were entirely different. A detailed account of both "pathways" to street-level prostitution are described below.

Figure 5.2: Economically-Motivated Prostitution

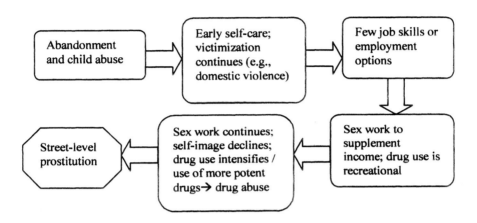

Chemical Dependence and Economic Structures

Forty-one participants (95%) reported that they had been, or continued to be, dependent on illicit drugs. The majority of these women (41%) reported addiction to crack cocaine. Another 29% reported addiction to crack cocaine *in addition* to other substances. Aside from crack, drugs of choice also included: heroin, marijuana, amphetamines, and prescription medication, especially Ritalin.

Following the work of Potterat and colleagues[24] and Graham and Wish[25] as described earlier, I was curious as to the sequence and timing of sex work entry in relation to the onset of chemical use and abuse. Sixteen of the 43 women who were interviewed reported entering street-level prostitution to support a pre-established addiction. However, 17 other women reported engaging in prostitution *before* becoming drug addicted. For these 17 women, drug dependence evolved following prolonged exposure to the sex industry. It is noteworthy also that eight additional women reported that entry into prostitution and chemical dependence occurred simultaneously.

Addiction-Motivated Prostitution
Addiction to crack, it was explained, does not occur "progressively." Most reported knowing they were hooked to the drug after either the first or second use. "One hit is too many, one thousand hits are not enough," a phrase repeated by several participants, clearly articulates the immediate potential for addiction to this powerful stimulant as it produces something akin to "...an orgasm of the brain."

Rachel was one of the 16 women who entered prostitution to support a pre-existing drug addiction. She was 41-years-old when I interviewed her in prison. Rachel was raised in an upper-middle-class family. She attended modeling school, married in her late 20s, had two children, and worked in her family's lucrative used-car business. Certainly, Rachel's past defies prediction that she would one day be trading sexual services on the streets. At age 33 however, a friend introduced her to crack; she had no idea what it was. She explained how crack "didn't do anything for me" on that first try. Two weeks later, she tried it again. That time "it got me real good." She reported the financial impact of being a crack addict: "I used to bitch about spending $40 a week on a bag of pot and now, shit, going through $500 in one day on crack doesn't even phase me." Before long, Rachel was using crack cocaine on a daily basis. She spent nearly $60,000.00 on the drug over a six-month period of time. Then, to finance her growing addiction, she sold her jewelry, furniture, and even her car– it was a brand new Jaguar. Two years after her first experimentation with crack cocaine, Rachel was divorced, had lost custody of her children, had sold all material possessions, and was involved in the street-level sex trade. Crack, she admitted, "is pure evil."

Erica's involvement in prostitution was also addiction motivated; although circumstances culminating in her sex work differed considerably from those described by Rachel. Erica was raised by a drug -addicted mother. She tried cocaine for the first time at age 15. She was in her own home and in the company of her mother. She dropped out of school in the tenth grade and, by age 17, was dating various dope dealers. She traded sex to support an aggressive addiction to crack cocaine. It was at that point in her life that "formal entry" into prostitution began, before then, she explained: "It was prostitution– but I wasn't smart enough to get paid for it. I was basically giving it away to get high." She continued, "I was 23 before I realized that I could actually get into a car, get cash in my hand and get back out and have my own money."

Erica never used condoms when she prostituted because "The only thing that was important to me was the addiction." She was not shy in admitting that she regularly traded sexual services in direct exchange for crack cocaine: "Yeah, I would suck somebody's dick for $20 worth of crack if I'm jonesing." An interesting contradiction emerged however. On the one hand, she readily admitted to engaging in prostitution activities and to being a "strawberry" (i.e., trading sexual services for drugs). However, she refused to label herself as a "prostitute" and stated, "I wouldn't do it [sex work] when I'm not addicted. That is it. I am not a prostitute."

Financially-Motivated Prostitution

It is important to note that drug addiction was not the primary motivation for initial sex work entry among the majority of participants. Most first exchanged sexual services due to financial need. Eight of the 43 women, in particular, reported engaging in "survival sex" (i.e., exchange of sexual service for material possessions) as youth while on the run. Prostitution, it was noted, "is quick and easy money. Tax free." The risk however, it that "...it could cost you your life, and it does cost you your self-worth, that's just automatic."

Although many women reported initiating sex work out of financial necessity, the connection between drug use and street-level prostitution cannot be ignored. Eighty-nine percent of those women whose prostitution entry was economically motivated reported becoming regular drug users as their time in prostitution continued. To put it plainly: only two women, out of the entire sample of 43, *never* developed a drug addiction.

Still, in contrast to the research reports of Potterat and his colleagues[26], most of the women who participated in this investigation indicated that prostitution preceded drug addiction. Kendra provides a case in point. By age 20 she had two children and was living in the basement of her mother's rented house. When asked to describe how she became involved in prostitution, she explained that, after "aging out" of the foster care system she:

> ...started going back over to my mom's house. She was having guys come over and she would be like, 'Well, they want to do this and that. And they're going to give you some money. Or, you don't have to do nothing and I will just have your brother go in and take his [the man's] wallet.' So I just started to do stuff like that, and then it just became the easy way of getting money.

Later, after moving out of her mother's residence, the process continued: "If I needed something, like my rent needed to be paid, I would have a man come over and I would proposition him." There was no short supply of willing men ready to assist. Kendra would typically "proposition" men in the most benign of places, such as "Shopko, while shopping, or anywhere like that. And somebody says 'What's your number– blah, blah, blah, and this and that'." From there, conversation would ultimately focus onto how they could best meet each other's needs.

Kendra never dated men younger than she was, most were at least 20 years her senior. In fact, at age 22 Kendra had a child with a man who was 63. These types of arrangements continued, Kendra reported, for approximately six years. She eventually became friendly with the "dope men" and often allowed them to borrow her car for drug runs. In turn, they gave her crack. The drug became more important than paying the bills and all income generated from prostitution was used to fund her addiction. It was then that Kendra slid into street-level sex work.

Similarly, Jenna initially entered prostitution to earn hard cash for necessary items. After being kicked out of her foster home at age 16, she and her infant daughter moved in with her 22-year-old boyfriend. As a high-school drop out, Jenna's employment options were limited to fast-food service. Her boyfriend sold drugs. She reported being "okay with that. His money paid rent, mine paid for everything else." She avoided involvement in his illegal affairs and explained, "We never had that much [drug] traffic [at home]. He would leave and go to the street to do his thing." Jenna was 18 when she first engaged in sex-for-money exchanges. The money was very attractive to an 18-year-old mother earning minimum wage. Her boyfriend, she explained, never found out. She described her introduction to prostitution:

> There was an older guy that lived next door to the apartments we stayed in. He
> would always give me the eye and one day he said 'come over to my house' and
> I came over there and he had $50 there. He said, 'Just relax' and I did. I did not
> think it was that bad. And maybe a month or two later, I'd do it again.

Her relationship with the neighbor continued on and off for over a year. The man,
Jenna guessed, was about 50-years-old.

Jenna's addiction to crack cocaine began innocuously enough; her boyfriend
concealed crack in one of her cigarettes, knowing she would smoke it. She recalled:
"It was great, it was wonderful, beautiful. I wanted more. When they say the first
time gets you, it does!" Within a few months she was voluntarily smoking crack in
a pipe "and was stuck ever since." She managed to maintain a job, with supplemen-
tal income from "dates." Interestingly, Jenna did not become involved in street
prostitution until she was 28-years-old; she was only 29 at the time of our interview.
When asked to describe her attitude about street-level sex work, she replied, "[It is]
part of survival, part of doing what is necessary."

Sharia, like Kendra and Jenna, initially entered prostitution to make money.
After witnessing her mother's slow death from cancer and her father's immediate
remarriage, Sharia ran away at 15 and never returned. By 16, she was a mother
herself and explained, "I did not have very much of a teenage life. And by the time
I turned 17, I was pregnant with the second child." She married the father of her
second baby and together they had two more children. The man was malicious and
beat Sharia regularly. Leaving him, however, was not an option. "It was the end of
the 1960s, wasn't many shelters around for abused women–and so I basically took
it." Sharia's experiences were not unlike those of other victims of domestic
violence. She explained:

> I used to leave him–back and forth, back and forth– and he would talk me into
> coming back. And my self confidence was down real low. He used to say 'You're
> not a beauty queen. Who wants a woman with four kids'?

After enduring a decade of physical, verbal, and emotional assaults, Sharia obtained
the courage to leave him for good.

Prostitution began when she was 25-years-old because "I didn't want my kids
to grow up without anything." Earlier in chapter four, I described the work of
Potterat and colleagues[27] who report that *exposure* to significant others involved in
the prostitution sub-culture may entice, and even encourage, entry. Sharia's
situation clearly illustrates this concept. She was indoctrinated into prostitution by
her own kin; her older sisters showed her the ropes.

I started hanging out with my older sisters and going out to bars and meeting guys. And I had a high way of living. I wanted to have the best of things for me and my children. And I had a good job at Blue Cross and Blue Shield, but I still wanted more.

She recalled her attitude at the time:

It was like, 'I am not going to deal with any man unless he can help me with my kids.' So it basically started off that way, but then it gradually started adding up to where if he wants me sexually he is going to have to pay–he is going to have to pay first. So it started in that way, not really going out and soliciting. And if guys called I let them know: 'Hey- I got four kids and I need some help.'

Perhaps as a result of the verbal degradation suffered during her marriage, Sharia described receiving *psychological rewards* from the sexual exchanges, not just monetary payment.

I think that basically in my heart I had this feeling from the abuse that if they [men] wanted me they are going to have to pay for it. They are *gonna have to earn me* [and] this went on for a few years.

Unlike Jenna and Kendra, Sharia did not go to the streets not because of drugs, but because of a man. She described him as "was street smart, [but] I wasn't. He started teaching me about being street smart. As for soliciting prostitution– he was showing me easy money."

However, similar to the others, Sharia began abusing drugs, and then became chemically dependent. Her first addiction was to prescription medication. This was followed by alcoholism and a rapid downward spiral ensued:

When I started using [crack] at the age of 35, my kids were gone [grown up]. I had made my kids my life and when they moved away... I guess I'm a care taker and I didn't have any one else to take care of and I started feeling a lot of that pain. I had too much time on my hands and I felt like I needed something stronger to medicate. I got introduced to crack through one of my sisters.

Within two years, she was "using 24-7" and "totally addicted." She continued using, heavily until she was sent to prison for possession of a controlled substance. Crack had been a driving force in her life for over 13 years. Speaking with authority, Sharia noted, "You just don't use drugs that length of time, go down hill and hit bottom for no reason. You have to be hiding something, killing the pain."

The life stories of many of the other women interviewed as part of this investigation mirrored those of Jenna, Kendra, and Sharia. Drug use was frequently described as an experimental or recreational pastime in the beginning. However, with time and extended exposure to the sex industry, drug of choice became more potent and use more frequent. Crack cocaine became a salvation for many, in that it brought relief from deeply buried pain. But it carried an exorbitant price tag.

Sam, whose journey to the streets paralleled that of Sharia, provided an astute, insider's perspective on the complex interplay between drug addiction and prostitution:

> I think it *is* possible to prostitute without drugs if you've never done them before. Once you get started on the drugs though, I think it's *impossible* to go back to just prostituting. It would take a real strong person to prostitute without drugs, if they've done them before. [emphasis added]

Crack's Influence on the Sub-Culture of Street-Level Prostitution
Earlier, I noted the work of Maher[28] who described the pervasive impact of crack cocaine on the sub-culture of street-level prostitution. Maher's work is not an anomaly. The women who participated in this investigation described experiences similar to the women in Maher's study. Specifically, participants reported that the widespread use and easy access to crack cocaine had significantly altered the street-prostitution sub-culture for all involved, not just the addicts or the street-hustlers. Three factors contributed to the churned and contaminated environment.

First, it was explained that crack-addicted prostitutes would do "anything at any cost" to satiate their addictions. As a consequence, the going rate for sexual services had plummeted; it was difficult making money working the streets. Cheyenne illustrated with the following: "I thought it [prostitution] was disgusting, but it was cool because it was quick money... I never did anything for $20 like others will do." And then continued, "I mean– prostitution is degrading enough, but if you're gonna do it get paid for it." Marlee felt similarly and described a particularly memorable situation. She had taken a break from prostitution for about a year and then returned to the streets hoping to make some fast cash. She immediately ran into a former client. In negotiating a price, he suggested $20 for fellatio, a service she had previously performed for him for $200. Astonished by his suggestion, she told him, "You are crazy! You cannot even *look at me* for $20!" Needless to say, her re-entry into the sex industry was short-lived. Talisha, too, felt the economic strain from the changing street sub-culture. She reported, "With tricks, it is just not the same. They are not paying what they used to. Used to get tricks to pay $50 or $100. Now, they want to give you $5 and $10."

Second, it has been argued that prostitution, generally speaking, is hierarchically organized and that street-level prostitution is the lowest, most degrading form of sex work. Interestingly, as part of my investigation I learned that another hierarchy exists as well, a hierarchy *within* the street-level prostitution sub-culture. This hierarchy is based on the actions of the women themselves. Specifically, "strawberries," or women willing to provide sexual services *in direct exchange for drugs* (i.e., sexual service→crack payment) had earned the worst reputations among other street-working women. Strawberries, it was noted by many, engage in the lowest form of degradation. Cheyenne believed "If you're doing it [prostitution] because you're a crack whore, that's just the lowest of the low."

To an outsider, the actions of a strawberry may not seem too unlike the actions of other prostituted women who provide sexual services, receive monetary payment, and then immediately purchase drugs with income generated (i.e., sex→money→crack). To an insider however, monumental differences exist and the two situations are far from alike. Handling money, it appears, implicitly *legitimizes* the actions involved to earn that money. It was further explained that strawberries (or "crack heads") had stigmatized street-level sex work and incurred shame and humiliation on all street-level prostituted women.

Finally, as a direct result of the pervasive presence of crack cocaine, the streets had become infiltrated by drug dealers and dope pushers. Vast quantities of the drug, and the potentially lucrative business of dealing, resulted in an explosion of street crime and violence; street-level sex work has become notoriously dangerous for all involved.

Summary

To briefly summarize, two primary patterns emerged in relation to the women's *initial* entry into prostitution. Approximately one-third began using drugs heavily and very early in their lives (e.g., mid-adolescence). As their addictions soared, their ability to legally support themselves plunged; particularly lacking education or marketable skills. After losing, or selling off, all material possessions, their chemical addictions drove them to the streets where the demand for sexual services was guaranteed.

A somewhat larger group of women entered prostitution slowly, through covert avenues carefully orchestrated to earn money. Income generated from sexual services was used primarily for survival purchases such as paying bills and purchasing food. Sometimes the money simply provided a more comfortable existence. These women were not typically chemical-free, however, drug use was a recreational activity. Alcohol and marijuana were popular during the initial stages of prostitution entry.

Chemical dependence, however, is an equal opportunity demon. With extended involvement in the sex industry, more potent mind-altering substances became necessary; escapism was the ultimate goal. Those whose prostitution activities had once paid the rent, eventually began hitting the "pipe" (i.e., the crack pipe) and then the streets.

Of all 43 women who were interviewed, only two reported never being chemically addicted at some point in their lives. Similar to the findings of Maher[29] and Feucht[30], the impact of crack cocaine on the sub-culture of street-level prostitution had not been subtle. Simply put, the tricks were getting cheaper, the addicts more desperate, and the violence more rampant and severe. Through direct and indirect routes, the street-level prostitution sub-culture had been indelibly altered by the presence of crack-cocaine.

Relationships with Pimps, Partners, and Clients

Pimps

Despite the popular image of streetwalking prostitutes' lives controlled by pimps, only 17 (39%) of the 43 women who participated in this investigation reported ever having a pimp. Five women had children with men whom they described as their pimps, and three reported relationships with pimps lasting more than a decade.

Pimps were frequently described as having several women working for them at once. For the pimp, street-level prostitution was a money-making venture. Pimps with a cadre of prostituted women were, it was explained, physically and verbally abusive to and sexually involved with all of them. The situation is referred to as a "stable." It was not uncommon for the stable to travel from state to state, luring new women into the group with promises of easy money and, more than anything, a sense of belonging and purpose. Relationships between the women comprising the stable were not characteristically friendly, but largely based on competition, jealousy, and suspicion. Needless to say, such social dynamics created a status-based hierarchy among the women. The first woman working for the pimp had the highest status and most authority over the others. Trina explained:

> There was a time when he [her pimp] had seven other 'hos besides me, and two or three of them were living in the basement. And he'd say, 'I got to leave tonight, I got to go spend some time with so and so.' And he'd take one of them to a motel and spend the night with them. I didn't like that a bit. I was real jealous and I wanted him all to myself. I'd let them [the other women] stay for a little while, but then after about three months I'd be like [to the women] 'You know you don't mean nothing to him don't you?' And, 'you know that he loves me and that he got a baby and two other kids that call him daddy don't you?'

Like Trina, Talisha also had children with a man whom she referred to as her pimp. Also like Trina, Talisha reported feeling little affection toward the other women working for him. However, her stable-mates served a special purpose: the more women working for her pimp, the less money she had to earn herself. Because she benefitted from the other women's presence, Talisha exerted personal effort to increase the size of the stable.

> I brought girls home and he would get money from them too. I would bring girls home. Call it "catching'hos" or whatever you want to call it. I bring them home and they make money so I don't have to do as much work. Then I sit back and they can make the money.

When the pimp left town, Talisha was in charge of the other women. She collected the money they earned and monitored their behavior. When the pimp returned, she gave him all income that had been generated in his absence. She provided additional information about her living situation:

> I had my little ho sisters living with me, too. I had my own set up because the kids and I, we might be living in a motel or something that had a kitchenette, and they [the other women] would be living in the next room. We were always together.

Despite being "always together," the other women were not to be trusted, according to Talisha, because:

> They were like back stabbers, you know? You really couldn't trust them. If you did something, like you went somewhere or did something that you knew he [pimp] wouldn't approve of, they'll cross you out just so they can get good merits or spend some time with him.

Still, she took pity on one of the other women in the stable and "helped her get back home because he [pimp] kept jumping on her [beating her up]."

Georgette had also been a member of a stable. However, her experiences with the other women were quite different. Rather than being the "main" woman with the most status, she was the youngest and newest addition to the group. When she joined, she was only 18. "I was like the baby of the group. The rest of them was like late 20s, early 30s. And they looked at me as the baby." Her initial role was to drive the women around while they picked up "dates" and then drive them back. She was with the group for five years, and would have continued her involvement had her pimp not gone to prison. Others also reported involvement with pimps. However, not all were part of a stable and many of those relationships only lasted for a brief period of time. Thus, it is important to *not generalize* the experiences of these three women as illustrative of all pimp-prostitute relationships.

Hooking Up with Pimps. As the women explained, prostitute-pimp relationships most often began in one of two ways. The first involves women who are slightly older, wiser, and already involved in the sex industry. Through on-going sex work, a woman may become introduced to a pimp. He may or may not initially identify himself as a pimp. A woman seasoned in the sex industry would typically be drawn to a pimp because of his charisma, such as his "gift of gab," wealth, and the respect he received from others. In this type of scenario, the woman would voluntarily enter a sexual and business relationship with him. She would prostitute for him by earning money for desirable commodities, and perhaps also for drugs. If she was the "first" or main woman entering the stable, she also helped recruit new faces to increase profit and reduce her own work load. The amount of money generated by women working as part of a stable is difficult to calculate, although several participants who had done so reported driving luxury vehicles, wearing expensive clothing, and donning exquisite jewelry. Still, according to Talisha, "Fast cash don't last long."

Patti agreed, noting "I made lots of money in prostitution. I spent lots of money."

The second process by which someone begins working for a pimp involves young females, usually runaways, who are befriended by men who are, typically, much older. These men prey on the young, naïve girls by providing survival necessities including food, shelter, and clothing. Within a week or two, the girls discover that they are indebted and expected to return the favors.

Barb met her first pimp when she was only 14. As a run-away, she often hung-out at the bus station because "It was a fun and exciting place to go." It was there that she began conversing with her soon-to-be pimp. The man was not a complete stranger. In fact, he had been acquaintances with Barb's father and she remembered that she "had met him earlier, at a Christmas party... Anyway, he was one of them perverts down at the bus station waiting for young girls." He enticed her with talk of "a car, money, blah, blah, blah," and convinced her that "everything will be alright." She admitted: "I had no clue. I really thought he was being a friend and trying to help out. Of course, at the time, I thought 'well cool'." It was only later that she realized strings were attached.

Tori also became involved with a pimp while on the run. She was 16 and, like Barb, was picked up at the bus station. She recalled:

> He was preying on young girls at the bus station and that's how I got started. He gave me a place to stay and then kinda roped me in. And then it was like 'You can help me now.' I think it was like on the fourth or fifth day. And you feel kind of obligated. And, well, I didn't want to go home.

Four others reported meeting their pimps in a similar manner. They were all between 14 and 16 years old when they were manipulated into prostitution service, and all were on the run.

Living up to their reputation, pimps were characterized as violent and intimidating; drugs were sometimes used to control and manipulate "their" women. Yet, several women reported that they were in love with their pimps, too. Emotional attachments, in addition to fear, maintained their involvement with the pimps.

The relationships between the women, their pimps, and drug use deserves additional attention, particularly in light of research conducted by others. In the 1993 book *Crack Pipe as Pimp*[31], it is explained that women addicted to crack cocaine will spend most, or even all, income generated from prostitution or other illegal activity on drugs. Pimps would be working at their own demise if they allowed the women working for them to become drug-addicted in that all of the women's money would go to the crack dealer, not the pimp. Thus, pimps have a vested interest in keeping the women working for them away from drugs. Unfortunately, since I did not ask the women specifically about their pimps' attitudes toward drug use.

It is interesting to note however, that when asked whether they had worked for a pimp or not, three participants simply responded, "the rock [crack] was my pimp." Their lives, in other words, had been completely controlled by their addictions to crack cocaine, not a man.

Male Partners

Some women were involved with men who pimped them out by encouraging or forcing them to prostitute for money. Income generated was typically used to purchase drugs in that the men's chemical addictions were supported by their partners' prostitution. Cheyenne was a case in point. At 18, she and a girlfriend became acquainted with a man who ran a brothel out of his home. They began hanging out at the man's house. He "supplied the tricks, the condoms and the bedrooms" and kept $10 of any money earned by the girls. The house, said Cheyenne, was "just another house to go to, like a friend's house and you made money while you were there. It was cool." Before long, Cheyenne told her live-in boyfriend about the house and the money she earned. Surprisingly,

> He started sending me over there, making me go everyday. There were days that I just didn't want to go over there, but [we] needed rent money and he wasn't making enough money on his dope because he was smoking it all. He'd be like, 'Well, Chey, we need some money,' so I'd go over there and get the money.

On days when few customers visited the house, Cheyenne would simply "go to the streets."

The man who pimped Bryn was her own husband. During the initial years of their marriage, money was hard to come by. Still, they both managed to find work, albeit, low paying jobs with little room for advancement (e.g., babysitting or lawn-service). After having three children, the economic strain was oppressive despite governmental assistance. According to Bryn, prostitution provided "Money. I never did it for drugs back then." She further recalled:

> That's mainly why I started doing it, to just pay the bills. We were smoking pot at the time, but it wasn't no heavy thing. Then, further on down we did get into the cocaine and it got to be for the habit, not the bills. You know? So the more the habit, the more the money, the more the work [prostitution].

She described her husband's role in her prostitution involvement:

> It was my husband who wanted me to do it and it got to the point where he would have just a really bad attitude and wanted to shove and hit on me. And then it got to the point where I said 'fine.' So I went and did it. It continued day in and day out. I mean, there was times I was sick and he wanted me to go out, it just got tiring.

The relationship between Bryn and her husband, as one might imagine, was irreparably damaged. She explained her feelings toward him and his exploitation of her, with the following:

I guess that's when I lost all the respect for him, you know? Because we were doing good and we both had jobs. I guess to him he was money hungry and knew that I could make him money real fast. And when you get into the drugs it doesn't matter where you have to go to get the money. And so that's where I think that I lost all the love and respect for him.

At least ten of the women interviewed reported engaging in street-level prostitution while involved with, or married to, a male partner. Several of the women reported that their partners had been clients at one point–men they had actually met while working the streets. Kiley and her boyfriend met "on the stroll [the 'ho stroll]." "It was" she explained, "a difficult relationship. We fell in love. He was a client and there was something special about him." At the time she met him she was three months pregnant; he was the only person present when her son was born. They had been together for over two years.

Rachel, too, had developed an on-going, intimate relationship with a man who had once been a client. The biggest difficulty in their relationship was their differing views on her prostitution.

I told him, I said, 'Don't try to change me right away. This has been my life for the last seven or eight years.' And he'd say, 'Rachel, I don't want a girl that's doing that. I don't want a prostitute, it's either them [the tricks] or its me'.

Despite his urging, Rachel continued to prostitute and they remained together.

When asked to describe how a marriage or similar relationship is maintained when prostitution is involved, Amy explained, "They're dysfunctional. They [the men] are usually using and so they want you to go out prostituting so they can have dope." This statement was reiterated by numerous others. Some indicated that their partners would babysit their children while they worked the streets for drug money. However, not all men who knew about the prostitution encouraged or agreed with it. Erica, for instance, stated that her partner "hated it" that she engaged in sex work for drug money. She reported further, "I would give him permission to lock me up at night with some coke, and then he would go to bed, and that way I wouldn't go out prostituting. I wouldn't take off. I was that out of control."

Participants were adamant in distinguishing relationships between men who were *partners* from those who were *pimps*, although the differences are quite subtle to an outsider. Both partners and pimps were characterized as prone to physical violence and abuse, both fathered children of the women, both were aware of the women's prostitution and drug related activities, and often, both partners and pimps introduced the women to the streets and forced their continued involvement. The primary differences included that: (1) pimps typically *required* that the women make a specific amount of money, (2) the women gave all of their earnings to their pimps who, in turn, provided shelter, clothing, and other commodities, and (3) the pimps often had several women working for them at once with whom they were also sexually involved. Those women whose partners were aware of their prostitution reported determining the amount of money they made and controlling, at least to some degree, how that money was spent. Furthermore, although the women were obviously sexually involved with others through their prostitution activity, they tended to believe that their male partners were monogamous and *not* sexually involved with anyone but themselves.

Clientele

In addition to describing relationships with pimps and partners, the women also provided a wealth of information about the men they met on the streets, namely, the clients and tricks who solicited their services.

Ten participants reported having "regulars" or specific men that they "dated" on a consistent basis. Maintaining regulars was beneficial for a number of reasons. First, regulars provided a constant and steady source of income; money from regulars was virtually guaranteed. Second, because of the on-going nature of their relationships with regulars, trust was implicit and therefore, risk of physical harm minimized. Third, it was generally agreed that regulars paid more than the "going rate" for services rendered. Tami described one of her regulars as a commercial pilot who visited her three times a week:

> ....and all I would have to do was wear a long dress, high heels, and then I would urinate in a cup and he would jerk off. He'd pay me $300. That's it. That's all he wanted to do. Then we'd drink wine and have dinner together.

It is important to note that the very nature of these relationships implied value and worthiness. That is, regulars were interested in a particular *woman*, not just *any* woman, or they would not have continued to visit the same person again and again. Thus, I suspect that regulars provided the women a sense of self-worth and virtue, perhaps invoking feelings that few had ever experienced.

In contrast, the negative side to dating regulars was that, once they found a woman they liked and felt comfortable with, the men's "requests" could turn kinky–even bizarre. Alli recalled,

> I would always ask for specifics–you know? Like 'What exactly are you looking for? What is it you want?' You know? Because some people be real fucked up. Like this one man I met. He used to just want me to ride around in the car with him. He would want me to bring out lingerie for him and he would put the lingerie on and just want me to, you know, jack him off.

In recalling her years on the streets, Amy referred to one of her regulars as simply the "icky man." When asked to elaborate she stated, "He was just icky. He took a bath but he didn't clean his clothes real well and his skin was scaly, real scaly. *And he was just the icky man!*" Similarly, Rachel exclaimed, "You wouldn't believe the shit we see!" Tami concurred. I asked her to describe the "weirdest" regular she'd ever encountered. She immediately responded: "Oh Lord!" and then proceeded:

> I had this lawyer in Nashville Tennessee and he would be dressed in a three-piece suit and underneath he wore a black negligee, fishnet pantihose. And he would have me strap on a dildo. I didn't have to get undressed. I stayed fully dressed. And he wanted me to talk to him like he was a dog–like he was worthless, he was nothing. Fifteen minutes and he'd be gone. He'd beat off while he sucked the dildo I was wearing. I am serious! And he was a high paid lawyer in Nashville!

In contrast to those women who dated regulars, some participants reported seeing each client only once; dating the same man on a regular basis personalized the work to a level beyond which they were comfortable. Trina's situation is illustrative. She initially entered prostitution after two painful marriages: her first husband had been killed and her second had cheated on her. She reported, "I was just licking my wounds. I was just like, this [prostitution] is the perfect relationship. I don't have to fall in love. I don't have to be heard." Kiley felt similarly: "I did not keep regulars. It was nothing I wanted to do. I didn't want to get into it, I didn't want to get into business like that."

The amount of time spent with individual clients, as well as the amount of money earned from each encounter, varied considerably depending on several factors, including: the type of service requested, the "going rate" on the streets for that particular service, and whether the woman was "jonesing" for drugs or not. As noted earlier, as the women's addictions escalated, they were willing to provide more explicit and degrading services for less money in return.

Feelings Toward Clients. The women reported that, unless their clients were "regulars," they knew very little about the men they "dated." Still, the majority of the women *believed* that, by and large, the typical clients were married men. Some, like Bridget, gauged a client's marital status by his actions.

> If I came across a guy that was real shaky, or really didn't know what the hell he was doing, I would assume him married. I would say [to him], 'Hey, you're okay there, you're cool! We'll hurry up and get this over with. You don't tell your wife and I won't tell her either'!

Yolanda felt similarly. She wasn't interested in knowing personal details about her clients. She conveyed her feeling toward tricks: "You [client] can use me, I'll use you, and we'll just leave it at that."

Others were less nonchalant and actually quite disgusted by the moral double-standard they experienced. That is, as prostitutes they were stigmatized by society. However, the men who were soliciting their services (i.e., the "demand" side of the equation) were frequently married or otherwise involved in intimate relationships. The tricks were leading double lives. They were acting the role of the upright, morally righteous citizen, when in fact they were cunning and deceitful. The women at least were honest about who they were and what they were doing.

One participant stated, "Mostly everyone I met was married. I never seen many during my prostitution life that wasn't married. I can say that about 99% of married men are unfaithful. One percent faithful." And Kiley had become completely disgusted with the tricks she encountered. She described one who left her feeling nauseated. He actually took her to his home and into his daughter's bedroom where the sexual exchange occurred. Cammie's experiences were similar. Many of her "regulars" were married men; she was astounded at their boldness. She exclaimed, "I'd go to their house! I mean–and their wives would be gone on business trips or whatever!" She continued: "I don't hate men, but I don't have a lot of respect for them–men who are supposed to be husbands and daddies and all of that." Marlee simply commented: "All men–ain't none of them no good. I'm serious, okay? They all cheat."

Logistics of the "Game"

Interestingly, several of the women mentioned that they rarely, if ever, engaged in sexual intercourse. They explained how the "game" was really a lesson in manipulation and deceit, the primary objective of which was to obtain as much money as possible without actually providing sexual services. Kiley described her indoctrination into the rules of the "game":

> I come to learn through prostitution that you have to be able to play the game. There's a lot of manipulation, a lot of lying and dishonesty and stuff. I kinda dummied-up, you know? As degrading as it is, you want to avoid having to do the actual intercourse or sex act or whatever it is at all cost– for me anyway. And I find that to be true for other women as well.

To play the "game," Kiley described obtaining her client's money up front, before engaging in any type of sexual activity. With money in hand, she would then run away. Sometimes she would tell the client she would be "right back" and then "run like hell." Jenna described similar tactics. "It [prostitution] is a quick way to get money. A lot of times I would con the money out of people. I'd say 'let's go by my house' and I would get out of the car and run." Georgette too, reported that "As I got older it wasn't about sex anymore, it was about taking the money and just haulin' ass." Similarly, Ellen avoided sex with clients to any extent possible and reported:

> I'm addicted to making money, but I would prefer that nobody touch me. And in prostitution, the ladies that do that, they don't like it, you know? They are hurting inside, you know what I'm saying? It's something they have to do. But they don't like it. And I don't like people putting their hands on me, touching me. 'Stop touching me!' You know? You'd rather go to the point of robbery instead of having sex with them.

But robbery or similarly manipulative behavior, as one might suspect, could quickly turn deadly. Talisha described "conning" one trick out of his money. The trick chased her down, and, once caught, threatened to kill her. She gave the money back. Likewise, Bryn explained how her behavior changed considerably after realizing the potential danger involved in conning tricks.

> It first started off to where I'd just rob them, I never dated them. I used to rob them. And then it got to the point where I thought I could get really hurt bad. So then I just started trickin' em. You know, having sex or whatever.

Interestingly, when asked if she ever "ran" with a trick's money without providing agreed-upon services, Michelle replied, "I never took the money and ran. I never did that." Yet, she continued: "sometimes, in the process of doing whatever I was doing, I would somehow *get* the rest of their money." The manner by which she "got" the rest of their money was never explained.

In contrast, Amy was completely opposed to playing the con game. As a Black woman she did not believe in living up to the reputation that Black women had earned on the streets.

> Black girls have a bad reputation. White girls "do" most of the tricks. Black girls are out to get the money and, if they can, they rip them [tricks] off. And I don't think that's right. I mean if you say you're going to do it, do it. It can't take that long.

Additional logistics of the "game" were explained. Some participants refused to date particular men. Their decisions appeared to be made based largely on racial stereotyping. Black men, it was generally agreed, liked to spend more time with women and, because of this, some felt it was economically inefficient to date them. Talisha remarked,

> I started out with Black men, and then I started dating white men and that's all I would date is white men because they were more respectful. Black men wanted to have sex with you all day and the white men—you be through with it. They be done with you.

In other words, if one could quickly turn a trick, earn money, and then move on to the next, why spend more time with any one than was absolutely necessary? The economics of the game demanded fast turn-over.

Patti also spoke of client preference based on racial characteristics. However, an interesting twist emerged. She reported only "dating" white tricks, and, like the others, her reasoning was due to logistics and timing. But her intimate relationships were always with Black men. "That's all I had was white tricks. I wouldn't do Black men because they took too long and wouldn't pay enough. But as far as my personal relationships—it was Black men." She continued, "I hate people, but I hate white men specifically. I can't stand the thought of looking at a white man and thinking that I could sleep with him [as opposed to having sex with him]. I can't deal with that. I can't."

Moreover, given popular media images, it is typically assumed that street-level sex work occurs only at night. Surprisingly, it was learned that business is also very good in the mornings. Catching the rush-hour traffic, typically between the hours of 5:00 a.m. and 9:00 a.m., was preferable for many. I asked for clarification and participants explained that married men, or those involved in similar relationships, avoided suspicion from their partners by picking up sex workers *in the morning on their way to work*, rather than in the evening or late at night. Not only was the business decent, risk of injury was significantly reduced. One participant, in particular, reported only working during daylight hours: "I was too scared, I wouldn't do it at nighttime." Erica, too, preferred picking up clients in the daytime "because it was safer and quicker. If they're on their way to work in the morning they got to get to work or if they're on their lunch break they only got so much time."

Condom Use

Only a fraction of those interviewed reported using condoms regularly. Yolanda noted always using protection and then stated, "I've been with 178 different men and I've never had one disease." Another insisted, "I was always very clean. Very, very clean to the point that I wasn't going to get any kind of disease." Interestingly however, in my interview with Talisha, she exclaimed: "Anyone tells you they use condoms all the time—they are lying!"

Most of the women, including Tami, reported infrequent condom use. Still, she was aware of the potential dangers associated with unprotected sexual practices. "I'm not going to lie. I didn't always use them, no. I've been blessed with that. I caught Hepatitis C and I'm real lucky I haven't got HIV." Bridget reported that she never used condoms, largely because the tricks didn't like them. They complained that "condoms take away the feeling." Several participants noted that their clients *refused* to wear condoms and some tricks paid extra money if they could engage in sex *without* them.

> Yes, some of them would pay more. And the sad part is they'd look at me and say 'Well, I'm married.' And sometimes I'd look right back at them and say, 'Yeah, but I'm not. What makes you think that I haven't got something'?

A small number of the women indicated that they only used condoms with tricks whom they did not know. They never wore them when engaged in sexual activity with "regulars," with their pimps, or with their male partners. The fact that those men (i.e., "regulars," pimps, and partners) most likely slept with other women, many of whom were also prostitutes, did not seem to be a concern.

Finally, those participants who described working for drugs or drug money were the least likely to use condoms. These women reported not caring about whether they used them or not; pregnancy or exposure to a sexually transmitted disease such as HIV, was of little consequence. "I just did not care anymore" commented Cammie. Similarly, when Landis was asked if she used condoms, she stated, "Never" and then continued, "when I was younger I wasn't really aware of them–of the problems [STDs/HIV]. Later I learned about the disease [HIV] and everything, [but] I didn't care if I had it or not, I didn't care if I died." Still, regarding the health dangers associated with prostitution, Bryn commented:

> I wouldn't recommend nobody else doing this [prostitution]. I have this friend and she told me her life story. She has AIDS and she contracted it from a trick. When she told me, it really broke my heart. Because her life was me– it was my life! No, I wouldn't recommend this for anybody.

Pregnancy

It was not surprising to learn that six of the women had become pregnant by tricks. "Trick babies," and the women who bore them, were considered very low status. Their reputation was similar to that of "strawberries." Some participants explicitly reported that the fathers of their children were *not* tricks, or if they were tricks that they had developed on-going relationships with those men. In other words, they wanted to be clear that their children were not *really* "trick babies." Both of Amy's sons had been fathered by tricks.

> I would never refer to my kids as trick babies and if somebody did I would go off, but that's what they are, okay? That's what they are. But they're mine and I love them with all my heart. I also think there's a lot of babies born to women who don't use protection when they date and I think they need to put a stop to that. I know one girl that dates and she's got like six kids. And that's stupid. And they're on welfare. Give them a hysterectomy or tie their tubes.

Pregnancy, as noted in chapter four, had little impact on prostitution activity. Twenty-two women became pregnant and carried those pregnancies to term *after* entering the sex-industry. For those women, life largely proceeded without interruption. One participant reported that her pregnancy *attracted* clients. And another continued to meet a particular "regular" throughout the entire term of her pregnancy: "As I got further along we quit having sex and I just [performed oral sex]. But he was always there."

Summary

In a recent book, *The Prostitution of Sexuality*[32], it is reported that 80% to 95% of all prostitution is pimp controlled. Such statistics were not supported in this investigation, as less than half of the women I interviewed reported working for a pimp. Still, pimps managed to maneuver their way into the lives of some. One strategy, employed with seasoned sex workers, involved the use of charisma, charm, and business savvy. Demonstrated ability to make money was a critical component to maintenance of pimp-prostitute relationships. Still, it cannot be denied that emotional attachments emerged between several of the women and their pimps. These relationships were not necessarily short-lived; some women were with their pimps for extensive periods of time.

The second 'pimping' strategy was employed with young girls, typically runaways, who were new to the streets. These tactics involved the use of manipulation and deceit. Pimps wore masks of concern, offered assistance, and generously provided necessities of survival. The generosity never lasted long and the pimps soon demanded that their "favors" be returned. The women complied; they had no choice. It is important to note that the women who were *manipulated* into service by pimps did not speak of emotional attachments to them. Still, regardless of the strategy used to ensnare the women, and regardless of the women's age or experience, pimps were described as explosive with a propensity for violence.

The women also provided detailed information about their experiences with clients. Numerous benefits to keeping regulars were noted, as were the potential risks. For some, sexual involvement with strangers was preferable to on-going engagement with someone familiar, as maintaining "regular" would personalize sex work to a level beyond which they were comfortable.

Alfred Adler[33] believed that being able to laugh at ourselves, and at our life situations, is an important ingredient for strong mental health. Although the women's mental health, per se, was not assessed, it was clear that many were quick witted and comical. Sense of humor was most evident when discussing clients–and especially the men's quirky, kinky requests and idiosyncratic behaviors. Laughter, as well as tears, were frequently expressed throughout my interviews with these women. It is, I believe, quite hopeful if not remarkable, that many of these women had *not* been thoroughly jaded by their life experiences. Unlike Char, who described no longer having "feelings," many others retained their capacity to feel, to express emotion, and to laugh.

The women's relationships with male partners, distinct from relationships with pimps or clients, were complex and, for some, difficult to comprehend. Male partners were described as just as brutal and unpredictable as pimps and strangers. Several male partners had introduced their girlfriends or wives to the streets and many had directly or indirectly supported the women's sex industry involvement. Perhaps the question many readers are asking themselves is: Why do women stay with men who encourage or even force their prostitution? An equally valid question, certainly, could also be asked: Why do men prostitute their partners? Re-framing the question removes the totality of blame from the women and opens the issue to greater scrutiny from a broader, gender-inclusive perspective.

Relationships with Fellow Street-Workers

Lacking unconditional regard from male partners, one might surmise that women prostituted on the streets would turn to each other for emotional intimacy and support. Unfortunately, this was not characteristically the case. Popular images of street-level prostituted women often depict female street-workers as traveling in groups or cliques, such as one might find in a shopping mall or on a college campus. The data do not support the image. It was commonly explained that women on the streets behave toward one another much like women comprising a "stable."

Comradery and cooperation are in short supply within the sub-culture of street-level prostitution. The majority of the women described operating under an assumption of mistrust and suspicion toward *everyone*, including other prostituted women. Perhaps out of necessity, self-interest was the "Golden Rule" because "everyone on the streets is out for themselves." Kiley described other female sex workers as "sly, terrible. You can't trust them. There's always a catch." Cheyenne concurred: "You can never trust another girl who's doing the same thing [prostituting] you are. We're all out there trying to get money."

Interestingly however, Cheyenne had to *learn* to be mistrustful. She described one incident which forever colored her perception of other prostituted women. She was new to prostitution and met up with another girl. As they walked the streets together, their attention turned to a potential trick. He drove past them slowly, circled the block, and then returned several times to leer. Cheyenne thought he was a cop. The other girl allayed her fears, stating "No, that's not a cop, he's a trick. He's a good payin' trick." Cheyenne, who was determined to earn some cash, flagged the man down, got in his car, and was immediately arrested. It was Sergeant Cole from Vice.

> That's how I got my first prostitution charge. One thing you don't do is you don't ask another hooker 'Is that a cop or a trick?' 'cause if they're a good payin' trick that girl ain't gonna tell you cause she wants that money herself.

Bridget agreed. When it came to working the streets for money:

> It's each for her own. They [other street-workers] don't care. They'll say 'I got your back.' [But] you ain't got my fucking back 'cause the minute you say you got my back, that's when I'll get ready to get locked up. I never really liked to travel the streets [with others]. I like to be by myself when I'm out there.

Jenna concurred, noting "I stood by myself a lot. I wasn't a crowd -pleaser. I always was by myself." When asked if the women on the streets looked out for one another, Kendra likewise responded, "Hell no! I always stuck by myself. They [women] are crazy out there!"

Jackie's opinion was that prostituted women *interacted* with one another, it was simply kept at a minimum and largely centered around police activity. "You know, if we see each other we'll be like 'The cops are out thick today' or 'Be careful 'cause the cops are doing their stings tonight' or something like that." But according to Jackie, they prostituted women do no offer assistance or *warn* one another of dangerous tricks. "I wouldn't have told nobody [about danger]. Let them find out on their own."

In addition to commenting on the deceit and manipulation characterizing relationships between prostituted women, many also described intense competition. For Amy, relationships with other sex workers consisted of "a competition thing. because I'm heavy and most the girls were real skinny." She was not alone in her assessment of the influence of physique on catching clients. Marlee, too, described how size, in addition to race, impacted the potential amount of money a woman might earn.

> If you're white, you'll get more money. If you're a Black girl they'd [tricks] be afraid of you. And then white men don't really like women with big butts. They don't. Black men like women with big butts. White men don't. I could make more money than the rest of the girls out there 'cause I'm small.

According to Michelle, competition certainly existed between the women on the streets, but personally, it wasn't an issue. "This might sound conceited, but I only had competition with one other woman. The rest—there was no competition at all." Sam largely agreed with the opinions of the others; competition existed, cooperation was scarce, and self-interest ruled relationships between women on the streets. Nonetheless, she claimed to be different. She did not fit the typical mold because:

> I looked out for people. I was different from a lot of the crack smokers and a lot of the prostitutes. I had so many tricks that I was giving them away to other women, you know, and talking tricks into taking them. Like, some tricks wouldn't date Black women, and I'd say 'Oh, but she is cool,' you know? So she could get some money. I was just real generous. I didn't feel like it was a competition for who could get the most, I just wanted friends.

Like Sam, Marlee was not confrontational with other women she met on the streets. In fact, she described feeling concerned about others, especially the younger girls she encountered.

> I don't want to encourage nobody to do it [prostitution]. I mean, because it's dangerous. I remember one time this girl was talking to me because she wanted to go out there. I told her, 'You know you're gonna go to jail.' I was telling her all the things she needed to know, and I scared her. Well, I thought, maybe if someone would have told me those things I wouldn't have been out there. It's not a life to have. Even when I saw young girls I would say, 'You need to go home girls, what you doing out here? Don't do this. This is not a life, really, it's not'.

Despite Sam's desire to "make friends" and Marlee's attempt to discourage others from prostitution, the sheer reality is that these two women were, at least in this regard, in the minority.

On the other hand, not all of the remaining women spoke of competition and callousness when discussing relationships between prostituted women. Several participants fell somewhere between the two extremes. A few noted "having friends" or being friends to some extent with others similarly prostituted on the streets. However, they noted that when friendships emerged, such relationships were between two or three other women only. Cliques of street-workers did not characterize the experiences of the majority. Moreover, if friendships existed, they typically began in an environment *other than* the streets, such as in jail, prison, or detox. Importantly also, once drugs entered the mix, any and all friendships were governed by principles of survival: It was each for her own.

Discussion

Following the theoretical guidance of ecological systems theory[34], this chapter was designed to provide information about the social and cultural milieu of street-level prostitution. According to Bronfenbrenner, human development is unquestionably impacted by the significant people comprising our social networks, and the cultural norms which govern interaction between and among them in various contexts. To this end, my interviews with prostituted women allowed a bit of insight into the significant people involved in the "game" and the norms, values, and mores which provide color, substance, and definition to the sub-culture of street-level prostitution.

Several assumptions, derived from media images and urban legend, were largely unsupported by the women's experiences. For instance, cliques of women do not prostitute together. In the street-level sex industry, allies are rare. Reports further indicate that the street-level sex industry is not pimp-controlled, at least not in the Midwest. However, I venture to guess that prostitution works quite differently, at least in this regard, in larger cities. Moreover, women involved in prostitution are rarely believed to be married or involved in marriage-like (i.e., co-residence) relationships. However, several participants were married or co-residing with male partners during their tenure on the streets. Some were legally married to their pimps.

The street-level sub-culture was also described as rapidly changing. The "new" girls, it was noted, are motivated by addiction, not money. Thus, sex-for-cash is no longer a lucrative business on the streets. The "new" pimp may very well be the drug man or dope pusher who has a vested interest in maintaining prostituted women's drug addictions. The traditional pimp, the entrepreneur with a "stable" of women working for him, may be going out of business[35].

Although the sex-industry itself is hierarchically organized, several hierarchies also exist *within* street-level prostitution venue. "Crack whores" (i.e., strawberries) occupy the lowest-status rung on the reputation ladder. Miller[36] and others[37] describe similar findings, noting that prostitutes who exchange sex for money, rather than sex-for-crack, experience less stigmatization and a greater sense of dignity. However, additional distinctions also emerged. Women who became pregnant from a male intimate were given greater status than those whose children were the product of indiscriminate sexual behavior with clients. Women who bore "trick babies" received little respect. Both types of women (i.e., strawberries and those with "trick babies") lacked self-control and self-respect. Strawberries were at the mercy of their addictions; women unaware of their babies' fathers were characterized as equally reckless and repugnant.

Interestingly, another hierarchy was also described. Women who allowed themselves to become overpowered, both physically and psychologically, by their pimps were regarded by some with sympathy; but by the majority with disdain. Michelle reported,

> Ain't no man gonna take what I laid down for, you know? For what I used *my* body to get. I never understood why women would go out and do all this and that and then give the money to a man!

Her view was not unique. Women who controlled themselves, their own money, and their prostitution activities were implicitly regarded as "higher status" than those controlled by pimps. Although not overtly stated, this view was implied in the fact that the women were very quick to distinguish *partners* who pimped them out, from men who were "pimps," despite the very similar behavior of both. Even Marlee preferred that her husband be called a "hustler" rather than a pimp, despite his having an entire stable of women working for him.

Apparently, issues of power and control underlie the status differentials among women prostituted on the streets. In subtle ways, it was conveyed that women able to retain *self-authority* and who were not governed by their addictions, by a pimp, or by complete self-disregard, were also able to retain a sense of pride and personal integrity; these women occupied the highest echelons of the street-level prostitution hierarchy.

Notes

1. Bonnie Bullough and Vern L. Bullough, "Female prostitution: Current Research and Changing Interpretations," *Annual Review of Sex Research* 7 (1996): 172.

2. Karen Hardman, "A Social Work Group for Prostituted Women with Children," *Social Work with Groups* 20, no.1 (1997): 20.

3. Frederique Delacoste and Priscilla Alexander, *Sex Work: Writings by Women in the Sex Industry* (San Francisco: Cleis Press, 1998).

4. Ine Vanwesenbeeck, "Another Decade of Social Scientific Work on Sex Work: A Review of Research 1990-2000," *Annual Review of Sex Research* 12 (2001): 285.

5. Thomas E. Feucht, "Prostitutes on Crack Cocaine: Addiction, Utility and Marketplace Economics," *Deviant Behavior: An Interdisciplinary Journal* 14 (1993): 91-108.

6. James A. Inciardi, "Crack, Crack House Sex, and HIV Risk," *Archives of Sexual Behavior* 24 (1995): 249-269.

7. Feucht, "Prostitutes on Crack," 91-108.

8. John J. Potterat, Richard B. Rothenberg, Stephen Q. Muth, William W. Darrow, and Lynanne Phillips-Plummer, "Pathways to Prostitution: The Chronology of Sexual and Drug Abuse Milestones," *The Journal of Sex Research 35* (1998): 333-40.

9. Nanette Graham and Eric D. Wish, "Drug Use Among Female Arrestees: Onset, Patterns, and Relationships to Prostitution," *Journal of Drug Issues* 24, no. 2 (1994): 315-29.

10. Jean Faugier and Malissa Sargeant, "Boyfriends, 'Pimps' and Clients," in *Rethinking prostitution: Purchasing sex in the 1990s*, ed. Graham Scambler and Annette Scambler (New York: Routledge, 1997), 121-36.

11. Lisa Maher, "Hidden in the light: Occupational Norms among Crack-Using Street-Level Sex Workers," *Journal of Drug Issues* 26 (1996): 143-73.

12. Paul J. Goldstein, *Prostitution and Drugs* (Lexington, MA: Lexington Books, 1979).

13. Feucht, "Prostitutes on Crack," 91-108.

14. Maher, "Hidden in the Light," 143-73.

15. Maher, "Hidden in the Light," 144.

16. Gaetana DiChiara and Alan North, "Neurobiology of Opiate Abuse," *Trends in Pharmacological Sciences 13* (1992): 185-93.

17. Glen R. Hanson, Peter J. Venturelli, and Annette E. Fleckenstein, *Drugs and Society*, 8th ed. (Ontario, Canada: Jones and Bartlett Publishers International, 2004).

18. Hanson et al. "Drugs," 287.

19. Dorothy Hatsukami and Marian Fischman, "Crack Cocaine and Cocaine Hydrochloride," *Journal of the American Medical Association* 276 (1996): 1580-1588.

20. DSM-IV-TR. "Substance-Related Disorders." In *Diagnostic and Statistical Manual of Mental Disorders*, 4th ed., Text Revision [DSM-IV-TR]. (Washington, DC: American Psychiatric Association, 2000), 223-50.

21. Marian Fischman, and Chris E. Johanson. "Cocaine," in *Pharmacological Aspects of Drug Dependence: Towards and Integrated Neurobehavior Approach Handbook of Experimental Pharmacology*, ed. by Charles R. Schuster and Mike Kuhar (New York: Wiley, 1992), 159-195.

22. Neil Swan, "31% of New York Murder Victims Had Cocain in Their Bodies," *National Institutes of Drug Addiction [NIDA] Notes* 10 (March/April 1995): 4.

23. Ed Neukrug, *The World of the Counselor*, 2nd ed. (Brooks/Cole, 2003).

24. Potterat and others, "Pathways to Prostitution," 333-40.

25. Graham and Wish, "Drug Use Among Female Arrestees," 315-29.

26. Potterat and others, "Pathways to Prostitution," 333-40.

27. Potterat and others, "Pathways to Prostitution," 333-40.

28. Maher, "Hidden in the Light," 143-73.

29. Maher, "Hidden in the Light," 143-73.

30. Feucht, "Prostitutes on Crack," 91-108.

31. Mitchell S. Ratner, *Crack Pipe as Pimp: An Ethnographic Investigation of Sex-for-Crack Exchanges*, (New York: Lexington, 1993).

32. Kathleen Barry, *The Prostitution of Sexuality*. (New York: New York University Press, 1995).

33. Harold H. Mosak, "Adlerian Psychotherapy," in *Current Psychotherapies*, ed. Raymond J. Corsini and Danny Wedding (Brooks/Cole, 2000), 54-98.

34. Urie Bronfenbrenner, "Ecological Systems Theory," In *Six Theories of Child Development: Revised Formulations and Current Issues*, ed. Ross Vasta (Philadelphia: Jessica Kingsley Publishers, 1989), 187-249.

35. It is possible that sex-for-cash is still common in largely cities. Importantly though, *The Prostitution of Sexuality* (documenting 85% of prostitution as 'pimp controlled') was written in 1995. The culture may have changed dramatically since then.

36. Jody Miller, "Gender and Power on the Streets: Street Prostitution in the Era of Crack Cocaine," *Journal of Contemporary Ethnography* 23 (1995): 427-52.

37. Margarat R. Weeks, Maryland Grier, Nancy Romero-Daza, Mary Jo Puglisi-Vasquez, and Merrill Singer, "Streets, Drugs, and the Economy of Sex in the Age of AIDS," in *Women, Drug Use, and HIV Infection*, ed. by Sally .J. Stevens, Stephanie Tortu, and Susan L. Coyle (New York: Haworth Medical Press, 1998), 205-29.

Entrance to the prison where 16 women were interviewed.

Control Center at the Iowa Correctional Institute for Women; guard smoking in background.

Waiting for customers on the "ho' stroll"; it's 6:00 a.m.

Not an unusual sight on the "ho' stroll." Police presence is thick day and night.

Char was living here, with an abusive husband who pimped her out for drug money, when interviewed in 2001.

Back side of an apartment building located just north of the "ho' stroll."

Two women looking for customers on a slow weeknight.

Chapter Six

Violence and Victimization

People are like stained-glass windows.
They sparkle and shine when the sun is out,
but when darkness falls–their true beauty is revealed
only if there is a light from within.
                                        –Elizabeth Kübler-Ross

Street-level prostituted women are particularly vulnerable to the threat of physical and sexual victimization[1-3]. The sheer scope and magnitude of violence against women prostituted on the streets has increased dramatically over the past decade, paralleling the street-culture crack epidemic[4]. Still, "physical and sexual violence towards prostitutes has seldom been the focus of public or academic interest"[5]. The marginalized status of prostituted women, some argue[6-7], largely accounts for the lack of attention to or concern for their physical and emotional well-being. In an earlier chapter, I described the participants' experiences with childhood victimization. Physical, emotional, and sexual abuse were frequently reported. Indeed, victimization of various types characterized the formative years and early familial environments of most of the women who participated in this study. Unfortunately, the women's adulthood experiences mirrored those of their childhoods. Although as adults, the perpetrators of violence against these women changed, their experiences with various forms of violence and exploitation remained consistent.

In this chapter, the violent sub-culture of street-level prostitution is described. This chapter begins with an overview of the academic literature documenting sex-industry violence. This is followed by personal accounts of violence, as experienced and described by the study's participants. Violence experienced at the hands of clients, partners and pimps is presented, as are strategies taken by the women to reduce risk of physical harm. As part of my research, I collected self-report survey data from each of the 43 participants; the third section of this chapter presents results from *quantitative* data analyses. Stress theory, which provided the theoretical model for framing my approach to studying street violence and self-preservation strategies, in particular, is also explained.

Review of Current Literature

National and international organizations, such as the American Medical Association (AMA) and the World Health Organization (WHO), are attracting widespread attention to the public-health concern of violence against women[8]. Recognition that female victimization represents transgressions against *human rights* and constitutes serious risk for physical and emotional problems has fueled the attention. It is important to note that one of the eight most prevalent forms of global violence against women is violence against *prostituted* women[9]. Victimization against women involved in the sex industry is endemic and pervasive.

Victimization implies an interpersonal power differential in which one party dominates another[10]. MacMillan[11] notes that violent victimization includes interactions in which individuals are unable to prevent or protect themselves from attack. Thus, "victimization has implications for one's sense of agency, self-efficacy, and perceptions of others in the social world"[12]. Moreover, violent victimization may have profound psychological consequences[13-15] and significantly alter long-term developmental trajectories[16].

All people are *not* equally at risk for violent victimization. Compared to men, women are significantly more likely to experience physical and sexual assault. Moreover, women involved in heterosexual intimate relationships are more likely victims of violence than are those involved with same-sex partners[17]. Certainly also, exposure to and involvement in environments characterized by crime and deviance increase victimization risk[18]. The street-level sex-industry, as one such environmental context, breeds violence and exploitation. Street-level prostitution presents significant personal risk[19-21], particularly when drug-use is involved[22]. Yet, despite efforts by renown advocacy groups such as WHO and AMA to recognize violence against women as human rights transgressions, "societal attitudes concerning prostitutes continue to be that they are unrapeable, do not suffer physical attack, [and that they] deserve violence inflicted upon them, or that no harm is done when [they] are hurt or killed"[23].

Victimization of Prostituted Women

Street-level sex work is inherently dangerous; male violence against female street-workers is endemic[24-26]. In an investigation including 16 prostituted women, Miller[27] found that 93% had been sexually assaulted, 56% had been robbed, and 44% had been forced or coerced into engaging in sexual activities with self-identified police officers. Physical assault with weapons was widely reported as well; the women in her sample described being beaten with objects and stabbed with knives. Miller's participants further reported kidnaping, strangulation, and being abandoned in remote regions. Unfortunately, the incidence and severity of violence experienced by the women who participated in Miller's study is not unique. Silbert and Pines[28,], as well as others [29], report exposure to and intensity of violence among street-level prostituted women similar to those described by Miller.

In an investigation comparing violence among women prostituted on the streets with those working in safer, "indoor" environments such as brothels, Church and colleagues[30] found that street-level prostitution was associated with higher levels of violence perpetrated by clients than the effects of the city, drug use, or age that the women began prostituting. Without question, the street-level sex industry is replete with danger and treachery. As one might expect, clients/tricks are not the only sources of crime directed against prostituted women. Pimps and intimates, including husbands and boyfriends, are frequently implicated in the rapings, beatings, and deaths of female sex-workers[31]. However, reference to female sex workers abandoning the streets due to personal safety concerns could not be located in the existing literature.

Self-Protection

Williamson and Folaron[32] examined the extent to which street-level prostituted women took measures to protect themselves from harm. Although only thirteen women were included in their study, results were intriguing. The women described operating largely under "instinct." That is, the most frequently mentioned survival strategy included the use of intuition to "read dates"[33]; the women relied on gut-level feelings of danger or lethality. Other strategies included: relying on God, meeting the date in a familiar spot, and planning forms of escape should an encounter turn dangerous. Interestingly, the women in Williamson and Folaron's study also reported dating "regulars" as a technique to ensure personal safety. Interestingly too is that, among those women interviewed by Williamson and Folaron, "All... stated that they warned other prostitutes about a potentially dangerous date"[34]. As noted in chapter five, the majority of women who participated in my investigation reported that they would *not* warn other prostituted women about dangerous clients.

Developmental Consequences of Violence

Physical and emotional consequences of street-level violence have been the focus of a few recent studies. In particular, symptoms of post traumatic stress disorder (PTSD) have been examined among prostituted women. PTSD is a psychiatric disorder the may occur following the experience or witnessing of life-threatening events, such as military combat or violent personal assaults such as rape[35]. PTSD is characterized by a cluster of symptoms, including sleep disturbance, nightmares, flashbacks and extreme agitation and anxiety[36]. In their investigation, Farley and Barkan[37] examined violence experienced by prostituted women across the life-span in relation to experiences of PTSD. Results revealed that adulthood experiences of PTSD were related to childhood physical abuse *and* to the occurrence of rape in adulthood. Importantly also, the more types of violence that were reported (e.g., childhood sexual assault, adulthood rape, physical assault) the greater the severity of PTSD symptoms. Farley and Barkan's investigation is particularly valuable on two accounts. First, they identify challenges to *mental health*, not just physical health which has traditionally received the greatest amount of attention in studies with prostituted women. And second, their investigation was framed within a developmental model. That is, present circumstances, as well as historical events, were calculated in assessing PTSD symptomology.

Victimization Across the Life-Span: Adulthood Experiences with Violence and Abuse

In the pages which follow, the women's adulthood experiences with violence, as inflicted by clients, pimps, and intimate partners, is presented. Self-protective preservation strategies employed by the women to reduce the potential of harm are also discussed.

Clients/Tricks

Street prostitution, some believe, is a form of self-destruction. It would be difficult to argue otherwise given the life-threatening risks posed by the sub-culture of street-level sex work. "Dating," in the context of the "game," refers to picking up clients. Thirty-two (73%) of the 43 women interviewed as part of this investigation reported having been subjected to multiple forms of battery and assault while dating. Some had been violated on multiple occasions and in multiple manners. Their experiences are not unlike the prostituted women interviewed by Miller, Williamson and Folaron, or Silbert and Pines, in that my participants also described being beaten with objects, threatened with weapons, abandoned in remote regions, strangled, and raped.

Rape

Eleven women reported having been raped. Four of them had been raped on multiple occasions and three others had been gang raped. Char, as one particularly tragic example, had lost count of the number of times she had been raped. She had even "been raped twice in one night," yet she "kept on going [continued working the streets]." Char was not alone in this regard. Tami had also been raped multiple times, as had Talisha. When asked about her experiences with street violence, Talisha responded:

> Yes, I've been raped. That happened to me everywhere I went. It happened to me in Colorado, Utah, and Texas. But when I was in Texas I had a gun put to my head, got raped and robbed– You just give them what they want and you pray they don't kill you.

Despite what she had endured, Talisha put her experiences in context and provided an astute comparison:

> I feel I have been abused somewhat, my body as far as tricks goes and getting raped and stuff like that. I feel my body has been abused. But I thank God I'm not all cut up in the face. I feel like I have been blessed because some women I see that tricks cut them across the face and some got scars on them that you can see. You always think you got the pain. But mine is not nothin' compared to some of the women I have talked to.

Perhaps Bridget was one of the women Talisha was referring to. Like the others, Bridget was asked about frightening situations encountered on the streets, to which she responded, "I do recall a life/death situation." She then explained an incident in which she had been "picked up" by several men in the same vehicle. They drove her to a remote area and then proceeded to gang rape her, one by one, in the back seat of the car. The nightmare continued:

> I remember this like it was yesterday. I was there in the back and all of a sudden this guy comes around and punches the fucking lights out of me. He came around from the front and just went BAM! Then, he told me to get the fuck out. I was bleeding and everything, and you know, I was so glad [they left] they could have killed me. That was the worst situation. That was the worst thing that ever happened to me since I been out there prostituting.

Bridget was no longer angry about the incident. She had made amends in her mind by rationalizing,

> They had probably had something done to them some time and they just took it out on me. I've heard that happens before. You know, where some trick gets robbed and they come back and take it out on somebody else.

Erica had also been raped by a trick; she was only 17 at the time. When asked to explain how she returned to the streets after the ordeal she stated: "I just looked at it as not getting paid." Her response was chilling, and likely a coping mechanism or form of cognitive maneuvering which allowed her to return to the dangerous street environment without paralyzing fear and perhaps, also, with some level of personal dignity intact.

Erica was not alone. Most of the women reported using "denial" to cope with life threatening situations. However, there was one woman who was unique. At the time she was interviewed, Jenna had only been off the streets for two months. She sought help because of a particularly terrifying incident: she had been raped in an abandoned warehouse and held there, against her will, for more than two hours. It was, admittedly, the most frightening experience of her entire life. The incident compelled her to seek help and leave the streets.

Other Forms of Bodily Injury

Rape and sexual assault were not the only forms of brutality inflicted upon these women by their clients. Tami summed up her experiences: "There were times when the only way out of a situation was by the grace of God." To no surprise, given the work of other researchers, physical injury from violent customers carrying weapons or objects used as weapons, was commonly reported. One participant had nearly had her ear torn off by "...some type of weapon. They hit me with something, it sounded like a gun shot. My whole ear almost came off and I was left for dead." And Sam had been beaten with a tire iron; her wounds required 150 stitches to repair. I asked her about fear, or if she ever felt as if her life was in danger, to which she replied: "I didn't even care. I didn't even care. I didn't think about it." Sam went back to the streets the very same day she was beaten so brutally.

Vehicles were sometimes also used as weapons to inflict injury. Both Candace and Patti described near-miss incidents in which tricks attempted to run them over and Chancey had been thrown out of a moving car by a disgruntled client. Yet, in addition to instruments of opportunity, like tire irons and vehicles, knives comprised the weapons of choice by angry, malicious tricks. Talisha, for instance, had been stabbed and nearly killed by one client. She remarked, "You'd think that death call would've been enough for me to stop. But it wasn't."

Several women had been hospitalized due to the maliciousness of others. In a bizarre incident, Anna bought crack cocaine that had been diluted with rat poison. She spent 10 days in a coma, on life support, and was genuinely surprised that she was alive to tell her story. And Tami, too, had also been hospitalized due to the intentional actions of others. She explained,

> I was in a coma for three days in Nashville. I had gotten beat, my jaw was broke in two places, I had four fractured ribs [and] all I remember was he was a black man in a maroon car.

She described her memory of the event:

> I got in the car with him. I fought with him. I got away and he chased me down. And the last thing I remember is the boot coming toward my face–and it was in a residential area! When I came out of it [coma] I had two black eyes, my nose was swollen and my face–I probably looked like the elephant man. They [doctors] wanted to bolt my jaw back together. I said 'No– by the Grace of God I was brought here on earth and by the Grace of God I'll go. Nobody is going to touch my face.' It was bad. It was really bad.

It would be difficult to delineate the entire scope of bodily injury inflicted upon these women by crazed tricks. There were many, many variations of the same corrupt and hateful theme.

Particularly disturbing is that these women had no recourse– no form of legal action or retaliation against the men who brutalized them. Participants rarely reported crimes of victimization to authorities. Of all the women interviewed, only three had *ever* reported episodes of abuse or violation inflicted by clients to law enforcement. When asked to explain why she did not report crimes against her, Tami remarked:

> Society and law enforcement consider a prostitute getting raped or beat as something she deserves. It goes along with the lifestyle. There's nothing that you can do.

Talisha's experiences with the police largely confirm Tami's statement. Talisha described how she *had* contacted the police on two different occasions to report crimes against her. The police offered little assistance. "They really didn't give a damn. [They] figure you're out there, so take the consequences." Similarly, Cammie contacted the police after being beaten. She believed she "was just a street rat to them." In other words, paralleling the experiences of Talisha and Tami, the authorities offered little help and dismissed her as if she were not worth their time. An obvious problem in contacting police is that the women themselves were engaging in illegal activities. Several were fearful that, if they were to contact law enforcement for assistance, that they would be arrested for prostituting.

Self Protection
Like Williamson and Folaron[38], I too was curious as to whether the women employed self-protective strategies for harm reduction and purposes of survival. Self-protective maneuvers seem particularly critical given the apparent reluctance of law enforcement to act in defense of prostituted women. I found that the women engaged in a variety of cognitive and behavioral strategies aimed at self-preservation. Intuition, similarly described by Williamson and Folaron, was commonly mentioned by the participants in this investigation. Some also reported that they would *never* accept a ride from, or travel anywhere with, a trick because getting into someone's vehicle was an open invitation to injury. Instead, they preferred to meet their dates in designated areas. According to Tami, "There isn't a man on this earth except for God that can watch your back when you get in a car and drive off."

Although Anna did not have a policy against traveling with clients, she engaged in self-protective strategies nonetheless. She explained, "I wouldn't let them take me far away. I always stayed in the area that I knew. And if I even thought they were even attempting to get weird, I would get out." Three participants had done just that. They jumped from moving vehicles because they sensed danger. Several women also reported that they completed sexual exchanges in visible areas– such as near street lights or busy roads as a means of lessening danger posed by unpredictable clients.

Rachel's strategy involved selectively choosing her dates. "I wouldn't just pick up any Tom, Joe or derelict out there. I am picky." She was not alone, several regarded themselves as quite "picky." Jackie, for instance, would not date "white men driving red trucks." Moreover, maintaining a group of "regular" clientele helped reduce risk of bodily harm. Barb explained,

> Basically, because of that [regulars], I just never went through a lot of the stuff
> that the other girls out there, or that my sister, went through. You know, they get
> beat up and go through a lot of trauma. I never went through a lot of that.

Interestingly, in their discussion of survival strategies employed by prostituted women, Williamson and Folaron made no mention of the *women's* use of weapons. In contrast, nine women who participated in my study described working the streets while armed. Two of the participants, Alli and Kendra, carried box cutters although neither had ever had to use them. Alli remarked, "Thank God I never used it! Never! I never ran into anyone who tried to force themselves on me or nothing like that." Three others carried a gun, Anna kept a razor, and three additional women reported carrying knives at various times while working the streets. And, opposed to most, Marlee did not believe in concealing the fact that she carried a weapon. "I carried a knife–and I let it be known." Finally, and as mentioned in chapter five, several women only worked the streets during daylight hours as a means of self-protection.

Regardless of strategy used, physical safety was not guaranteed. "Any time you're out there on the street," noted participant, "your life is in danger." Moreover, despite the potential for physical assault and injury, eight women actually thrived on the "excitement" of the lights and sounds of the streets. Chancey remarked, "It was a high just getting home alive some nights." Perhaps these eight women were natural risk-takers and adrenaline junkies. Perhaps, had they not been prostituted on the streets, these women would have been sky-divers or extreme-sports enthusiasts. On the other hand, perhaps they had become so emotionally numb that life-threatening situations were *necessary* in order to feel any sensation at all.

Still, even those attracted to the glamour and excitement of the streets admitted that the walkways and alleys held a much darker side. Although Sam was "...addicted to the prostitution too, to the excitement, not just the drugs. I just loved it out there," she continued by explaining a recent experience:

> We had a class [at WellSpring] and they played tapes and we had to write down
> how we felt while we were listening to the songs. And they played 'Roxanne, you
> don't have to put on that red dress tonight,' and a vision came to me. I was
> walking down the street at three or four in the morning and it was drizzling and
> one car was going by every half hour, just lonely as could be. And it made me
> realize how lonely that life really was, that it wasn't anything exciting. It was
> lonely. It was very lonely.

Summary

The participants relayed horrific stories of abuse suffered at the hands of strangers. Physical and emotional scars, the consequences of multiple forms of bodily injury, were in no short supply. Many participants had been raped; some had been sexually assaulted on several occasions and others by multiple people at once. Additional forms of brutality were also inflicted, with and without various types of weaponry. Several women were surprised they were still alive. The majority reported taking precautions, at least intermittently, to protect themselves from harm. Strategies for self preservation included relying on intuition, carrying weapons, and refusing to travel in clients' vehicles. Nonetheless, those women "catching tricks" in order to feed a relentless drug addiction took the greatest risks with their own lives. The drugs often compelled risk-taking behavior by lowering inhibitions and altering decision-making abilities; but, more importantly, by the time the women's lives had reached ground zero, they reported little reason to live. If they lost their lives to the streets, they explained, so be it.

Numerous participants reported thriving on the danger inherent in street-level sex work. They were allured to the "excitement" and the "glamour" of street-prostitution. They experienced emotional highs after surviving life-threatening encounters. Such situations provided an adrenaline rush. Perhaps as a consequence of extended emotional numbing, the autonomic responses to near-death experiences reminded them that they *were* still alive. Concern or fear for one's own personal safety was the exception, not the rule. Romero-Daza and colleagues[39] report findings from research conducted in Connecticut that is quite similar to results of this investigation. Geographic location, it appears, is irrelevant and violence against prostituted women by clients is the norm, not the exception.

Male Partners and Pimps

Clients, one might imagine, are the most treacherous players in the "game" of street-level prostitution. Because clients are typically strangers, it is natural to assume that their anonymity allows for the infliction of greatest harm against the women they solicit on the streets. In other words, lack of emotional attachment coupled with the low probability of future encounters or legal consequences of their actions, might compel predators toward greater brutality and viciousness against the women unfortunate enough to "date" them.

Despite the savagery which characterized some clients, pimps and intimate partners, including husbands and boyfriends, comprised the source of the *majority and most severe* forms of abuse inflicted upon these women. Strangers were not the greatest threat to these women's physical safety, but instead, the most dangerous men appeared to be those the women allowed to enter their lives as companions and sources of support.

Nearly every woman interviewed mentioned violence as a defining feature of their intimate relationships with male partners. Patti, as but one example, summarized her experiences: "Every man that I have ever been involved with, not the tricks, but every man that I have been in a personal relationship with has turned violent after I made a commitment." In fact, one of those men beat her with a lead pipe. She spent three months in the hospital from internal bleeding, broken ribs, and a cracked jaw. Like Patti, many others described involvement with a succession of violent, abusive men. Candace indicated that she had been "in a whole bunch" of violent relationships, in fact, "every one I've ever had." She then stated, "They [the men] say I do stuff to *make them* hit me, like cussing them out or all kinds of stuff that ain't true."

Angel also reported that most of her boyfriends had been extremely violent. The cops had arrived on her doorstep multiple times due to neighbor intervention. She described one particularly violent boyfriend by saying, "Yeah, he used to beat the shit out of me. He beat the hell out of me." When asked if she'd ever been hospitalized, she responded,

> No, but I should have. I had to see an eye specialist because he hit me in the back of the head so hard it blackened both my eyes. They did a CAT scan– thought there might be damage back there [to the optic nerve].

Despite the incident, Angel continued her relationship with the same man.

And Barb, who was pregnant with her seventh child when she was interviewed, described the fathers of each of her previous six children as prone to violence and explosive behavior. The father of her oldest three, whom she met when she was only 15, was particularly abusive.

> Kerry got really, of course, on the abusive side with everything. I probably called the police fifty million times. The whole police station knew us. We'd move to different addresses but they always came on a regular basis. And they'd be pulling him off me, and they'd [police] be like 'Was he drinking tonight?' and I'd be like 'No, he don't drink.'

When Barb was six months pregnant with their last child, she was "beaten on a daily basis. I almost lost her [the baby]." Although that relationship ended soon afterwards, a string of equally abusive boyfriends followed.

Twelve of the women reported being hospitalized for injuries received from beatings by their male partners. Rachel, for instance, moved in with a man she met during treatment and explained, "Everything was great, we were going to meetings and everything." However, soon after, they both began using again and then "Things just got progressively worse and he beat me and he left me for dead. He tried to bite my ear off, tried to set my hair on fire, he knocked all my front teeth out." Needless to say, the relationship ended and she went back to the streets. The streets were actually a safer place for her.

Similarly, one of Cheyenne's boyfriends was so violent that he broke her eardrum. In reference to this man she said,

> He was like somewhat of a pimp, but a love affair on the side. But more of a pimp, you know? He had his bad spots, but he also had his real good spots. He made sure I was eating, he made sure I had a place to stay. You know, I'm just dependent on men, and whether it be good or bad, I'm dependent on them. I want to be loved.

Another woman described being beaten with a shoe for not telling her partner she was pregnant. And yet another stated that her boyfriend "brought me home a disease once, and then beat me for it." And Cammie, who was only 18 at the time she was interviewed, described how her boyfriend beat her until she was nearly unconscious and then drove her around a graveyard describing how he was going to bury her alive. She reported constantly having "[strangulation] marks on my neck or bruises on my face...what is really sad is that I expected that, I didn't think there was anything better for me."

In addition to violence from intimate partners, pimps were also prone to physical, verbal, and sexual assault. That pimps control the women who work for them through the use of intimidation and violence has been well documented by other researchers [40-41]. What is largely missing from many of those accounts, however, is the women's reactions to and feelings about their abusive pimps.

Talisha, who was with her pimp for over a decade, described him in terms that fit the typical stereotype. Their relationship was rocky; he would be "Jumping on [beating] me or disrespecting me–having sex or something with another one of his women in the next room. I call that disrespecting me." Like many women embroiled in abusive relationships, Talisha would leave him for awhile, but eventually, she "...would come back or leave and he [would] come and get me. I used to leave him all the time he'd come back and get me."

Trina's pimp was similarly "disrespectful." Yet, in order to recruit new women into the stable, she was responsible for conning them into believing her pimp was a kind and generous person.

> I'd be like [to the other women], 'Are you going to get with my man? He's so good and he's so sweet and he do this and he do that for you.' And then I'd be like, 'Do you want to meet him?' And they'd meet him and he'd be real nice and polite. Huh, yeah, right! Until he got them for about a month or so and then he'd become the real Gregory. He'd always be like 'Bitch!' I thought 'bitch' was on my birth certificate!

Gregory beat Trina often, including "when he got drunk, or mad, or anytime he felt like it. He didn't care. But I thought that meant that he loved me. That was the message I got as a child because my dad used to beat my mother."

Summary

The sub-culture of street-level prostitution is comprised of treachery and danger. Violence against prostituted women has been well-documented in the United States and internationally[42-44]. However, as evident in this study, tricks (i.e., clients, customers) present minimal risk to prostituted women compared to that inflicted by partners and pimps– the very men who comprise their support networks. Without question, participants experienced more frequent and more severe forms of violence from men who were "intimate partners" than from those who were clients or strangers.

Williamson and Cluse-Tolar[45] draw parallels between pimp-controlled prostituted women and women experiencing domestic violence by intimates. Both types of relationships, they argue, are ultimately based on power and control; and, more importantly, both types of relationships fulfill certain needs which may include a sense of love and belongingness. When a prostituted woman's primary source of social support is her partner or pimp, men who benefit greatly from her prostitution activities, the challenges for her in leaving the sex industry rise exponentially. An *emotional* bond ensnares her within the "game." Additionally important is that women who have experienced an entire life of victimization are most at risk for remaining with abusive men and least likely to expect or demand to be treated differently.

Supplemental Information:
Stress Theory, Survey Analyses, and Results

In addition to verbal reports, self-report questionnaires were also employed as part of this investigation. Participants completed six survey instruments designed to assess *stressful life events, depression, locus of control, impulse control, social support, and coping strategies*. These instruments were used to test stress theory as an organizing framework for better understanding sources of stress and mechanisms of coping with potentially stress-inducing situations among this unique population.

Stress Theory

According to stress theory[46-48], an individual faced with a potentially stressful event (e.g., interpersonal conflict) reacts first by making a *primary cognitive appraisal*. As part of this appraisal process, the person labels the event (e.g., the conflict) as: irrelevant, benign/positive, or stressful[49]. Next, *secondary cognitive appraisal* occurs in which the individual evaluates her *internal* and *external* resources. Internal and external resources are assets available that provide *options* for managing the "event." Internal resources refer to personal attributes (such as feelings of self-worth or efficacy). External resources refer to factors outside the individual, and may include, for instance: assessment of one's social support network or material resources. Events are perceived as "stressful" based on unique perceptions of an event as exceeding or taxing one's internal and external resources[50]. Coping strategies (e.g., asking others for assistance) are behaviors or cognitions used by an individual to alleviate anxiety or to reduce the impact of stress-inducing experiences. Although coping strategies are tactics used to minimize stress, they need not be conscious or effective. Denial and drug use are considered coping responses[51], despite their potentially destructive long-term effects. Stress theory is depicted below in Figure 6.1.

Figure 6.1: Stress Theory

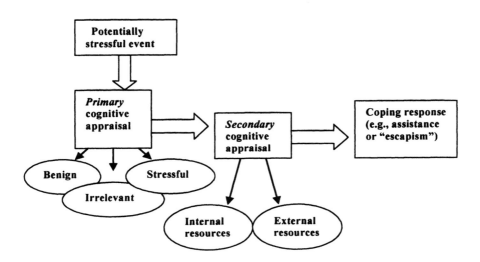

The six survey indices (refer to chapter two for detailed information on each) were applied to the theoretical model in the following manner:

▸ potential *stress-inducing circumstances* were operationalized (or measured) through the life events survey;

▸ *internal resources* were operationalized with three instruments: depression, locus of control, and impulse control;

▸ *external resources* were assessed through the Norbeck Social Support questionnaire; and

▸ a *coping* inventory was administered to assess five unique strategies used to cope with potentially stress-inducing situations, including: (1) social actions (i.e., talking to someone), (2) escapism (e.g., eating, using drugs), (3) externalizing (e.g., acting out, yelling), (4) internalizing (e.g., keeping feelings to self), and (5) active (e.g., doing something about the situation).

Based on stress theory, six hypotheses were formulated:

(H1) Emotional and practical support will be *positively* associated with *proactive* coping strategies (e.g., seeking assistance from others, taking action).

(H2) Passive (e.g., internalizing) or potentially harm inducing (e.g., escapism) coping strategies will be *positively* associated with depression and *negatively* associated with emotional and practical support;

(H3) External locus of control will be *positively* associated with depression and *negatively* associated with emotional and practical support;

(H4) Life events will be *positively* associated with external locus of control;

(H5) Lower levels of impulse control will be *negatively* related to social coping strategies (e.g., seeking assistance) and *positively* related to both escapism and an external locus of control; and

(H6) Coping responses will be determined *first* based on internal resources (e.g., depression, locus of control, impulse control) and *second* based on external resources (i.e., social support).

Results from Quantitative / Survey Data Analyses

Prior to running analyses to test the hypotheses, it was first necessary to statistically compare those women who were associated with WellSpring ($n = 26$), to those who were incarcerated ($n = 14$) and those who were recruited through word-of-mouth ($n = 3$). The purpose of these comparisons was to ensure that the women involved in intervention were not different, statistically speaking, from those lacking formal intervention services. Significant differences between these two groups could signify biases that would need to be addressed when interpreting results of data analyses.

Comparisons were thus made on all survey indices (e.g., depression scores, locus of control, social support) and the following demographic variables: age, education, number of children, and age when the women began prostituting. Only one significant difference emerged. Participants located through the WellSpring program were slightly less educated, by two years, ($M = 8.5$ years, $SD = 5.1$) than those lacking formal assistance in exiting the sex industry ($M = 10.5$ years, $SD = 3.4$) ($F = 5.32$; $p < .05$). Because of the minimal group differences, data from all 43 participants were compiled for the remaining statistical analyses.

Hypothesis Testing: Correlational Analyses

Hypothesis One: Emotional and practical support will be positively associated with proactive coping strategies (e.g., seeking assistance from someone else, taking action).

As evident below in the correlation table (see Table 6.1), partial support was found for the first hypothesis. *Emotional support* was significantly and positively associated with two proactive coping strategies: talking to someone ($r^2 = .30$; p<.05) and taking action ($r^2 = .32$; p<.05). *Practical support* was significantly related to taking action ($r^2 = .32$; p<.05).

Although not hypothesized, practical support and emotional support were also positively related ($r^2 = .95$; p<.01). This association is not a complete surprise for two reasons. First, emotional and practical support are both *subscales* (or sub-types) of the overall *social support* variable. That is, they both measure unique types of support, but are nonetheless two aspects of the composite *social support* construct. Second, it is quite likely that network members who provide one type of support (e.g., emotional) also provide other types of support (e.g., practical).

Hypothesis Two: Passive (e.g., internalizing or keeping feelings to oneself), or potentially harm-inducing coping strategies (e.g., escapism) will be positively associated with depression, and negatively associated with emotional and practical support.

Partial support was found for hypothesis two. Referring again to Table 6.1, it is clear that, although neither escapism nor internalizing was related to depression, *escapism* was significantly and negatively associated with *talking to someone* ($r^2 = -.53$; p<.01) and *taking action* ($r^2 = -.35$; p<.05). In other words, those utilizing escapism (e.g., using drugs) as a coping technique were significantly *less likely* to seek assistance from support network members or to utilize active strategies in efforts to reduce or minimize stress. Said differently, those employing self-destructive coping techniques tended to *not* use proactive, positive coping strategies (e.g., utilizing their support networks by seeking assistance from others).
Furthermore, escapism and internalizing behaviors were positively associated ($r^2 = .52$; p<.01) indicating that those using "escape" strategies were also more likely to internalize events when faced with difficult situations.

Moreover, although not predicted, active strategies were positively associated with talking to someone (e.g., seeking assistance) ($r^2 = .58$; p<.01). The significance of this association is not surprising as "talking to someone" might be perceived as a form of "taking action" (i.e., one must take action when asking others for assistance). Thus, a confounding effect may have occurred between these two *types* of coping. The results are nonetheless important in that seeking assistance and taking action are both considered *constructive* coping strategies compares to passive-oriented, and potentially *self-destructive*, techniques involving escapism and internalizing.

Variable	Variable Associations										
	1	2	3	4	5	6	7	8	9	10	11
1. Escapism	----										
2. Talk to Someone	-.53**	----									
3. Internalize	.52**	-.09	----								
4. Externalize	.14	-.04	.01	----							
5. Take Action	-.35*	.58**	.15	-.20	----						
6. Emotional Support	-.10	.30*	-.09	.08	.32*	----					
7. Practical Support	-.06	.29	-.09	.08	.32*	.95**	----				
8. Depression	.13	-.10	-.07	.23	-.29	-.20	-.19	----			
9. Life Events	.35*	-.41**	.33*	.13	-.21	.05	.11	-.04	----		
10. Locus of Control	.26	-.21	-.01	.16	-.23	-.31*	-.30*	.59**	-.15	----	
11. Impulse Control	.22	-.37*	-.33*	.17	-.49**	.01	.02	.23	-.01	.34*	----

*p < .05; **p < .01

Table 6.1. Correlational Analyses: Variable Associations and Their Significance

Hypothesis Three: External locus of control will be positively associated with depression and negatively associated with emotional and practical support.

Table 6.1 illustrates results offering support for hypothesis three. *[External] locus of control* was significantly associated with *emotional* (r^2 = -.31; p<.05) and *practical support* (r^2 = -.30; p<.05) and positively associated with *depression* (r^2 = .59; p<.01). These results indicate that those individuals lacking a sense of personal control over their own lives (i.e., an external locus of control) were *more likely* to indicate depressive symptomology and *less likely* to report receiving emotional or practical support from social support network members. It is quite likely that individuals with an external locus of control perceived that they would not receive help from network members, even if they asked. Another possibility is that those with an external locus of control believe that they are largely at the mercy of *external forces*, such as fate or luck, so why bother trying to change stress-inducing circumstances?

Hypothesis Four: Stressful life events will be positively associated with external locus of control.

Hypothesis four was not supported (r^2 = -.15, ns). That is, simply experiencing *more* stressful life events was not associated with having an *external locus of control*. Interestingly however, the number of life events was significantly associated with three types of coping. Specifically, the greater the number of life events reported, the more likely participants were to use *escapism* (r^2 = .35; p<.05) and *internalizing* behavior (r^2 = .33; p<.05), and the less likely respondents were to cope by *talking to others* (r^2 = -.41; p<.01). Participants reporting more stressful life events, in other words, were also more likely to report *coping* with those events using potentially harm inducing behaviors (i.e., escapism and internalizing) and less likely to use potentially *constructive* coping techniques.

Life Events. Additional analyses were run to determine the most commonly reported "life events" experienced within the past year. Arguments or fights with parents (noted by seven women), experiencing the death of a close friend or family member (noted by six participants), having a close friend or family member seriously hurt or injured (which occurred to five participants), becoming involved in counseling or therapy (five women), and decreasing use of alcohol or drugs (four women) were most common.

It is important to point out that the scale used to assess life events was a commonly used and well-regarded research instrument. However, it was not designed for use with this unique population of women. The *types* of life events included on the instrument are those that would potentially create stress among an entire spectrum of adults—not necessarily a population of street-level prostituted women. A more appropriate, population-specific instrument does not currently exist. Incidents such as being beaten by a client or pimp, raped, or conned out of money, (i.e., situations common among prostituted women), were not assessed through this instrument.

Hypothesis Five: Less impulse control will be negatively related to talking to someone and positively related to using escapism and having an external locus of control.

Further examination of Table 6.1 reveals that partial support was found for the fifth hypothesis. *Impulse control* was significantly and negatively associated with *talking to someone* ($r^2 = -.37$; p<.05) and positively associated with *external locus of control* ($r^2 = .34$; p<.05). These results indicate that individuals reporting *little* impulse control (i.e., those who act on the spur of the moment without thinking about the consequences of their actions) were *less likely* to talk to someone or seek assistance from another when faced with a stressful situation. Moreover, individuals lacking impulse control were also more likely to report feeling little control over their own lives (i.e., to have an external locus of control).

Hypothesis Testing: Multiple Regression Analyses

Hypothesis Six: Coping responses will be determined first based on internal resources (e.g., depression, impulse control) and second based on external resources (i.e., social support).

To test this hypothesis, separate hierarchical multiple regression analyses were used and two models were created. As illustrated in Model 1 (see Table 6.2 below), internal resources (i.e., depression, impulse control, locus of control) were entered into the analyses in Block 1. In Model 2, external resources (i.e., emotional and practical support) were entered into the analyses in Block 2. Analyses were conducted for each of the five coping strategies (i.e., escapism, talking to someone, internalizing, externalizing, and taking action). This statistical procedure allowed for determination of the amount of *variance* accounted for through internal resource variables. Variance assumed through external resource variables, above and beyond the influence of internal resources, could then be assessed.

Hypothesis Six was partially supported. Table 6.2 reveals the univariate statistics, R^2 changes from Models 1 and 2, and the standardized regression weights from Model 2. For *active* coping strategies (i.e., doing something about the problem), Model 1, including all three internal resources variables, had an $R^2 = .26$, an adjusted $R^2 = .20$ F (3, 39) change = 4.49, significant at the p<.01 level. *Impulse control* evidenced a negative significant regression weight. These findings indicate that low (or less) impulse control is negatively associated with using active (i.e., doing something) coping strategies.

Model 2, with external resource variables added, had an R^2 change = .10, F (3, 39) change = 5.95, p < .05, with practical support and impulse control having significant regression weights. Emotional support did not contribute to variations in choosing active coping strategies. For *social* coping strategies (e.g., talking to someone), Model 1, with internal resource variables (Block 1) had an $R^2 = .14$, an adjusted $R^2 = .11$, F (1, 41) change = 6.38 (p < .01). Impulse control had a negative significant regression weight, indicating impulse control was negatively associated

Table 6.2. Summary of Results from Regression Models

Coping Strategies	Internal & External Resources	R^2 Change Model 1	R^2 Change Model 2	Standardized Weights Model 2
Do Something		.26**	10*	
	Depression			-.14
	Locus of Control			.12
	Impulse Control			-.49**
	Practical Support			.33*
	Emotional Support			----
Talk to Someone		.14	.09*	
	Depression			.08
	Locus of Control			-.02
	Impulse Control			-.38*
	Emotional Support			.31*
	Practical Support			----
Internalizing		.12		
	Depression			-.06
	Locus of Control			.15
	Impulse Control			-.36*
	Emotional Support			----
	Practical Support			----
Externalizing			.06	
	Depression			.19
	Locus of Control			.01
	Impulse Control			.12
	Emotional Support			----
	Practical Support			----
Escapism			.09	
	Depression			-.06
	Locus of Control			.24
	Impulse Control			.15
	Emotional Support			----
	Practical Support			----

* $p < .05$; ** $p < .01$

with talking to someone, but not the two other internal resources (i.e., depression as an indicator of well-being or locus of control).

Model 2 retained all three internal resource variables (i.e., depression, locus of control, impulse control) and emotional support, when external resource variables (Block 2) were added in the analysis (R^2 change = .09, F (3, 39) change = 5.95 (p < .05). Emotional support had a positive significant regression weight and impulse control had a negative significant regression weight, indicating higher levels of social coping was significantly related to impulse control and perceived emotional support. Simply stated, after controlling all internal resources (i.e., depression, locus of control, and impulse control), perceived emotional support was a *significant predictor* of using *social* coping strategies in potentially stressful situations.

Hierarchical regression models for *internalizing, externalizing,* and *escapism* did not exhibit significant R^2 change and F values. External resource variables were excluded from the models for these coping strategies. For *internalizing,* the R^2 change was .12, and the F (3, 39) change was 1.80 (p > .05). For *externalizing,* the R^2 change was .06, and the F (3, 39) change was 0.89 (p > .05) and for *escapism,* the R^2 change was .09, with an F (3, 39) change of 1.28 (p > .05). None of the internal or external resources were significantly associated with using escapism, internalizing, or externalizing coping strategies *except for impulse control.* Impulse control had a negative significant regression weight when analyzed with *internalizing* coping strategies.

Summary and Discussion

Certain populations, including women and individuals residing in deviant or crime-infested environments, are particularly vulnerable to the threat of psychological and physical harm. According to O'Neill, street-level prostituted women "participate in their own annihilation"[52]. This chapter delineates some of the processes by which "annihilation" may occur. Violence, brutality, and maliciousness inflicted by others, coupled with self-condemnation and destructive forms of escapism, create a physically and psychologically destructive environment.

Victimization may exert profound impacts on an individual's sense of security and agency, which may in turn diminish or challenge optimal well-being. According to stress-theory, assessment of threat or harm is an *individual-specific* process based largely on primary (i.e., cognitive registration of the event) and secondary (i.e., evaluations of personal assets and resources), which ultimately determine coping responses. The manner by which one copes with or responds to potentially threatening circumstances may or may not be effective, and may or may not present additional challenges to personal well-being. To illustrate, drug use by street-level prostituted women may serve as a form of "escapism." But for many, chemical addiction furthers the necessity of remaining on the streets to support one's drug dependence.

Importantly, verbal reports indicated three primary sources of violent perpetrators: clients, pimps, and partners. However, one cannot assume that violence inflicted by these three sources is equally damaging or threatening. Violence perpetrated by strangers likely has different physical and psychological consequences for prostituted women than violence from intimates. With intimates, one is much more likely to be *emotionally* connected to the source of harm.

Correlational analyses provided additional information useful for providing effective, comprehensive intervention on behalf of prostituted women (see summary of results in Table 6.3, below). First, assisting prostituted women in the formation of healthy social support systems (e.g., with mentors, sponsors, women who have successfully exited the sex industry) is critical. Turning to others for emotional and physical support was strongly associated with the use of constructive coping strategies. Moreover, lack of support, or having a weak social support system (or inability to access support network members) were related to negative coping strategies.

Of concern is the strong association between the use of escapism and internalizing coping strategies. Both reactions challenge the development and maintenance of healthy relationships and likely feed off of one another thereby creating a self-destructive cycle. Strong linkages to supportive individuals could interrupt the cycle and possibly promote the use of healthy behavior when faced with anxiety-inducing circumstances. Unfortunately, use of escapism through chemical dependence is pervasive among street-level prostituted women. Thus, drug addiction recovery may very well be the first line of defense for service providers attempting to assist prostituted women learn more constructive coping responses.

Interestingly also was that the number of life events was *negatively* associated with seeking assistance from others. Lacking causal data, it is difficult to interpret the meaning of these findings. However, it is likely that individuals may overwhelm support network members when they experience numerous stress-inducing events within a relatively brief amount of time. In effect, individuals may not be able to turn to informal sources of support as new events pile-up. On the other hand, it could be argued that, lacking rich emotional and practical support systems, individuals are more likely to take greater risks or to rely on themselves out of necessity, thus resulting in (or creating) an accumulation of stressful life circumstances and events. Regardless, correlational analyses reveal the need for intervention and prevention programs to provide prostituted women with education and practical guidance in establishing, accessing, and maintaining strong (and health promoting) networks of support.

Finally, contrary to the "Pretty Woman" myth, none of the participants had been "saved," however broadly defined, by Prince Charming (or Richard Gere). Most were severely and continuously victimized by the men in their lives. What is particularly disturbing is that the most severe violence against these women was perpetrated by the very men comprising their informal support systems during both childhood (e.g., fathers, stepfathers and brothers) and adulthood (i.e., husbands/boyfriends and pimps).

Table 6.3. Summary of Hypotheses, Results from Data Analyses, and Implications

Hypothesis	Results from Analyses	Implications
H1: Emotional & practical support will be (+) related to proactive coping strategies.	**Hypothesis was Supported.** *Emotional support* was (+) related to two *constructive* coping strategies: (1) talking/social seeking, & (2) taking action; *Practical support* (+) related to 'taking action'.	**H1 and H2:** Emotional and and practical support appear strongly related to *constructive* coping techniques. Use of *con-structive* coping techniques is related to less *destructive* (e.g., escapism) strategies. Creating strong interpersonal relationships is critical.
H2: Harm-inducing coping strategies will be (+) associated with depression, and (-) associated with emotional & practical support.	**Hypothesis *Partially* Supported.** Escapism was (-) associated with social/talking coping strategies and (-) associated with taking action.	See Above.
H3: External LC will be (+) associated with depression and (-) associated with emotional & practical support.	**Hypothesis was Supported.** External LC was (-) associated with emotional support and (+) associated with depression.	Prostituted women with an *external* LC are more likely to be depressed and lack emotional support from network members. Intervention focusing on personal agency is warranted.

Continued on next page.

Chapter Seven

Exiting with Optimism

The difficulty lies not so much in developing
new ideas, as in escaping from old ones.
— John Maynard Kynes

When interviewed, the majority (93%) of the women who participated in this research were no longer *actively* involved in the "game." Fourteen were incarcerated, so although they were not off the streets voluntarily, they were nonetheless out temporarily. All twenty-six participants recruited through WellSpring were seeking assistance in order to escape prostitution. The remaining three women, those recruited through word-of-mouth, were attempting to exit on their own without legal intervention or the assistance of formal services.

Thus, this investigation centered not only on prostitution *entry* but also on *exit* attempts and strategies. What factors or experiences compel women to leave street-level sex work? As part of this investigation, I was certainly curious to know the answers to this question, but to others as well. For instance, how did these women envision themselves in the future? What were their dreams and aspirations? And relatedly, what did they perceive as the biggest challenges or stumbling blocks to accomplishing their goals? These questions then, were posed to the 43 female participants.

Little is currently known or understood about processes involved when a woman attempts to leave the street-level sex industry. Only three studies could be located in which the exit process was explicitly examined. Spanning three different countries (Thailand, Sweden, and the United States), these studies provided a guide as I began my own investigation of the exit process. In this chapter, I summarize these three investigations and then provide a detailed account of the primary factors motivating my participants' attempts to exit prostitution. This discussion is followed by a brief synopsis of their future plans and goals.

Overview of Previous Studies Examining the Exit Process

The commercial sex trade has been implicated in the development of a severe HIV epidemic in Thailand[1] and thus, has received some recent attention by social science scholars in that country. Notably, Manopaiboon and colleagues[2] interviewed 42 current and former sex workers to determine factors facilitating and inhibiting their ability to leave the sex trade. Of the 42 women who participated, only 1 had *never quit* sex work, 25 had *quit and re-entered* at least once, and 16 quit the sex industry and never returned.

Three factors, prominent in the women's decisions to leave prostitution, were discussed. These included: (1) developing an intimate relationship, (2) developing negative attitudes toward sex work, and (3) fear of HIV/AIDS. Economics was a significant factor propelling women *back into* the sex trade after attempting to leave. Indeed, economics comprised "the main reason for initiating, remaining in, or returning to sex work"[3] among the Thai women who were interviewed. Interestingly, money garnered from prostitution activity was largely used to purchase material possessions (e.g., house, television), pay off debt, or to support family members. Drug-motivated prostitution was not mentioned by the Thai researchers.

It is important to note that prostitution is viewed very differently in Thailand than in the United States, largely due to work availability. Few employment options exist for women in northern Thailand, aside from farm work or street vending, and thus, the participants' families often supported their daughters' prostitution involvement. According to Manopaiboon et al., "[Participants] did not feel that they would be stigmatized because of their former career as a sex worker. They had done the work out of economic necessity and their community accepted that"[4]. Noteworthy also is that these sex workers were not specifically involved in street-level prostitution, but instead worked in a variety of other sex trade venues including karaoke bars and massage parlors, which may account for the visibly absent mention of either drug use or violent victimization among the prostituted Thai women.

Half-way around the world, in a Swedish investigation, Månsson and Hedin[5] interviewed 23 women who were currently, or had been, involved in the sex industry. Although many were street-level prostituted women, participants involved in other types of sex work (e.g., escort services) were also included. Two types of "break-aways" were described: those which happened quickly by women loosely associated with the sex industry, and those which occurred gradually, after years of exploitation.

Månsson and Hedin describe three different *turning points* that were significant in the women's decisions to "break-away" from sex work. One type of turning point involved eye-opening events, or experiences which made the women realize they needed a "real career". Another type of turning point occurred due to traumatic events involving severe violence and/or life threatening experiences. Finally, positive life events, such as falling in love or having a child marked turning points for other women. Based on the nature of their break-away experiences, the participants were divided into three groups: (1) those who transitioned directly into a new role involving work or study; (2) those who became involved in structured treatment (e.g., detox, an education program); or (3) those who developed a marginal existence characterized by un- or underemployment and welfare dependency with a high possibility of prostitution re-entry.

Månsson and Hedin further identified several challenges associated with exiting prostitution. Primary among these are working through the emotional experiences and feelings of shame associated with prostitution involvement which may involve acute anxiety and development of psychosomatic symptoms, living in a marginal situation while forging a new identity; and forming and maintaining intimate and close relationships, especially with men.

Finally, in a study conducted in the United States with street-level prostituted women specifically, Williamson[6] describes a five stage model of prostitution involvement, from entrance to exit. The five stages include entrance, social adjustment, social immersion, "caught-up," and re-evaluation and exit. Due to its relevance to the phenomena of *exiting*, the fifth phase warrants special attention. Re-evaluation and exit is characterized by life evaluation, intense remorse, and acknowledgment that sex for money, substance use, and the prostitution lifestyle must be abandoned.

Williamson[7] and her colleagues[8] describe three factors precipitating the exit decisions of street-level prostituted women. *Cumulative burdens* refer to the accumulation of emotional and physical trials associated with street-level sex work, such as acute traumas due to street violence and subsequent emotional consequences of victimization. *Restrictive factors* refer to challenges associated with physical deterioration resulting, most often, from long-term substance use and marginal health care. Finally, *relational factors* also influence exit decisions. Relational factors, according to Williamson et al., involve challenges associated with the loss or threatened loss of valued relationship(s) due to prostitution involvement.

Summary

Only a handful of studies have examined women's attempts to exit the sex industry. Only one of the three which could be located focused exclusively on women prostituted on the streets. Yet, this type of information is critical if intervention services are to effectively address challenges associated with the exit process as women attempt to forge new lives for themselves away from the "game." My investigation was intended to fill gaps in the literature and builds upon the work of others. In the pages which follow, results of this phase of my study are presented.

Exiting The "Game"

Participants who were voluntarily attempting to exit the sex industry were asked to describe the primary motives behind their decisions. In contrast, the women who were involuntarily off the streets by virtue of legal intervention, were asked whether they believed they would return to the sex industry once released from prison. Responses from the two groups are presented separately.

Voluntarily Attempts at "Exiting"

Among those who made a voluntarily, conscious decision to leave prostitution, five factors emerged as most influential in their decision-making processes, including: hitting bottom, experiencing life-threatening events, regaining custody of their children or the desire to be better parents, the changing street-level prostitution sub-culture, and spiritual awakening. It is important to note that these reasons were not necessarily mutually exclusive. Some participants described *multiple* reasons for wanting to escape the sex industry. Additionally, three WellSpring clients, Cammie, Cheyenne, and Lettie, reported that they were not "out" of the game entirely. These three women were maintaining "regular" clientele as a source of income. However, none of the three were prostituting on the streets at the time they were interviewed.

Hitting Bottom
Ten women described "hitting bottom" as the most compelling factor motivating their decisions to create new lives for themselves. Hitting bottom, it must be acknowledged, is subjective and thus referred to different things for different women. For some, finding oneself homeless or living in a shelter constituted the "bottom." For others, hitting bottom was synonymous with incarceration.

Bridget sought assistance after finding herself homeless with nowhere to turn. She was living in a homeless shelter at the time she was interviewed. When asked what motivated her to stay out of prostitution, she replied, "Knowing that if I go back, if I get high, I won't have a damn thing. I'll be right back where I started from and believe me, that's nowhere. I mean, I'm scared." Still, Bridget was not totally convinced that her attempt at change would be successful. When asked if she thought she would ever return to prostitution and drugs, she responded: "I hope not. All I can say is just live for today and just pray that God will continue to give me strength."

Tonya, Tori and Ellen described "hitting bottom" after being arrested, charged with solicitation, and spending time in jail. Although two arrests had motivated change for Tori, it took Ellen four times and Tonya seven different jail sentences to elicit an exit attempt. It was while in jail that they learned about WellSpring and were seeking assistance there.

Life-Threatening Events

Life-threatening events also prompted change. Char sought assistance from WellSpring after surviving not one, but two, near death experiences in rapid succession. In the first, she barely escaped a house fire and in the second, she ingested crack cocaine laced with poison. She was found in a gutter, barely alive. Marti and Jenna also survived life-threatening events. Marti had been stabbed by a trick and then thrown out of a window; Jenna had been raped at knife point and held against her will in an abandoned warehouse. She recalled how the incident motivated her to seek assistance: "I was raped, abused, and almost lost my life. Before, I was like, 'Who cares if I die?' But it wasn't till I faced death that I decided I had a reason to live."

Children and Parenting

Eleven different participants explicitly noted that their children provided the motivation they needed to make positive life changes. Most agreed that exiting was necessary if they were to ever regain custody of their children. Some simply wanted to be better parents. Lettie was one of only a handful of participants who had never lost custody of her children, despite her history of prostitution and an addiction to crack cocaine. She commented, "I have two wonderful kids..." and then:

> I missed a lot of their lives when they were young from being high. And I regret it. But I keep telling myself that they're going to need me more in the future—more in the future than in the past and that's what's keeping me going. Because I can't do nothing about the past and I can't do nothing about those times when my kids needed me and I was in trouble. But I can do something about the future. I can't kill myself because of my children and I can't go on getting stuck on the street because of my kids.

Sub-Culture Changes

Marlee and Talisha, as well as several others, indicated that changes in the sub-culture of street-level prostitution had been the primary factor motivating their exits from the industry. As described earlier, the inundation of crack cocaine had indelibly altered the context and culture of street-level sex work. Risks of injury or death due to rampant violence, coupled with strawberries turning tricks for pennies, made the "game" an unattractive endeavor. The pay off was not worth the risk.

Talisha described the process by which she made a final decision to exit by saying:

> You know what, I been robbed out there, I been robbed for my jewelry, I been robbed and raped. I had a gun held to me. You do this and you do that, that kind of thing and then the tricks got cheap.

She then remarked:

> You know, its okay to be out there. Today it ain't wise, but if that's the type of lifestyle you want to live. But for me– I guess I have gotten older and I'm like I want to settle down with one man, not having sex and being with this man and that man. I don't want that.

When asked if she was concerned that she might one day return to prostitution and drug use, Talisha replied, "Not back into none of that. No. I'm through with that. I really am. Because I hurt my family, I hurt my kids. I tore them apart."

Marlee's responses mirrored those of Talisha. She had witnessed enormous changes in the sub-culture of the street-level sex industry over the past decade. She no longer found the streets exciting. Instead, they were dangerous. Moreover, Marlee was income-oriented and could no longer make money in the "game." Also like Talisha, she described reaching a place in her life where she wanted stability, consistency, and the ability to retire comfortably at some point in the future. She explained,

> I regret that I went on the streets. Like now, I'm just now getting started in a [legal] job when most of my friends been on their jobs 15 years and are ready to retire. I know I regret that. I could have done something better with my life.

Marlee largely believed that prostitution was forever a memory of the past. "You know," she commented, "they say 'never say never' and I pray everyday that I don't have to. [But] when I make-up my mind to do something, I do it."

Spirituality/Religiosity

Spirituality, as defined by the Summit on Sprituality[9], is a "capacity and tendency that is innate and unique to all persons. Spiritual tendency moves the individual toward knowledge, love, meaning, hope, transcendence, connectedness, and compassion. Spirituality includes one's capacity for creativity, growth, and the development of a values system. It encompasses the religious, spiritual, and trans-personal." Spirituality is generally believed to be less formal than religion which entails a set of codified beliefs that connects a person to a God or gods and that influences her daily life[10].

Five participants spoke of spirituality and/or faith in a higher power as strongly influencing their attempts at lifestyle changes. For instance, although Erica had been unsuccessful in previous attempts at exiting the sex industry, she believed that this time would be different. She had turned to God for support and guidance and explained: "I had seven months of sobriety before this relapse, and this relapse lasted a year." She relapsed because"I wanted to use– that's the only reason. I truly thought I had been delivered from my addiction at one point in life. I had no desire to use what-so-ever." She was then asked what motivated her most recent attempt at sobriety, to which she responded "Myself" and then continued,

That desire to quit is always there, but to actually do it you have to be ready and God– it has a lot to do with God. It does. I knew I wasn't going to stay back out there [on the streets], I just didn't know when I'd be done.

Sam, likewise, reported that God's work had been the primary factor motivating her latest exit attempt. She described a dream she had while in jail, a dream in which she kept insisting that her ex-husband had to "repent" for the misery she had endured while with him. Remembering the dream when she awoke, she decided to write her ex-husband and to include a bible scripture. She picked up a Bible and in the process, asked God: "Well, what scripture should I give him [her ex]?" And then:

I opened up my bible and I came right to a scripture about repenting. You know, to give yourself to the Lord. That's what it was. That's what the scripture was: 'Give yourself to the Lord.' That really got me believing. What I believe is, I prayed, and I asked God to give me patience and to give me strength.

Although Trina never provided a specific "factor" or "turning point" that motivated her exit, she did explain how exiting was a *process* that began for her when she was jailed for prostitution. In jail, Trina began reading the bible and soon afterwards developed a romantic relationship with a detention officer. She was interviewed in an apartment that the two shared. God's hand, she believed, was helping her maintain sobriety. During the interview, Trina described her break from prostitution:

I have so much more to look forward to in life than drugs. I wasn't getting anywhere. I'm 35 years old and no dummy. I can go back to school, I know how to work, I'm not disabled. In a year I could have my license reinstated, a permanent job, have my kids and a relationship with them. Whereas with drugs, in a year where am I at? What do I do? I'll be somewhere getting high or prostituting.

She was then asked why *this time*? Why would this attempt at being drug- and prostitution-free be different from previous attempts? She replied, "Because I finally realized it. I guess it was God's calling." Trina's reasons for exiting included a smorgasbord of personal, economic, and relational issues that finally converged to provide the needed impetus to attempt the exit process once again.

Finally, a number of the other women who were interviewed reported that fear of HIV infection or other sexually transmitted diseases/infections (STD/Is) prompted, at least partially, their desire to make lifestyle changes. One participant simply "wanted a better life" than what the streets afforded.

Involuntary Exits

Fourteen women were interviewed while incarcerated in a women's maximum security prison. They had been incarcerated for an average of 14 months. Several had been in-and-out of prison on numerous occasions. One woman, Georgette, had spent a total of 21½ years in prison, with intermittent time on the streets. As noted in an earlier chapter, Georgette and her daughter Candace were both incarcerated in the same prison, for the same offenses.

Crimes leading to imprisonment included prostitution, drug use with intent to distribute, larceny, robbery, armed robbery, parole violation, and extortion. Although not an ideal spot for life-reflection, several participants nonetheless indicated that being imprisoned had been beneficial. For example, each of the 14 imprisoned women reported having been chemically dependent. Incarceration forced sobriety. Additionally, prison provided opportunities to obtain job skills (e.g., computer training) and educational advancements (e.g., GED course work) which many felt would assist them in obtaining employment once released. Moreover, the prison also offered self-help classes on a variety of topics ranging from anger-management to interpersonal skills building. Several of the women had completed these courses and found them personally valuable.

Their reasons for being off the streets were obvious. Legal intervention had derailed their lives, at least for a short while. Yet, just because their removal from society was a result of legal action, this does not imply that their removal was not welcome. Some were thankful for the reprieve from the streets. Anna reported, "You know, I kind of look at it now like it's probably a blessing that I'm here and not dead."

Seven of the 14 felt that prison had provided them an opportunity to re-evaluate their lives from a chemical-free point of view. Rachel, for one, was ready for a lifestyle change. Not only was she free of drugs but her boyfriend had also stopped using during her incarceration. She was hopeful that, upon her release, they could make a life together that wouldn't include prostitution or drugs. And Bryn, who had served six and one-half years, of a 25 year sentence for first degree burglary and prostitution, was convinced that she would never again abuse drugs. She was decidedly less certain about her ability to remain prostitution-free. She explained:

> I've really learned my lesson this time around. I came in here over prostitution and drugs. And I don't think I'll ever do it again in my life. You know, I mean I have that fixed in my mind right now. But that's not to say never. That I will *never* do it again. But I would never do it [prostitute] for drugs, like if I need money for my kids or something like that. I've been through a lot of hell, I just really want to change my life.

However, in order to make significant life changes, she had to make a clean break from her husband– the man who had pimped her out. According to Bryn,

He's been a big downfall in my life. So that's one thing I'll have to give up, is him. I mean I love him, but I don't see him in my life. Otherwise I will be back [in prison] and I'm not coming back here for him or nobody else.

Although Georgette had spent the last 21 years of her life familiar with the prison system, she was attending in-house drug treatment for the first time ever and reasoned, "This is the first time I've been to treatment and it's because I want to quit. I'm through. I'm tired." Angel also believed she was "done" with drugs and, when asked if she felt she would return to prostitution replied, "Lord I don't want to."

Not surprisingly, compared to their non-incarcerated peers, the imprisoned women expressed less confidence in their ability to remain prostitution and drug-free. Release from prison and the transition back into society would likely present tremendous challenges for some. Four participants admitted that the allure of "old playgrounds and playmates" would prove too tempting to abandon entirely. To illustrate, Patti was asked why she stopped using cocaine, to which she replied, "I haven't. I was forced to quit because I'm incarcerated."

Similarly, although Alli was not planning future involvement with the drug scene, she was less-than-certain that she would be able to remain chemically free upon her release. "I'm going to put forth a better effort than I did before. I know when I start having urges I'm going to do what I was told to do: call my Sponsor." She then stated, "I mean I can't say that I'm never [going to use drugs], but I'm going to say that I'm going to put forth an effort."

Summary

Motivation to exit the sub-culture of street-level prostitution was largely prompted by five unique, but oftentimes intersecting, factors. The reasons given by these women for attempting to exit the sex industry are quite similar to those reported by Williamson[11] in her study of street-level prostitution. Specifically, Williamson described *relational factors* (i.e., fear of losing an important relationship) as motivating women's exit from the street-level sex industry. In this investigation, participants also spoke of relational factors as paramount in their decisions to exit. They described wanting to regain custody of their children and to be better parents. Further, some also spoke of the need to exit in order to *maintain* intimate relationships with male partners. Rachel, for instance, risked losing her long-time boyfriend if she did not successfully exit the sex industry and remain drug-free. She was not willing to take the risk.

Williamson further described *restrictive factors* (i.e., physical deterioration) as prompting women's prostitution exits. In this study, several participants including Georgette, Marti, and Marlee, spoke of "being tired" and being "ready" for a new lifestyle. They spoke further of wanting *security* in the later phases of their lives and of the desire to retire at some point; prostitution would not allow for financial security in the future. Furthermore, Williamson's notion of *cumulative burdens* (i.e., accumulation of emotional and physical trials, including acute traumas) nicely corresponds to what several participants in my investigation described as "hitting bottom". Hitting bottom typically referred to being homeless or incarcerated; and another group described surviving life-threatening experiences.

Curiously, previous studies have failed to mention *spirituality* or connection to a higher power as motivating the exit process. In fact, regardless of whether the study was conducted in the United States (i.e., Williamson[12], Williamson and Folaron[13]), Thailand (i.e., Manopaiboon et al.[14]) or Sweden (i.e, Månsson and Hedin[15]), and regardless of *type* of prostitution explored (e.g., massage parlor, escort, street-level) religiosity/spirituality is visibly absent in published reports of the sex-industry exit process. Among the participants of this investigation however, God's power and influence was mentioned repeatedly.

Finally, in their classification based on the nature of women's "break-away" experiences, Månsson and Hedin describe women who transitioned directly into work or study, a structured treatment, or who developed a marginal existence with high risk of prostitution re-entry. Incarceration or imprisonment, was *not* mentioned as a "transitional" context in their investigation. However, among the women who participated in this study, incarceration was noted as a common place for the transition process to begin. Many of those interviewed reported that their time away from the streets, either in prison or jail, allowed reflection and prompted determination to leave street-level prostitution for good. Time off the streets appeared to provide a much-needed *transitional context* for making behavioral and cognitive changes necessary for a turning-point to begin.

Looking Ahead:
Aspirations and Challenges

Dreams are renewable. No matter what our age or condition, there are still
untapped possibilities within us and new beauty waiting to be born.
–Dr. Dale Turner

Generally, whether their exit attempts were voluntary and intentional or involuntary due to legal intervention, the participants shared similar hopes and dreams for their futures. They described wanting: to regain custody of their children back and to be better parents; a committed, monogamous relationship with a partner who provided unconditional love; a home and a physical space to call their own and which provided a sense of security; a strong relationship with God or a higher power; and a steady source of legal income and the ability to use their skills and talents in a meaningful manner. Their dreams are no different from yours or mine. These are the dreams of people who desire to love and to be loved, who desire to fit in and belong, and who desire to make a contribution to society through valued, purposeful work. Many were optimistic about the journey before them. Many believed, as Anna did, that "a bright future" was in the making.

Relationships

When asked about their futures, participants wanted, more than anything else, close intimate relationships. Children were discussed frequently. To illustrate, two of Sam's four children were still minors. One was in a foster group home and the other a detention center. More than anything, she hoped to one day have "...my boys back. I want to get my kids back. To have a normal life." She was not alone. Alli was "determined to get my kids back and to get my life back."

Like Sam and Alli, Bryn also spoke of relationships with her children and an intimate male partner. Her ideal future would be complete with a home of her own. As evident in her comment below, she was willing to wait many years if necessary, to see her dreams come to fruition.

> My dream life is to own my own house and to be married and to have a family of my own. I don't know if it would be ten years down the road or it might be fifty years down the road. But before I die, I want to own my own house and to have a husband that is going to love me and take care of me.

Like many others, Amy also spoke of her children with great eagerness and optimism. She was within two weeks of re-gaining custody of her sons who had spent the previous year in foster care. She not only wanted them back, but she also wanted to be a better parent, and someday, to have a home. Amy was pensive about marriage. She desired a committed, monogamous partnership but had reservations because she had "never been in a healthy relationship." Moreover, she had never witnessed role models who demonstrated strong marital bonds. She was afraid of repeating the same mistakes that she saw others make and was at a loss as to how to build and maintain a healthy, strong marital relationship. Still, the ideal man would:

> ...be someone who accepts me, that we can talk about whatever and he wouldn't throw anything about my past in my face, not be judging me, to just love me for who I am and for what I've lived through and where I've been and to be encouraging.

Bridget hoped to marry the father of her youngest child, a four-month-old daughter. While she was attempting to re-direct her life and exit the sex industry, the baby's father had full custody. And Barb hoped to keep the child she was carrying– the baby was due within two months of our interview. She was hoping to be a better parent in the future than she had been in the past, and leaving the "game" was necessary for that to happen. And Kendra hoped that leaving the "game" would help her earn the respect of her children.

Others also spoke of relationships. When asked about her plans following her release from prison, Georgette stated, "Right now, my grandkids are in foster care. They're with my cousin and all I want to do when I get out is get a job and get a place to stay and get my grandbabies back." She was then questioned about her daughter's ability to care for her own children, to which Georgette remarked, "She's got a two-year sentence and I don't think she's ready to act right and somebody's got to act right." Candace, who was also interviewed, envisioned herself attending school and becoming a cosmetologist. Finally, Jackie emphatically stated, "I know I'm going to be a better person when I get out of here. And not just for my kids, but for myself."

Although many spoke of their desires to renew relationships with children and build relationships with intimates, not everyone wanted marriage, or even a partner. Ellen is a case in point. When asked whether she envisioned marriage for her future she reasoned, "No I don't. I don't ever want to get married again, never, never, never. I just want to live the rest of my life around my grandbabies. My life is going to be around *real love.*"

Employment

Six of the women reported knowing exactly what their future careers would entail– they wanted to be counselors and social workers. It is no coincidence that many of these women hoped to be advocates on behalf of others. They had survived the terror and betrayal of childhood molestation, physical abuse, and blatant neglect. They had been violated on the streets by clients, and in their homes by their partners. Many of their lives had spiraled swiftly out of control. And they had turned to themselves, in order to regain their self-hood. It is because of their experiences that they believed they could effectively advocate on behalf of others.

Chrissy, who had completed two years of community college, was determined to return to school to be a social worker. Her choice of career was fitting because "I love people and I think my purpose here is to serve." Yolanda and Tami wanted to be counselors–Yolanda working with homeless women and Tami with troubled runaways. Cammie also described a desire to help others, but not as a counselor. Cammie's talents were elsewhere. She was a writer and an artist, and explained:

> I want to be a screenwriter. I want to write books, like self-help books about abuse and stuff like that. I mean, I want to write. I want to be heard. I want to be heard because I've experienced a lot and I've learned a lot and I want to do something where other women can someday learn from it.

Finally, Angel had owned and operated an escort service prior to her incarceration. In the future, she hoped "to own another business–a legal one!"

Spirituality/Religiosity

Reference to God or a higher power was not limited to these women's explanations for leaving the sex industry. Indeed, in discussing their futures, multiple women mentioned the desire to devote their lives to God. Sharia commented: "I have made up in my heart and mind that I want to serve the Lord the rest of my life, because He truly has delivered me." Erica also wanted to serve God; the exact capacity of her work was yet to be determined. Still, she explained: "Eventually, I see myself doing something for God, whether it be helping prostitutes like myself or drug counseling. I honestly don't know. Whatever God calls for me, just to do God's will." Like Sharia and Erica, Tonya similarly stated, "I see my self doing something for God." And Chrissy was quite clear that her life would be devoted to serving God. She commented:

> Right now, what I want is contentment–peace of mind. I want to be healthy, I pray and ask God to let me fall in love with Him. I want to fall in love with Him. I want to love God like I love myself. I am a self-centered, pleasure-seeking person. I wish that I could love God that way. And I think that if I could, all my troubles would be over with.

Chrissy was not looking for a panacea or a silver bullet to magically erase the troubling aspects of her life. Instead, she was searching for serenity and peace. She and many others wanted a new lease on life filled with opportunity and optimism. It is through God and spiritual healing, many believed, that their goals would be attained.

Ellen summed up the desires of many. She wanted more than a job, more than a loving family, and more than a stronger relationship with God: she wanted an entirely different life.

> I hope to change my whole entire life and to see life in a whole different perspective. I want to see things in a different way than what I've been seeing. I want to do things in a positive way. I think the way that I was living my life was negative. There was a lot of negativity around me. I just want to do things on a positive base [sic]. I was doing things without God. I was doing them to please myself and not God and I learned you have to have Him inside. And with His spirit inside, you can do all things.

Additional Comments

Several participants described conscious efforts *not* to think about the future; their goals centered on daily successes only. Jenna reported, "I can only go one day at a time. Recovery teaches that. But I look forward to committing myself for a year. I have never made it a year of sobriety and that's my goal, to get a year. That is a small goal." And, rather than discussing what she *hoped to have* in the future, Marti instead stated what she *did not want*: "No alcohol, drugs, men, or marriages."

It would be misleading to only mention those women who had plans of changing their lives by taking active steps to remove themselves from the "game." Not everyone provided hopeful or optimistic accounts of their futures and not everyone appeared ready to exit. In fact, Autumn and Patti described future plans that would likely result in prostitution re-entry. They were temporarily off the streets and out of the "game"due to incarceration, but primed to remain embedded within the sub-culture of street-level prostitution. Autumn's plans for the future included moving to Las Vegas and becoming a dancer. A lot of money could be made in this line of work, she explained. Without question, given her history of prostitution and chemical dependence, Autumn's dream of dancing on the Las Vegas strip may very well propel her immediate re-entry into the "game." She was not unaware of this risk. She anticipated my questions by offering the following qualifying statement: "[But], I'm not selling myself for money." Clearly, Autumn was well-aware of the risk imposed by her dream career. Like Autumn, Patti appeared ill-equipped or motivated to make lifestyle changes. She admitted: "I can tell you that I am *not done* selling drugs" [emphasis added]. Hustling, she explained, was just too lucrative to abandon.

Finally, the most heartbreaking and tragic statements that I heard from any individual who participated in this investigation, were spoken by Char. When asked about her future, she simply stated, "I'm going to be alone by myself with the devil." Char was convinced that, due to the physical abuse she had inflicted upon her youngest son, she was destined to spend eternity in hell repenting for sins committed. I questioned Char about her support system, and perhaps a love interest or partner to which she replied, "Ain't no normal person going to like me." She did, however, have one hope for her future: "to see my daughter happy."

Challenges

Most of the participants were quite cognizant of the challenges they faced in turning their lives around so that their exits would be permanent. Certainly, the women varied extensively with regard to how committed they were to making the significant lifestyle changes necessary in order to leave the "game" for good. Some, like Marlee, had been out of the sex industry for an extensive period of time by the time they were interviewed. They had made the initial transition into conventional society and were continuing to live their lives free of prostitution and drugs. However, many others had only recently transitioned out of the "game." It is logical to assume that certain factors, including the recency of one's exit, length of time involved in the sex industry, and presence of chemical addiction, would surely impact the number and severity of challenges faced by the women, and conse-quently, the personal reserves, and formal and informal assistance required if their exit attempts were to be successful.

Addiction Management
Chemical dependence is, unquestionably, strongly connected to street-level prostitution. For the majority of women interviewed, drug addiction did not propel their entry into the sex industry, but nonetheless *compelled* their continued prostitution involvement. Said differently, chemical addiction maintained involvement in street-level prostitution even if other factors (such as economic need) prompted initial entry. It is therefore not surprising that the majority indicated

that remaining drug-free was paramount to their ability to abandon the streets. Numerous women had attempted to exit previously, their efforts had been only marginally successful. Talisha clearly described how the "entry-exit-re-entry" cycle operated in her life:

> With me, it's [exiting] hard because with crack, I'd say 'Oh I'm through. I'm not going to mess with it,' and then I'd turn around and I'd start doing it again. I was doing really good but relapse is something else. You can't do it by yourself. You have to work programs, you have to go to NA and AA and you have to have a support system.

To manage her addiction, Talisha planned to work programs "probably for the rest of my life, more than likely." Ellen was similarly concerned, as the future she envisioned for herself also required sobriety. Still, when asked if she would ever use drugs or engage in prostitution again, she remarked "It depends on the need and my state of mind–depends on what state of mind I allow myself to get into and I hope I never allow myself to get into certain states of mind again." Clearly, she was hopeful about her future, but the door was open for relapse.

Chancey was unique in that she was not chemically addicted and had not used drugs in over 30 years, yet she prostituted regularly. Chancey described herself as "a sex addict." She had been clinically diagnosed with bi-polar disorder, obsessive-compulsive disorder (OCD), post traumatic stress disorder (PTSD), and she was prone to genital self-mutilation. Chancey's biggest challenge, she admitted, was maintaining her mental health. When not properly managed, her energies were channeled into recurrent and compulsive sexual thoughts and images. Without proper treatment, Chancey's risk for continued prostitution was high. She also believed she would battle exaggerated sexual urges her entire life. Chancey was willing to attend support groups, see therapists, and take medication. Unfortunately, receiving quality care and treatment for her unique ailments was proving difficult.

Support Systems

In addition to remaining drug-free, participants spoke of additional challenges they faced. One of these involved the ability to develop and maintain a healthy, non drug-abusing support system. Unfortunately for many, this meant maintaining distance from their *former* support systems– support systems that included friends and family. Ellen explained:

> My biggest challenge right now is to stop being around people that use. This is one of my biggest challenges because of the fact [that] there are people in my family who use and I have to stay away from people in my family for a long period of time.

Roxanne concurred:

I need a support system. I need to build a support system and I'm just not sure where to start. I definitely know that I need that. I'll see my family and stuff [once released from prison], but I've set boundaries and they are not a good support system. So what I need to do is figure out exactly what agencies to go to, NA and people like that. I don't have it in me to do it all by myself right now.

Application of Knowledge

Certainly, one of the *biggest* challenges facing these women was wanting to change, wanting to live a different life, and making a conscious, concerted effort to doing so. Roxanne agreed:

I believe that whether you're in prostitution or in drug addiction, or whatever, I believe that anyone can change and come out of it. But you have to want it. And I mean you really have to want it. And you just can't say 'Okay, the knowledge is out there.' I mean, in these courses and classes they'll teach you, they'll educate you about drug addiction or this or that and you can observe it all. But if you don't *apply it*, it's no good.

As someone who had been involved in prostitution for 16 years, who lacked family support, and who was also chemically addicted, Barb's challenges to successfully exiting prostitution were vast. In fact, rather than identify specific issues that might tempt her return to prostitution and drugs, she commented instead, "I'm avoiding problems. I'm just going to try not to make any mistakes. *If it looks familiar, I'm going to leave it alone.*"

Dating

Finally, despite the desire of several to develop monogamous, committed relationships, such aspirations came with challenges– one of which involved finding the right partner. The "right" man, for many, would be a person who was drug-free, Christian, and who refrained from any and all criminal activity. Finding this person meant socializing, meeting people, and becoming involved in the larger community. It also meant dating. Herein was an issue of great concern. Four women were afraid of dating. They did not know exactly what "dating" referred to or how to go about doing it. Amy, for instance, was ambivalent about dating. She admitted, "Dating is exciting. It seems exciting. But then I also think that they might want to have sex so then I don't want to date."

Dating is something most of us experience over and over again throughout our lives– often beginning during the adolescent period. For the typical adolescent, the second decade of life is a time of identity consolidation and working through various developmental issues (e.g., sexuality, education, career choices) that impinge upon one's sense of self. It is important to point out that adolescence is a critical stage of development for honing interpersonal skills and building confidence in mixed-sex social interactions. Adolescent researchers describe a common path leading to intimate, one-on-one heterosexual relationship formation[16-18]. The process begins with mixed-sex group activities that involve little contact between males and females. Group dating follows, in which boys and girls go out together spending time as couples and with the larger group. Casual, couple dating occurs next. This is followed by serious, monogamous dating. The awkwardness felt by youth as they maneuver the dating scene is often bearable because the experiences are common to all; friends and potential partners are equally naïve and inexperienced.

Thus, although the dating landscape is filled with potential land-mines and embarrassing moments, one does not transverse the journey *alone*. Support is available from peers, parents, and perhaps also from older siblings. However, for the majority of women who participated in this investigation, adolescence was far from typical. They did not experience a transition period between childhood and adulthood that fostered or promoted "normative" developmental experiences. Yolanda explained: "I've never really had a 'date-date' in my whole life without just first going straight to the sex." Despite their extensive sexual experience, participants often reported lacking confidence in cross-sex interpersonal and relationship-building skills. In essence, they were faced with the monumental task of jumping a strange and unfamiliar hurdle that most people, by their mid-twenties or thirties, have had extensive experience.

Discussion

Leaving the streets was a conscious decision made by the majority of participants. Twenty-six were actively seeking help through formal intervention services as part of WellSpring, three others were attempting to exit without formal intervention. Among the remaining 14 women, exiting the sex industry was precipitated by imprisonment. None of the women who were interviewed as part of this investigation had *planned* on prostituting. They reported never imagining that they would succumb to the sub-culture of street-level prostitution, to chemical dependence, to violence and brutality, or to the degradation of selling themselves on the streets to passers-by. None reported "prostitute" as a long-term career goal. And, according to Amy, "Anybody that says that they like doing it [prostitution] is in denial." Thus, it is not surprising that they dreamt of better lives. Many believed that peace, serenity, and contentment were on the horizon.

Alfred Adler[19] argued that life presents challenges in the form of five *life tasks*. The first he referred to as *society*. Adler believed that no one exists in isolation because we are each dependent on one another and further, we *need* social recognition for a whole and complete life. In fact, *social integration*, to Adler, was a sign of strong mental health. A related task involves having an *occupation or work role*. According to Adler, we are dependent on the labor of others, and in return, we must contribute to society through labor. Work is essential to personal feelings of worthiness, value and belongingness. Work provides integration into a larger social context.

The third task, referred to as *sex* by Adler, actually has a much broader meaning and includes *love and intimacy*. As social beings, we must form and maintain close, intimate relationships with others. Cooperation in our inter-personal relationships is vital. Adler wrote that we would do well to approach others as collaborators, not competitors as they are our *mitmenschen*[20], our fellow human beings and our equals. Love and intimacy between comrades then, is a critical component of wholeness.

The fourth life task consists of recognition of and attention to our *spiritual* selves. Each of us must deal with "the problem of defining the nature of the universe, the existence and nature of God, and how to relate these concepts."[21] And finally, we must learn to cope with *ourselves*. Dealing with ourselves, as described by Adler, consists of developing a personal identity, learning about ourselves as individuals, determining our role(s) in society, and developing and living by a set of moral convictions. Taken together, how we approach, work through, and define ourselves in relation to each of these five life tasks largely determines our *lifestyle*. It is through our personally unique lifestyles that we give *meaning to life*.

Adler's insight into the human condition is appropo for investigation of the present phenomenon, despite his writing about life tasks, lifestyle, and life meaning many decades ago. Did the women who participated in this investigation not describe, in their own words, needing to "deal with" at least one (and often several) of Adler's five *life tasks*? Did they not speak of the need to love and be loved, of the need for intimacy in their lives and the dire need to develop new ways of relating to their children and partners? Did they not hope to participate in meaningful work and an occupation which would allow them to contribute talent and skill, in addition to their time? Did they not want to find a place in the larger cultural context, in conventional society, and to leave "old playgrounds and playmates" behind? Did they not speak of spirituality and the presence of God in their lives and the desire to be closer to Him and to follow His path? And finally, did they not speak of confronting their biggest demon of all, which was for many, themselves? The five life tasks described by Adler are not population specific. They exist for each of us. How we approach, process, interpret, and work through them however, is personally unique and subjective.

It is important to note further that Adler did not believe in the notion of "mental illness." People, according to Adler, were not "mentally sick" or "pathological." Instead, people became *discouraged*. Discouragement, he wrote, is a reaction to faulty learning, often from within the family of origin, that results in difficulty in dealing with one or more of the five life tasks[22].

According to Adler, overcoming challenges and promoting lifestyle changes, is best achieved through *encouragement*– through overcoming feelings of inferiority and discouragement, coupled with recognition and utilization of one's skills, talents, and resources. One can only hope that the formal and informal resources needed to do work through *discouragement* are available for the women interviewed as part of this study. If not, they may once again find themselves caught in the "entry-exit-re-entry" cycle, with unfulfilled dreams, feelings of self-degradation and failure, and notions of contentment and peace-of-mind forever elusive.

Notes

1. Bernhard Schwartlander, Karen A. Stanecki, and Tim Brown, "Country-Specific Estimates and Models of HIV and AIDS: Methods and Limitations," *AIDS* 13 (1999): 2445-58.

2. Chomnad Manopaiboon, Rebecca E. Bunnell, Peter H. Kilmarx, Supaport Chaikummao, Khanchit Limpakarnjanarat, Somsak Supawitkul, Michael E. St. Louis, and Timothy D. Mastro, "Leaving Sex Work: Barriers, Facilitating Factors and Consequences for Female Sex Workers in Northern Thailand," *AIDS Care* 15 (2003): 39-52.

3. Manopaiboon and others, "Leaving Sex Work," 48.

4. Manopaiboon and others, "Leaving Sex Work," 48.

5. Sven-Axel Månsson and Ulla-Carin Hedin, "Breaking the Matthew Effect- On Women Leaving Prostitution," *International Journal of Social Welfare* 8 (1999): 67-77

6. Celia Williamson, "Entrance, Maintenance, and Exit: The Socio-Economic Influences and Cumulative Burdens of Female Street Prostitution," *Dissertation Abstracts International, A: The Humanities and Social Sciences* 61 (2000): 773-A.

7. Williamson, "Entrance, Maintenance, and Exit," *Dissertation Abstracts.*

8. Celia Williamson and Gail Folaron, "Understanding the Experiences of Street Level Prostitutes," *Qualitative Social Work* 2 (2003): 271-87.

9. Summit on Spirituality, *Counseling Today* (1995), 30.

10. Gerald Corey, Marianne Schneider Corey, and Patrick Callanan, "Issues and Ethics in the Helping Professions," 6th ed., (Pacific Grove, CA: Brooks/Cole, 2003).

11. Williamson, "Entrance, Maintenance, and Exit," *Dissertation Abstracts.*

12. Williamson, "Entrance, Maintenance, and Exit," *Dissertation Abstracts*

13. Celia Williamson, and Terry Cluse-Tolar, "Pimp-Controlled Prostitution: Still an Integral Part of Street Life," *Violence Against Women* 8 (2002): 1074-92.

14. Manopaiboon et al., "Leaving Sex Work," 39-52.

15. Månsson and Hedin, "Breaking the Matthew Effect," *International Journal,* 67-77.

16. Jennifer Connolly, Wendy Craig, Adele Goldberg, and Debra Pepler, "Conceptions of Cross-Sex Friendships and Romantic Relationships in Early Adolescence," *Journal of Youth and Adolescence* 28 (1999): 481-94.

17. Marilyn J. Montgomery and Gwendolyn T. Sorell, "Love and Dating Experiences in Early and Middle Adolescence: Grade and Gender Comparisons," *Journal of adolescence* 21 (1998): 677-89.

18. B. Bradford Brown, "You're Going Out With Who?": Peer Group Influences on Adolescent Romantic Relationships," in *Contemporary Perspectives on Adolescent Romantic Relationships*, ed. Wyndol Furman, B. Bradford Brown, and Candace Feiring (New York: Cambridge University Press, 1999), 291-329.

19. Harold H. Mosak, "Adlerian Psychotherapy," in *Current Psychotherapies* (6th ed), ed. Raymond J. Corsini and Danny Wedding (Belmont, CA: Brooks/Cole, 2000), 54-98.

20. Mosak, "Adlerian Psychotherapy," 57.

21. Mosak, "Adlerian Psychotherapy," 59.

22. Mosak, "Adlerian Psychotherapy," 70.

Section Three

Follow-Up and Application

Chapter Eight

Three Years Later:
A Longitudinal Investigation

It is good to have an end to journey towards,
but it is the journey that matters, in the end.
                                    –Ursula Le Guin

Understanding women's reasons for entering and maintaining prostitution involvement, as well as strategies employed to exit the sex-industry, is absolutely necessary for creating effective prevention and intervention services, and advocating on behalf of a unique population of marginalized women. Yet, the majority of research has focused on prostitution *entry* and *maintenance* (i.e., why they remain involved). Only a handful of studies have addressed women's attempts to *exit prostitution*. These studies were described earlier and include the work of Williamson[1] and her colleagues[2] in the United States, the work of Manopaiboon et al.[3] in Thailand, and the work of Månsson and Hedin[4] in Sweden.

Limitations of Earlier Studies

Prior studies examining the exit process are limited on two accounts. First, two of the three investigations (i.e., those conducted by Manopaiboon et al., and Månsson and Hedin) included participants involved in a variety of *types* of prostitution. Only the work of Williamson is exclusively focused on the street-level prostituted women. Street-level sex work is qualitatively different from other forms of prostitution (e.g., brothel or escort service work). It is therefore reasonable to assume that differences also exist in exit strategies and challenges between women engaged in street-level versus other forms of sex work. Thus, maintaining *distinction* between various forms of prostitution is important.

Second, each of the previously mentioned studies utilized *cross-sectional* research designs. That is, data were collected at one point in time only. Despite the

163

wealth of information obtained, *developmental processes* cannot be adequately assessed from cross-sectional work. For example, Månsson and Hedin[5] interviewed 23 women with prostitution experience. They were grouped as follows: (1) those who transitioned into a new role (e.g., work or study); (2) those who became involved in structured treatment; and (3) those who developed a marginal existence. The data suggest that the third group of women are at greatest risk for prostitution re-entry. Yet, lacking developmental data, it is not possible to determine which of the women will or will not re-enter. Exiting prostitution is a process, not an event, which often involves numerous "exit-re-entry-exit" cycles[6-7]. Longitudinal data (i.e., data collected through time), provides information critical for documenting the entire cycle– and thus, for delineating specific factors that promote and/or challenge a woman's ability to remain permanently free of the "game." Such information could prove quite valuable for creating effective intervention and service delivery programs.

Longitudinal data from street-level prostituted women are visibly absent in the literature. Longitudinal research is intensive and time consuming. Academics are pressured to continuously publish research results and longitudinal methodologies make continuous publication difficult. Also, street-level prostituted women comprise a transitory, difficulty-to-access population. Maintaining contact with specific prostituted women through time presents enormous challenges that consequently render quality longitudinal work onerous, at best. Even among scholars with the desire, time, and ability to conduct longitudinal research, there is certainly no guarantee that participants can be found weeks or months, much less years, later. My goal in conducting a follow-up study of street-level prostituted women was to begin to address the gaps in the scholarly literature. I hoped to obtain *process-oriented* data that would allowed for the entire "entry-exit-re-entry" cycle to be documented among a single group of women. This chapter describes results of my efforts.

Phase Two:
A Longitudinal Investigation

Given my interest in human development, it seemed only natural that I would embark upon a longitudinal investigation. Thus, three years after conducting in-depth interviews with 43 street-level prostituted women, I attempted to re-locate each of them for a follow-up interview. My primary goal was to determine the extent to which they had been successful in their efforts to *exit* the sex industry and to explore factors which promoted and challenged their exit attempts. Thus, beginning in 2001, I began a long and exhaustive search for the original 43 women. I found 19 and 18 agreed to be interviewed for a second time. To achieve my research goals, interviews focused on developmental processes and life experiences in the three year period of time spanning the first and second interviews.

Methodology

Eighteen women (i.e., 42% of the original sample of 43) participated. They were located using the same strategies that I had used earlier (i.e., in 1998 and 1999). First, the director of WellSpring was contacted. She then contacted nine women who had remained involved with WellSpring. They were given my name and phone number and then contacted me.

I also returned to the maximum security women's prison where 14 women had been originally interviewed. Three of the 14 were located and interviewed in prison. I also contacted the parole officers of seven others. One woman was found through her parole officer and she agreed to be interviewed. The five remaining women were located through word-of-mouth.

Data collection proceeded much like it had during the original interviews. The procedures and goals were explained to each of the 18 women. They also completed a series of self-report survey instruments and then engaged in an in-depth, tape-recorded interview. Interviews lasted approximately 75 minutes and focused on factors that facilitated and/or challenged their exit successes. All interviews were conducted in private locations and all of the participants, except those who were incarcerated, received monetary compensation. The tape-recorded interview data were transcribed and then analyzed using Thematic Analysis.

Data Analyses and Group Division

This investigation was intended to explore the exit process, with attention devoted to experiences and events which promote or inhibit exit success. To this end, the 18 participants were divided based on whether or not they had remained free of prostitution, drugs, and other criminal activity over the course of three years spanning the two interviews. Two groups emerged. Five women had successfully avoided prostitution, drug use, and other forms of illegality. The remaining 13 had experienced significant setbacks in their exit attempts. Nine had returned to both prostitution and illicit drug use, one had returned to prostitution only, and three others had violated parole and been re-incarcerated. Thus, at both points of contact, three women were located and interviewed while serving prison terms. All three described extensive involvement with the legal system for a variety of offenses (e.g., prostitution, shoplifting, forgery, assault, and the possession and distribution of a controlled substance). These three women are included here because, despite their avoidance of drugs and prostitution, their developmental trajectories indicate individuals functioning on the periphery of society. Their ability to function within the boundaries of conventional society, outside the prison walls, had not been successful. Data from the two groups of women were analyzed separately.

The Sample

At the time of the follow-up interviews, participants ranged in age from 33 to 59 years (M = 41 years). Most were Black (*n* = 10) or non-Hispanic White (*n* = 5).

Many ($n = 7$) were divorced and had children ($n = 17$). Of 49 children born to these women, only seven lived with their mothers. On average, the women first entered the sex industry at 20.7 years of age (range = 11 - 31 years) and all but one ($n = 17$) reported current or prior drug addiction. For most ($n = 10$), drug abuse began at concurrent with or after their entry into street-level prostitution. Column one (of Table 8.1, below) presents demographic data for the 25 women who were interviewed once (1998/1999). Column two presents demographic statistics on the sub-sample of 18 women at the original data collection period (1998/1999) and column three provides demographic data obtained at the follow-up interview (2001/2002).

Testing for Sample Biases

Statistical comparisons were performed between the 18 women located and interviewed twice and their 25 peers who could not be located for a second interview. Chi-Square tests were used to examine differences in race, marital status and drug use; t-tests allowed for comparisons on age, age of entry into prostitution, years involved in the sex industry, number of children, and years of education. The 18 women who participated at both data collection points were significantly more likely to be single ($\chi^2 = 3.6$, df = 1, p =.06) and Black ($\chi^2 = 3.7$, df = 1, p =.05) than the 25 other women. The group of 18 was also significantly older (M = 37.6 years versus 30.3 years, SD = 6.4) (Z = -3.22; p<.001) and had spent an average of 6.4 more years involved in the sex industry (M = 15.2 years versus 8.8 years, SD = 7.1) (Z = -2.24; p<.02). The two groups were not significantly different on the number of children they had, total years of education, or use of drugs.

Exiting The "Game" of Street-Level Prostitution: The Road to Recovery

Among the 18 women who completed the follow-up interview, only five had remained free of prostitution, drugs, and other criminal activity in the three years preceding the follow-up interview. Four themes emerged as prominent factors influencing their exit successes, including: formal support services, renewal of significant relationships, employment and economic self-sufficiency, and involvement in a church community. These themes are described below, with background information presented first to contextualize their life situations.

Brief Background

When I first interviewed Amy, Kiley, Marlee, Yolanda and Rachel in 1998, they had been out of prostitution for an average of 3 years (range = 3 months - 8 years).

Table 8.1. Demographic Data: Sample at Both Data Collection Points

Variables	Time 1 (n = 25)	Time 1 (Subsample) (n = 18)	Time 2 (Subsample) (n = 18)
Age			
Mean	30.3	37.6	41
Range	19 - 42	30 - 56	33 - 59
Race/ethnicity(n)			
Black	8	10	10
White	15	5	5
Native American	2	3	3
Marital status(n)			
Never married	16	6	5
Married	5	5	2
Divorced	3	6	7
Separated	1	1	4
Residence(n)			
Shelter	7	7	2
Friends	2	1	0
Prison/Jail	11	5	7
Partner/husband	2	4	3
Alone/with children	3	1	6
Education:			
Mean	10 yrs.	11.7 yrs.	11.7 yrs.
Range	7th - 2 yr. coll.	9th - 2 yr. coll.	9th - 2 yrs. coll.
GED(n)	7	7	9
Mothers(n)	21	17	17
Total Children	56[a]	49[b]	49
Mean	2.7	2.8	2.8
Range	1 - 5	1 - 7	1 - 8
Child Residence(n)			
Mother	6	3	7
Father	7	12	11
Extended Kin	13	8	4
Foster Care	13	11	1
Adopted	8	3	8
On Own/Other[c]	6 / 3	10 / 2	13 / 5

Continued on the next page

Table 8.1. Continued

Variables	*Time 1 (*n* = 25)	Time 1 (Subsample) (*n* = 18)	Time 2 (Subsample) (*n* = 18)
Age Prostitution Entry			
Mean	18.4	20.7	20.7
Range	13 - 31	11 - 31	11 - 3
Time in sex industry[d]			
Mean	8.8 yrs.	14.8 yrs.	16.4 yrs.
Range	6 mos. - 25 yrs.	1yr. - 44 yrs.	2yrs. - 47 yrs.
Drugs[e](*n*)			
Drug abuse[f](*n*)	23	17	17
Pre-prostitution	8	7	7
Concurrent	5	3	3
Post-prostitution	10	7	7

*These 25 women could not be located for a follow-up interview; data are from the original (1998-1999) data collection; their demographic data are included for comparison purposes.
[a]Does not include total pregnancies; several reported miscarriages or abortions.
[b]Barb had an eighth child and Talisha lost a child (i.e., murdered) between the original and follow-up interviews. Thus, the total number of children remained the same (i.e., 49), despite the *range* change.
[c]Includes individuals living in mental health facilities, incarcerated, and who are homeless.
[d]Includes streetwalking, nightclub dancing, and involvement with Sugar Daddies.
[e]Drugs of choice include crack cocaine, methamphetamines, alcohol, and heroin.
[f]Substance addiction was determined by self-report, it was not based on clinical criteria.

They entered the sex industry at 23.2 years of age (range = 18 - 31 years) and had been involved in prostitution, at that time, for an average of 9 years (range = 1year - 16 years). Four of the five had been drug addicts. Also in 1998, three of the five lived in homeless shelters, one was incarcerated, and another lived with her husband in a home they owned. All of the women except Marlee had biological children, although none retained custody of their kids; Marlee's step-daughter lived with her. Only two were employed.

When interviewed for the second time (between 2001 and 2002), four of the five reported significant life changes. Amy had completed all state-mandated requirements and regained custody of her two sons. Yolanda had graduated from a treatment program, lived alone in an apartment, and was employed full-time at a dye manufacturing plant. She attended school part-time and had regular contact with her two children. Kiley was employed full-time as a sales coordinator, had recently purchased her first home, had regained custody of her oldest child (her youngest two had been adopted), and was attending school part-time. Rachel was married to her long-time partner, living in an apartment, working full-time, and shared custody of her two children with her ex-husband. Among the five women, Marlee's situation had changed the least between the first and second interviews. She was still married, living with her husband, and working full-time. However, her step-daughter was no longer living in her home.

Decisions To Exit

The five women described significant events culminating in their decisions to exit the sex-industry. *Hitting bottom* motivated exits for four. Yolanda and Kiley hit bottom when they were viscously attacked by clients; neither thought she would survive. Yolanda sought immediate and voluntarily entered a 9-month structured, residential treatment program. Although the incident did not propel immediate action for Kiley, it did initiate the exit process. She recalled,

> I just got tired. I started going to detox more frequently. Then, the last time [at detox], it just happened like that [snaps fingers]. I just reached out and asked if there was a bed in long term care.

Amy described *hitting bottom* when she lost custody of her children because of her addiction to crack cocaine. Interestingly however, Amy's initial response to losing her children was denial and *increased* drug use. Within 6 months of their absence however, she was participating in an in-house treatment program. "CPS [Child Protective Services] made me," she stated. "They said 'you have to go to treatment to get your kids back'." Rachel also described hitting bottom. She was sentenced to prison for four years on multiple drug and solicitation charges. "As much as I hate to say it," she remarked, "something good comes out of something bad. Prison did save my life. It really did. I was out there killin' myself." At the time of her imprisonment, Rachel had a $500/day addiction to crack cocaine and had nearly overdosed on three separate occasions.

Unlike the others, Marlee exited due to the declining economic viability of street-level prostitution. For years, street-level prostitution had been a lucrative endeavor for Marlee and her husband (he was her pimp). However, the wide-spread presence of crack cocaine had dramatically altered the prostitution economy. Marlee explained:

> The girls out there now are *not* like we used to be. They're out there for drugs. That's why the business is so bad. It's not even worth it. They're crack heads and will do anything for a little bit of money... they're not *real* ones [prostitutes].

In addition to economic changes in the street-level prostitution sub-culture, Marlee's step-daughter moved into her home. The incident impacted many areas of Marlee's life. She admitted:

> I stopped doing a lot of things because of my step-daughter being here with me. How can I tell a child 'you need to go to school, get a good education, go to college, get a good job' when she's looking at you saying 'well you don't work and we don't live bad,' you know? We was showin' her there's another way to do this [make a living].

It is important to note that Amy, Kiley, and Rachel had all attempted to exit at earlier points in their lives– but all had returned to the streets. Furthermore, it is impossible to say with any certainty whether any of these five women will return to prostitution in the future. Nonetheless, they had successfully avoided the sex industry, substance use, and criminal activity for a significant amount of time– in fact, by the time they completed a follow-up interview, they had been drug-free and out of the "game" for about six years[8]. In analyzing the data, four primary themes emerged as significant in their exit successes.

Formal Support Services

Formal support services were critical during the initial exit stage. With the exception of Marlee, residential treatment and continued professional services provided necessary support at a cross-roads in these women's lives. For instance, after being raped by two men, Yolanda went to great lengths to find structured treatment. Because services were not available in her community, she moved to a city 300 miles away to obtain residential care. She also received group and individual counseling through WellSpring and believed "Counseling is key. Counseling teaches you to think for yourself. Your counselor is not there to think for you- but to give you the tools to think for yourself."

Kiley and Amy also entered residential treatment. Kiley's lasted 6 months and Amy's was twice as long. Kiley participated in Alcoholics Anonymous (AA) and Narcotics Anonymous (NA), and both women received individual and group counseling through WellSpring. Also, after Amy regained custody of her two boys, the three voluntarily attended family therapy.

Like the others, Rachel also took advantage of formal services. While in prison, she enrolled in every class that was offered. The teacher of the substance abuse class "...was excellent– she made a big impact on my life... I'd like to thank her, you know?" After her release, Rachel entered a 4-month residential work-release program and, despite being a shy person, she excelled in her weekly AA and NA meetings: "It got to where I was talkin' more than anybody else at the meetings... and they asked me to start chairin' the meetings!" Rachel also reported to a parole officer who played a valuable role in her successful exit.

He tells you what you need to hear, not what you want to hear. He told me, 'I didn't ask to be brought into your life, you put me in your life.' He was kinda like a counselor. He was not only a parole officer but a friend. He made a difference in my life.

Formal services, including structured treatment, safe housing, and individual and group counseling were described as particularly important during the first year of the exit process. However, merely attending professional meetings, educational programs, or support groups is not sufficient for lasting behavioral change. All five women agreed that individuals ultimately determined the extent to which their exit attempts would prove successful. Marlee commented: "If you wanna be nothin' all your life, I guess that's what you're gonna be." In other words, personal choice is paramount; without commitment to change, formal services and professional supports will make little difference. In addition to formal support services and personal choice, informal support from significant others who denounced life in the "game" was further mentioned as essential for long-term abeyance.

Significant Relationships
These five women received substantial support from informal network members. Given their unique life circumstance, *sources* of informal support differed markedly between them.

Family and Male Partners. Rachel and Marlee frequently referred to various family member support as vital to their exiting. Marlee explained, "It was easy for me to get off the streets because of my mother. I wasn't raised to be a hooker, I had a beautiful mom; she never smoked, drank or anything. So I lost myself for awhile, but I'm back!" Rachel spoke of the support she received from her father and siblings; although her relationship with them had been rocky during her time on the streets, when she decided to exit, they fully supported and stood by her.

Aside from biological kin, both women described their husbands as their most critical sources of emotional support. Interestingly, both women had also been involved in prostitution *with their husbands.* Marlee's husband had been her pimp and they exited the sex industry *together.* In a similar vein, Rachel's husband was a former trick, and heroin and crack addict. They met five years before Rachel was imprisoned; crack use had been a daily ritual for them. However, during Rachel's imprisonment, he quit using drugs and gave Rachel an ultimatum: she had to choose between him or the "game." She chose him and commented: "He is my biggest support— he has strength that's unbelievable."

In contrast, Yolanda, Kiley, and Amy reported physical and emotional cut-off from their families of origin due to severe and sustained childhood abuse. "Family" for these three included their children and church groups only. Interestingly also is that all three described apprehension about romantic relationships and general *distrust* of men. Kiley believed that avoiding men was critical in her escape from prostitution:

> It is important to be in touch with yourself and be relationship free– from men especially. They [counselors] suggest going through recovery relationship free, and I firmly believe that. It takes a lot of energy to go through recovery... and men will manipulate you.

All three described years of experience with dysfunctional relationships. They admittedly lacked role models of strong partnerships and were uncertain about the likelihood of ever developing and maintaining healthy, intimate relationships.

Children. These five women discussed their children frequently throughout the interviews. Amy and Rachel, in particular, reported that the desire to be better parents was significant to their exiting success. Rachel readily admitted that parenting and the "game" cannot co-exist. She explained, "[Before], I had them [her children] physically, not mentally. I was not there, ya know? They'd sit out in the living room and I'd stick my arm in the bathroom door and get shot up with a needle." She continued,

> I am trying to be the mother I was supposed to be all along. The main reason I have stayed straight is– I look at my kids. I know the kind of person I was before I started on crack, and I'm not bragging– but I was a hell of a woman. I lost my self respect. When I lost my kids I lost my self respect. I lost everything.

Since exiting, the parent/child relationship had changed dramatically for Amy as well. By 2001, she and her children had been reunited and living together for nearly 3 years; but the transition was difficult. Amy remembered:

> I was afraid that everything I was doing was wrong, and if I got a little bit angry they [sons] would say 'that's old behavior'– that I was returning to my old behavior. Because when I was using, I got mad a *whole lot*. So they were scared of my going back to 'old behaviors'.

It took time and concerted effort, but Amy eventually regained her children's trust. She explained the process:

> I went to all my meetings, and when I told them 'I will be back in an hour' I was back in an hour. Because they didn't trust me. I think they were afraid to come home because I never showed them any security. They had a lot of fears. We did a lot of therapy.

Old Playmates. In addition to describing efforts to maintain and strengthen relationships with certain network members (i.e., family, partners, and children) these five women also described distancing themselves from others—namely, old playmates. To illustrate, when asked about contact with former acquaintances, Amy remarked,

Every once in awhile I believe that God will have someone stop in the gas station [her place of employment] and I will be there. And it is either to show me what it will be like if I go back out there [on the streets] or to show them what their future could be like if they would get God in their lives.

She then described a specific encounter with a former client:

There is this one guy named Jerry. He came by [place of work] one day and asked me if I still worked [prostituted] part-time. I said, 'No Jerry, I don't think God would approve of that.' He said, 'I didn't think so.' And I haven't heard from him since.

She continued, "I don't see many [old playmates] but I am not afraid to face these people of the past." Rachel, too, had sporadic contact with former clients while working as a waitress.

There was this guy that kept comin' in there that was a trick of mine... He would step on my feet 'Hi baby' and make little remarks. I couldn't do it. I would actually ask the other waitresses to take his table.

Rachel noted further, "When I used to hunt for my [drug] dealers I couldn't find them for nothin'. But when I got out of prison the first two weeks I ran into every dealer in town... I told em' I was straight and to put the word out." Marlee and Kiley described similar encounters. None of these four women initiated contact with "old playmates" and if chance encounters occurred, their interactions were limited and prolonged conversation was avoided. They indicated further however, that they were not "afraid" of former acquaintances. Instead, they felt that they were far enough removed from the "game" that its lure had diminished. Yolanda's situation was unique in that she moved to a new city after deciding to exit. She believed the move was critical to her exit success because: "I had a fresh new start in a new town. And I set up boundaries."

The Church Community

All five women described, at length and spontaneously, belief in a "higher power" and the importance of organized religion for their successful exits. All also described spiritual journeys which began slowly but gained steady momentum. Rachel, Amy and Marlee reported childhood introductions to "religion," but only as adults did belief in a higher power become central in their lives. Rachel recalled,

The religious seed was planted a long time ago, my mom used to take me to church. Then, while I was hooking— I used to stand outside this church and just cry. I saw a guy one time going to the church, I said 'Would you pray for me? I really don't want to do this, but I don't know how to get out of it. I'm not strong enough'.

After her prison release, Rachel found God and explained,

> I'm not a bible thumper– but I look at my kids, I look at my husband, I look at where I was and I've got God so much in my life right now. I couldn't do it without Him. I really couldn't.

Amy described a similar journey and attributed equal credit to God for her ability to exit prostitution. She was introduced to religion through a co-resident at a treatment facility. A particular interaction between them had made a profound impact on her.

> I was always talking about my kids [to the co-resident] and wondering if they were okay and blah, blah, blah and she told me 'You need to give your kids to God because you can't take care of them. You never did take care of them.' And it was sad, but it was true. I learned I had to focus on myself and my recovery. In order for me to be a whole person, I had to recover first.

Similarly, after exiting the industry, Marlee described sporadic church involvement at her husband's urging, followed by steady attendance, and then regular participation in bible study and prayer meetings. She described the shift in her life focus and personal values:

> I used to want a lot of money. Money does not make you happy. I remember one time I had $6,000 in cash and all my bills were paid. I was sitting in the bathtub crying. I didn't understand then why I was crying, but there was a void in my life. It was God.

Kiley and Yolanda were equally invested in their church communities. Both attended services regularly and participated in bible study groups. Yolanda was also an active member of church choir and "praise team."

Without question, the most prominent and consistent theme to emerge during interviews with these five women centered around the church. As their time out of the sex industry continued, their reliance on the church for inspiration and support increased exponentially, while their use of formal services slowly diminished.

Economics / Employment

The ability to legally earn a living wage is paramount to sustained removal from the sex industry. If one cannot afford the basic necessities of life, illegal schemes and income-generating ventures abound– particularly for women with connections to the street sub-culture and its expansive drug-trade. That said, employment was discussed frequently throughout the interviews. Despite extended absences from the job market, all five secured legal employment. Participants' first jobs typically included entry-level work (e.g., factory, fast-food) that evolved into higher-paying and higher-status positions. For instance, when interviewed in 1998, Amy worked in the fast food industry, by 2001 she managed a gas station. Despite no prior training, she proudly noted being hired for the management position because she was persistent and learned quickly. Kiley too had experienced benefits of work commitment; in three years she had earned enough money to buy her first home, whereas during our original interview she noted being in debt by thousands of dollars. Similarly, Rachel frequently worked 14-hour days and proudly described her parole officer's reaction:

> He started seein' my paycheck stubs where I'd have so many hours and he says, 'Well how in the– how come you're doin' that? Habba dabba.' And I said, 'Isn't that what you want?' And he says to me,'Yeah, but don't burn yourself out.' And I said, 'Just let me do what I gotta do'.

Economic viability not only allowed for daily subsistence, but also appeared to promote self-confidence. For instance, Yolanda noted being "hired on the spot" after completing an application and taking a test. She was hired as a receptionist, "...but they couldn't keep me busy. So now I run their hydro-berg machine and several other machines." She continued, "I'm developing skills. It feels good." Like Rachel, it was not unusual for her to work long days and earn over-time.

Employment opportunities appeared particularly significant during the initial exit stage for Yolanda and Kiley, both of whom lacked extensive informal support. Kiley noted, "I was paying off my bills instead of getting high." Likewise, Yolanda replaced her addiction "by working." All four women appeared to thrive on their work-related responsibilities, skill development, and ability to demonstrate competence and reliability. Their employment records were a source of pride.

In contrast, because prostitution had been lucrative for Marlee, the transition to legal employment was financially disappointing.

> It was kinda difficult when I started back [legal work]. I used to look at a check and would be like, 'Uh– I can't believe this is what won out [over prostitution]'! But now, I thank God for the little checks I get.

She then explained the sheer practically of legal employment:

> Before, I just lived day by day– didn't think about the future. And here it is I'm just starting to work– and keep in mind just about ready to retire. You can't hustle all your life. What are you gonna do when you get too old, you know? You can't draw social security. I don't have really anything in social security and I'm 40 years old! So I'm really mad at myself about that.

Summary

During the initial exit period, four of the five took extensive advantage of a variety of professional services (e.g., residential treatment, AA/NA, counseling/therapy). Use of formal support was, generally speaking, intense during the initial year of the exit process. With time and increased confidence, reliance on informal support increased and use of formal services diminished. Importantly, these women had severed all ties with "old playmates"; maintaining sobriety and freedom from the sex industry demanded this. Their informal networks consisted of people who would not tolerate life in the "game." Loss, or threatened loss of significant relationships (whether with partners or children), was central to exit success. Additionally, they described developing new support systems and connections to conventional society as they increasingly immersed themselves within various church groups. All described being impacted by a "higher power."

Employment was necessary for subsistence but also appeared to fill a void, particularly during the initial exit stage for those whose informal support systems were sparse. The work arena provided a context where these women obtained new skills and received recognition for what they could do (i.e., abilities, commitment) and not who they were (i.e., such as from significant others or church friends). They reported that their lives were dull, comparatively speaking; and that their time was spent at work, attending religious services, or at home. Still, they were content, a feeling impossible to capture when immersed in the "game." Rachel "...wouldn't change my life right now for a million dollars," a sentiment applicable to all five.

The "Entry-Exit-Re-Entry" Cycle Continues

Thirteen additional women participated in a follow-up interview. Unlike the five women discussed above, their attempts to remove themselves from prostitution, drug use, and illegal acts had not been wholly successful. Data analyses revealed that relationship loss, economic adversity, diminished use of formal services, and mental illnesses challenged their abilities to make significant life-style changes.

Significant Relationships & Emotional Attachments

Eleven of the 13 described how *relationship loss* triggered a return to "old behaviors." Further analyses revealed two sub-themes, namely loss of a new or anticipated relationship, and loss of long-term, enduring relationships.

Loss of New/Anticipated Relationships

Unlike Kiley, who heeded the advice of her counselors to remain "relationship free" during treatment, four women began relationships with male partners during the initial exit period. All four described re-entry into prostitution and drug use as precipitated by the cessation of these relationships. Sharia's situation is illustrative. When originally interviewed (1998), she was involved in structured treatment and only weeks away from graduation. However, she became involved with a fellow treatment participant, a minister, and dreamt of becoming a "preacher's wife." When interviewed in 2001, she recalled:

I thought at the time [1998] that my life and everything was going great. I was clean. I felt good about myself. I felt good about my life. My kids felt good about me, my family, everybody. And I was in love.

Within months of program discharge, the minister began using drugs again and then became violent. Sharia turned to her sister, an active drug addict, for refuge. Days later she too was using drugs; prostitution soon ensued. Sharia stated, "There's a lot of things that you shouldn't do during recovery that I did do because I thought I could handle this. But anything small can get you back to relapse."

Similarly, during the initial exit stage, Trina, Char, and Lettie also began new intimate relationships, all of which ended and left them feeling unworthy and rejected. Char explained how she "...met a man" before graduating from the WellSpring program. He was a user, "So I did what he did." When asked what could have prevented her from relapsing, Char flatly stated, "Some man who loved me," and then continued, "I thought he did but I must be crazy." When interviewed in 2001, Char was married to physically abusive man who pimped her out for drug money.

Like Marlee and Rachel, Lettie was also married to a man who was well-aware of her prostitution and drug-addiction. In distinct contrast from Marlee and Rachel however, Lettie's partner was not a source of emotional support or inspiration and her marriage was failing. She explained:

We are still together, but not really [separated]. He has a lot of dysfunctions.... He brings me down. If there is a cliff and I am about to jump he will say, 'No, go over there where you can jump higher. Jump where it is higher and then you'll hit those rocks'.

She then explained events culminating in her relapse:

I fell in love with this guy [not her husband]. I felt 'Oh my God, he really likes me' and then for a single no show [he failed to show up] I took that to heart and thought I must be dirty. I must not be worthy of being loved.

Drugs created the perfect escape and prostitution provided a context and environment where she was accepted– a place where she *belonged*. She stated:

I know certain places that I can go and get money because those people still like me. I know I can just go there and get money and all I have to do is lay on my back.

Lettie's desire to fit in and "belong" so to speak, was not unique. In subtle ways, Char and Sharia described similar needs and all invested hope in the development of new, intimate relationships as realizations of those desires. Relationship failure, and subsequent feelings of rejection, triggered their return to "old behaviors."

Loss of Long-Term Relationships

Seven others, including the three women who violated parole and returned to prison, also described relationship loss. Opposed to the loss of a new or anticipated relationship however, these women spoke at length of the loss of long-term, enduring relationships with male partners, children, and/or extended kin. Marti is a case in point. When interviewed in 1998, she was living with her ex-husband Alvin; they had lived together for over 25 years despite their divorce a decade earlier. He was, admittedly, her sole source of companionship and only friend. Within months of our initial interview, Alvin died. Soon after, Marti was forced to sell the home they had shared. The cumulative losses triggered an immediate urge to escape loneliness and severe depression. The result was drug relapse and re-entry into prostitution.

Four others experienced the death of loved ones between the initial and follow-up interviews. For Talisha, the death of a loved one was particularly devastating because she lost a child. Her 18-year-old son had been murdered. The trauma compounded when she turned to her husband for support and learned he was using crack cocaine.

> Crises like this [son's death] and it was really hard for me to deal with. I had a nervous breakdown and he [husband] wasn't there to help me. He was out on the streets. I'm trying to save him and I ended up using *with him*.

Prostitution involvement quickly followed as it allowed Talisha to maintain a chemically induced oblivion.

All three women who violated parole and returned to prison had also experienced the loss of long-term relationships in the three years preceding the follow-up interview. To illustrate, Georgette explained how, two weeks after being released from prison in 1999, her "mother" (i.e., biological grandmother) had died. Georgette was forced to sell the only home she had ever known and commented, "I've never really been out on my own... I lost everything out of my life, everything that I grew up with had just been wiped out."

Bryn and Jackie described similar experiences. Between the original and follow-up interviews, Bryn's father had died, her 19-year marriage had ended, and her relationship with her three children had become severely strained. In fact, she had neither seen nor spoken with any of her children in over a year. "That [relationship with her children] hurts me more than anything. My kids are grown. They were 4 and 1 when I started doing time, and now they're 18, 14, and 11." Still, like Rachel, Bryn believed there were benefits to prison:

> The way men treat their women, degrade them, letting them know they are a piece of shit– he is getting it through your mind that you can't have anybody else because no one else wants you. A lot of men, including mine, do that to women. To come up here [prison] and do some time is good for women to actually learn what is going on. Out there, they go straight to the drugs.

Her comment indicates that, despite 19 years with the same man, Bryn's marriage had been less than ideal. Others described similarly disappointing marriages, including Jackie, whose 13-year-marriage had also recently dissipated. To compound matters, Jackie's grandmother, the one person she felt "close" to, had died. She explained the cumulative impact "...I just didn't care about nothin' no more because I had just lost my grandma. My grandma was like my best friend, you know?"

Although death did not separate Bridget and Barb from their children, the parent-child bond was nonetheless threatened. When originally interviewed, both women were doing exceptionally well. They were living in "safe" settings, regularly attending WellSpring, and free of prostitution and drugs. Barb was pregnant with her seventh child, attending pre-natal classes, and was determined to be a good mother. Bridget believed she and her ex-husband would reunite and together raise their 4-month old daughter. By 2001 however, both women had returned to the "game." Bridget recalled the day she relapsed: "I was upset, lonely, hurt, angry, and I was fed up." Her ex-husband had denied her visitation with her infant daughter and was seeking legal action to bar further contact between them. She reacted with the familiar self-destructive behaviors of crack cocaine use and street-level prostitution.

Barb's situation was similar. She described how fear of losing her children triggered an immediate need to escape. Between 1998 and 2001, Barb had given birth to another child– her eighth. She retained custody of the youngest two only. Barb described how an accumulation of stressful events resulted in a "nervous breakdown" and she "started to crack up." Barb's sister intervened and took her two children. "It was the first time in over 4 years..." that she had been separated from the youngest of her eight kids. The incident triggered guilt and remorse for losing custody of the other six. She had vowed, she explained, to be a better parent to the youngest two than she had been with the older ones. After her children were gone, she went to a bar with every intention of picking up a "date":

> I figured I was just going to be on the street [prostituting]. I didn't have any idea what was going to happen after that. I felt like I had already failed at everything, so whatever happens– I deserve.

Economics

Among those wanting to work, securing legal employment did not appear problematic. In fact, 11 of the 13 women had been legally employed between the first and second interviews. Two clear distinctions emerged however, in how these women described income-generating ventures, compared to the five women whose exit attempts had been more successful. First, a clear lack of job-stability was evident; job-hopping characterized these women's employment patterns. It was not unusual for participants to describe working multiple jobs at various agencies within a few months' time. They described quitting their jobs for a variety of reasons such as: not liking the work, not "getting enough hours," or being inconvenienced by the location. Two of the 11 had been fired from places of employment for theft.

The second economic-related distinction between these women and their five peers involved their frequent use of illegal acts to obtain fast cash. Sharia described stealing merchandise "...at expensive stores, like Dillards" and then reselling those items to acquaintances. "I'd leave the tags on– so they know how much the clothes were." She continued, "I would get what people wanted- they would give me their lists." She might steal $500 worth of clothing, for instance, and then re-sell those items at half-price. Georgette manufactured a similar scheme of selling stolen items to friends and acquaintances, and three others simply resorted to stealing merchandise for themselves or forging checks if they couldn't afford desired items.

Relatedly, four other women either returned to the "game" between the first and second interviews, or noted that they would return to prostitution in the future, if finances became tight. Patti readily admitted that money earned from hustling was simply "too good to give up." She would not "...pass up no money, no kinda way." And Lettie explained how prostitution

> ...is just too easy. You try to ask somebody to give you some money to buy milk and eggs for your kids and they will say, 'I didn't have those kids for you. You need to get a job. But– we can go in the back room, okay baby?' That is a fact. A male will find money for a blow-job quicker than he will a pair of shoes for your kids. That is a fact. He is gonna find some money for that.

Formal Support Services

Twelve of the 13 women had been involved with some form of professional intervention since the initial interviews. In fact, seven of the 13 had received individual and group counseling through WellSpring, six had participated in various structured, residential treatment programs and eight had attended AA and/or NA. Chancey participated in all of these in addition to sexual addicts anonymous and obsessive-compulsive disorder groups. Moreover, two of the three incarcerated women had taken advantage of programs and classes within the prison system. However, they seemed to be of little value. Bryn commented, "I have taken almost every class they can offer me here [in prison] twice, three, four times... none of those classes can tell me how I am going to do my life."

Unlike those whose exits were successful, these women did not "work" their programs or fully utilize services offered. Indeed, seven stopped using their formal support systems prior to, or concurrent with, their relapses. Lettie stopped attending WellSpring shortly after returning to the "game" because she "...didn't want to disappoint them." And Sharia admitted that, despite having a "really good" probation officer, she "wasn't ready to stop using drugs. So I lied to her and avoided her and I stopped seeing her." Likewise, Trina stated "I wasn't ready [to quit]. I wasn't trying to deal with my issues. I wasn't saying 'I am through,' nor was I staying focused. I was not determined."

Several also described frustration with services that they had received. Four explained how the continuously changing staff at WellSpring and other human service agencies left them lacking stable, consistent care providers. Due to frequent turn-over, the quality of services had been substantially compromised. Three others explained that professional help for *prostituted* women, specifically, was not available. And two of the women refused to see counselors or other professional support providers due to fear of the consequences. Barb explained: "I am not going to risk losing my kids over something stupid like that [talking to a counselor]." She was fearful of arrest, or involvement from Child Protective Services, if she admitted the circumstances of her life to outsiders. Finally, Char was asked if she would seek out or use formal support services again, to which she replied, "No, they [service programs] don't work anymore."

Mental Health

Although none of the five who had maintained their exits mentioned mental health maladies, such was not the case with their peers who returned to prostitution or drug abuse. More than half of the 13 (54%) reported that they had been diagnosed with some form of mental illness. Bi-polar disorder, clinical depression, and obsessive compulsive disorder were mentioned most frequently. Three reported a long history of mental health difficulties. In fact, one had received electro-shock treatment and two had been institutionalized at earlier points in their lives. Interestingly, Chancey, who identified herself as a "sex addict," believed her return to the sex industry resulted from mental health issues and a medication mishap:

> I was put on some psycho-tropic medication which did a number on me– it made me paranoid and I became obsessed with sex. I was thinking about sex all the time. I couldn't get my mind off of it.

By her own account, Chancey believed she would never experience a "normal" sex life. Her sexual addiction had gone unchecked and untreated for far too long and adequate treatment was rarely forthcoming. She explained the impact on her life:

> I have no desire for a sexual relationship. I don't have anything to offer in the way of a sexual relationship. I could never have a normal sex life. I don't think that will ever happen for me. All I have ever done was to turn any part of sex into something dirty.

Later, when asked if she would return to the game, Chancey remarked, "It depends on what medication I'm on." Still, Chancey was more fortunate than others. Among the seven women with diagnosable mental illnesses, she was the only one receiving professional treatment.

Summary

Table 8.1, below illustrates the "entry-exit-re-entry" cycle as described by these 13 women. Four primary themes stood out as significant in their return to "old behaviors." In discussing their significant relationships, themes of loss or abandonment, largely due to death or feelings of rejection, surfaced frequently. In fact, 11 of the 13 described how their return to drugs, prostitution, or other criminal behavior was immediately preceded by stressful events or painful experiences with significant others. In discussing their interpersonal attachments and emotional connections, relationships with male partners and children were particularly problematic. In addition to experiencing the loss of significant relationships, these women frequently noted maintaining contact with or developing new relationships with people who tempted their return to prostitution, drug use, and other criminal activities (e.g., theft).

Figure 8.1: The "Entry-Exit-Re-Entry" Cycle

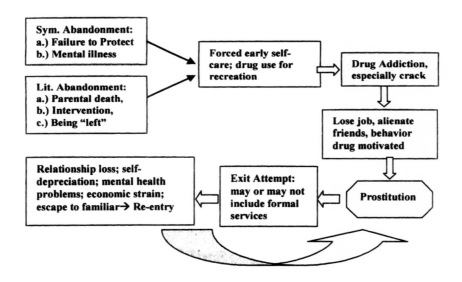

Employment, or other means of earning income, also emerged as a key theme in interviews with these women. Nearly all had been legally employed between the two points of contact. Even so, none described approaching employment as an opportunity to develop specialized skills or to learn a trade. Their employment histories were sporadic, at best, and several appeared to prefer the ready cash associated with illegal ventures to legal work. Significant also was the finding that seven of the 13 had been diagnosed with a mental health illness. Finally, one might speculate that formal services were unavailable to these women or that they lacked access to professional intervention. However, such was not the case. Twelve of the

13 sought assistance through a variety of community and professional services between the original and follow-up interviews. The formal support services available to and used by these women are quite similar to, and in some instances the exact same (i.e., WellSpring), as those available to and used by their "exited" peers.

Discussion

The purpose of this follow-up investigation was to begin to identify factors which promote and/or challenge a woman's ability to exit the "game" of street-level prostitution. Ecological systems theory[9] provided a framework for gathering data across multiple life domains– from family and institutional support, to employment patterns and religious leanings. Comprehensive data were collected to allow the lives of 18 women to be contextualized through time. The value of this work is twofold. First, long-term research with street-level prostituted women is rare; information gained provides a basis for new avenues of scholarship to be explored and gaps in the literature filled. Second, because two distinct groups emerged, comparison between those who had maintained their exits with those whose attempts had been less successful, was possible. Such data provide a basis for examining prominent factors that influence exit success and re-entry.

Three common themes emerged as influential for all of the women, regardless of whether or not they maintained their exit attempts, including: the significance of relationships and emotional attachments, formal support and professional services, and economics and employment. It is interesting to note that these same three themes were influential for all 18, yet the way the "exited" and "non-exited" women experienced each differed greatly. Among those whose exits had not been successful, experiences with significant others centered around issues of relationship loss and disconnect, rather than renewal and maintenance. Also, in direct opposition to the women who had successfully exited, many who returned to "old behaviors" reported maintaining contact with old playmates. Thus, in addition to experiencing emotional trauma of relationship loss or rejection, their informal networks often consisted of individuals actively involved in various illegal endeavors, including prostitution and drug trafficking.

Moreover, unlike Marlee, who focused on long-term financial well being, or the other "successful" four who perceived employment positions as opportunities to obtain skills and demonstrate competence, those who returned to old behaviors expressed limited patience with, or commitment to, legal employment. Short-term financial gain, rather than hard work and diligence, largely characterized their work ethic. Not surprisingly, illegal ventures often ensued.

Two additional distinctions surfaced as well. First, despite the consistency with which religion and spiritual re-birth were described by the five whose exits were successful, only two of the 13 others alluded to religion, God, or spirituality in any form. Second, mental health problems emerged as a theme among those whose exits were temporary, but not among the five women who had managed to refrain from drugs and prostitution. Although speculative, it is possible that the "successful" five failed to mention mental health problems because none had experienced any, or had experienced only minor mental health problems that had played little role in their ability to exit. On the other hand, perhaps some of the five had, indeed, experienced mental health difficulties, but received enough professional help so that their exit efforts were not jeopardized. Unfortunately, data needed to probe this issue further were not collected. Still, 54% of those who returned to prostitution, drugs, or other criminal behavior *spontaneously* mentioned diagnosable mental illnesses during the interview process. These numbers are too high to dismiss as mere chance. Thus, the information suggests a dire need for professional mental health services, including diagnosis and treatment, among street-level prostituted women. Additional research in this arena is sorely needed if intervention efforts are to effectively address the unique needs of this particular population.

In a related vein, nearly all of the women ($n = 16$) described involvement with formal support agencies including residential treatment, NA, AA, and WellSpring. Still, association with or use of such services was not sufficient to sustain lasting behavioral change, personal commitment is key. The women who successfully exited took it upon themselves to obtain knowledge, internalize information, and then apply newly acquired tools to their own lives. Their unsuccessful peers described, instead, an expectation that others were responsible for "fixing" their life situations or, more commonly, being uncommitted to making the necessary changes required in their lives differently.

The Stages of Change Model developed by Prochaska, DiClemente and Norcross[10] provides a framework for understanding an individual's readiness to change addictive behaviors. Prochaska and colleagues identified five stages of change experienced by clients with various forms of addiction. In the *pre-contemplative* stage, individuals are not aware of their problem and further, have no plans of changing their behaviors any time in the foreseeable future. Only at the insistence of others would individuals seek help during this stage. In the *contemplative* stage, individuals are consciously aware of their problem behaviors but have not made a commitment to address them. Individuals in this stage are considering behavior changes, but it may be a long time before action is taken.

Individuals in the next stage, *preparation*, have begun to make small changes in their behaviors and have intentions of making additional, perhaps larger changes, in the near future. The *action* stage often follows and is reached when individuals successfully change problematic or addictive behaviors. If change persists for more than 6 months, individuals have entered the *maintenance* stage. During this stage, the ultimate goal is to maintain behavioral and attitudinal changes made in previous stages.

This model appears to have broad applicability. Hood and Johnson[11] note, "These same stages of change pertain to clients with a wide variety of problems," (p. 70). When examined in relation to the women who participated in this investigation, the model informs understanding about the exit process. To illustrate, due to their extended absences from the sex industry for more than 6 months, the five whose exits had been successful through time could readily be identified as fitting within the *maintenance* stage. Further, examination of the model in relation to those who had returned to prostitution, drug use, or other criminal activity would result in some of the women, including Bryn and Sharia for instance, being placed in the *preparation or action* stages due to their conscious decisions to exit and the behavioral changes they were making in order to do so. Others, such as Char and Patti, would likely be placed in the *pre-contemplative or contemplative* stages. Patti was not interested in making life-changes that would effectively remove her from the "game." In fact, she predicted that "hustling" would be part of her future once released from prison. Similarly, Char was actively involved in drug use and prostitution when interviewed in 2001. She had no plans of seeking assistance to change her life and believed "programs" had nothing significant to offer her. (Table 8.2, below, summarizes the women's life situations at both points of contact and provides clues as to their "readiness" to change).

Development of a population-specific model that addresses the unique components of the prostitution exit process, that incorporates aspects of the Stages of Change Model, could prove valuable for service creation and delivery. Development of such a model might help identify key points of intervention within critical life areas informed by a woman's readiness to change. The data suggest that the initial stage of the exit process, what might be interpreted as the preparation stage, requires safe residence away from "old playmates," structured professional drug treatment, and mental health assessment and treatment. With time, movement into the action stage would necessitate additional forms of supports, including development or renewal of healthy emotional attachments to informal support systems (e.g., church groups and family), emphasizing re-integration and incorporation into the larger community. Development of employment skills and job training could be integrated into the action stage. The maintenance stage would consist of on-going individual and group counseling, mentoring, and systematic monitoring efforts to identify and address person-specific "triggers" or challenges facing the each woman in her unique life context.

It is important to note that models specific to the prostitution exit process must be created with individual differences in mind. The five who maintained their exit attempts varied considerably with regard to age, race, amount of time spent in the sex industry, family composition, and chemical addiction. Moreover, the one participant (i.e., Marlee) who made the easiest transition out of the industry and who required the least amount of formal assistance, was the one woman who had been immersed in the sex industry for the longest period of time. Her case history defies Månsson and Hedin's[12] conclusion regarding two types of "break-aways" in that Marlee was able to exit smoothly, developing a new identity and lifestyle, but could hardly be defined as "...loosely associated with the sex-industry"[13]. Several factors contributed to her relatively seamless exit: She had never been chemically addicted, street-level prostitution was no longer lucrative, and, perhaps most importantly, she exited with her husband and had a strong informal support network (e.g., family, church group) that did not condone criminal activity.

Table 8.2. Summary of Life Situations at Original and Follow-Up Interviews

Name	Original Interview (1998/1999)	Follow-Up Interview (2001/2002)
Prostitution and Drug-Free:		
Marlee	Living with husband; full-time employment; church involvement	Living with husband; full-time work, church involvement
Amy	Living in shelter; children in foster-care; employed at fast-food restaurant	Living in temporary housing with children; manager of gas station; church involvement
Kiley	Living in shelter; children in foster care; not working	Living in own home; custody of daughter; full-time work; part-time student; church involved
Yolanda	Living in shelter; working full-time; little contact with	Living in apartment; regular contact with children; full-time work; part-time school; church
Rachel	In prison	Married shared custody of children; full-time work; church
Returned to Both Prostitution and Drugs:		
Sharia	Residential treatment; engaged to minister	Living in shelter, attempting to exit again
Trina	Living with partner; attending WellSpring;	In prison
Char	Attending WellSpring;	Married to addict; actively prostituting and using.
Lettie	Married, living with kids and husband; using drugs	Separated; Living with children; actively prostituting and using drugs.

Continued on next page

Table 8.2: Continued

Name	Original Interview	Follow-Up Interview
Marti	Living with ex-husband; attending WellSpring	Attempting exit again; involved in work release; recently out of prison.
Bridget	Residential treatment; near program completion; working full-time.	Actively using drugs and prostituting.
Talisha	Residential treatment; near program completion.	Attempting exit again after relapse; residential treatment.
Barb	Attending WellSpring; Living with partner; some prostitution	Attempting exit again after relapse; living in apartment with two youngest children
Patti	In prison	In Prison; re-incarcerated after drug binge and parole violation

Returned to Prostitution Only, Not Drugs:

Chancey	Living in apartment; regularly attending Well-Spring.	Attempting exit again; Living in shelter; taking meds for mental health disorder

Law Violations / Did Not Return to Prostitution or Drugs:

Georgette	In prison	Violated parole; back in prison.
Bryn	In prison	Violated parole; back in prison
Jackie	In prison	Violated parole; back in prison

The data presented in this study, coupled with work revealed by other researchers, clearly speaks to the central role of relationship loss and renewal in the exit process. Further development of this concept could greatly enhance theoretical development and potentially aid intervention strategies. Assisting women in developing new informal systems of support or recovering from the emotional loss of significant others appears central for exit success.

Furthermore, it is important to note that leaving the sex-industry rests, at least in part, on having the ability to legally support oneself. Working minimum wage jobs with little room for growth in contexts that require and teach few transferable skills may prompt a return to "old behaviors" in an attempt to earn "fast cash." Employable skills and job training are necessary for women's long-term exits from the "game." Moreover, one of the most interesting, yet surprising, findings of this study involved the central role of religion, and integration into religious communities, among those whose exits were successful. No other study involving prostituted women could be located that addressed this issue. The door is certainly open for continued exploration of the role of religion in the exit process.

Compared to the five women who refrained from both prostitution and drugs, 13 other women had not been *as successful* in their exit attempts. Still, the fact that some women returned to the "game" (or to prison), does *not mean* that their exit attempts were not valuable or that progress was not made. To use an analogy, one might liken the "game" to a physically, emotionally, and sexually abusive partner. Imagine that, instead of attempting to leave the "game" a particular woman is attempting to leave her abusive husband or boyfriend. It is a rare situation indeed when a woman is able to walk away from her abusive partner, from a situation that is "familiar" and that provides a sense of "belongingness" and an identity, without looking back or ever returning. In fact, a woman will leave her abusive partner an average of 5-7 times before she leaves for good[14]. But each time she does leave, she becomes a little stronger, a little more confident, and a little more committed to making a permanent lifestyle change. The street-level sex industry exit process is similar. *Success* in exiting the "game," just as in leaving an abusive partner, is an amorphous beast and difficult to define. The phenomena are complex and the challenges significant, but change is possible as demonstrated by Amy, Marlee, Kiley, Rachel, and Yolanda.

Conclusion

The goal of the investigation was to examine, through time, the exit process of women involved in street-level prostitution, with particular focus on factors which facilitate and challenge permanent removal from the "game." Still, it would be unfortunate if the lives of the women themselves were unintentionally overshadowed by discussion of who "made it" out and who returned to prostitution or drug use. Too narrow a focus on outcomes (i.e., exit status) risks diminished recognition of developmental processes inherent in the "entry-exit-re-entry" cycle.

It was with great sadness that my search for the remaining 25 women, those whom I met in 1998 but could not re-locate in 2001, had to end. I think about them often. Despite it being 2006, I still contemplate whether or not they were able to make a clean break and create lives for themselves far and away from the "game." I wonder if, indeed, Tami had become a counselor for troubled teens as she dreamt of becoming; and, more importantly, if she finally found "serenity and peace of mind." I wonder if God's power had sustained Sam through the dark and uncertain exit process, as she believed it would. I wonder, too, if Cammie had developed her talents and become a writer who educated others through words and art, so that her troubles would not become theirs. Unfortunately, I must admit that the available data indicates that the odds are overwhelmingly stacked against them.

Notes

1. Celia Williamson, "Entrance, Maintenance, and Exit: The Socio-Economic Influences and Cumulative Burdens of Female Street Prostitution," *Dissertation Abstracts International A: The Humanities and Social Sciences* 61 (2000): 773-A.

2. Celia Williamson and Gail Folaron, "Understanding the Experiences of Street Level Prostitutes," *Qualitative Social Work* 2 (2003): 271-287.

3. Chomnad Manopaiboon, Rebecca E. Bunnell, Peter H. Kilmarx, Supaport Chaikummao, Khanchit Limpakarnjanarat, Somsak Supawitkul, Michael E. St. Louis, and Timothy D. Mastro, "Leaving Sex Work: Barriers, Facilitating Factors and Consequences for Female Sex Workers in Northern Thailand," *AIDS Care* 15 (2003): 39-52.

4. Sven-Axel Månsson and Ulla-Carin Hedin, "Breaking the Matthew Effect- On Women Leaving Prostitution," *International Journal of Social Welfare* 8 (1999): 67-77.

5. Månsson Hedin, "Breaking the Matthew Effect," 67-77.

6. Williamson, "Entrance, Maintenance, and Exit," *Dissertation Abstracts*.

7. Manopaiboon and others, "Leaving Sex Work," 39-52.

8. These five women had been out of the "game" and drug-free for an average of three years when first interviewed (1998/1999) plus an additional three years by the time they were interviewed for a second time.

9. Urie Bronfenbrenner, "Ecological Systems Theory." in *Six Theories of Child Development: Revised Formulations and Current Issues,* edited by Ross Vasta. (Philadelphia: Jessica Kingsley Publishers, 1989), 187-249.

10. James O. Prochaska, Carla C. DiClemente, and John C. Norcross, "In Search of How People Change: Applications to Addictive Behaviors," *American Psychologist* 47 (1999): 1102-14.

11. Albert B. Hood and Richard W. Johnson, "Assessment in Counseling: A Guide to the Use of Psychological Assessment Procedures," 3rd ed., (Alexandria, VA: American Counseling Association, 2002).

12. Månsson Hedin, "Breaking the Matthew Effect."

13. Månsson Hedin, "Breaking the Matthew Effect," 69.

14. Lenore E. Walker, *The Battered Women Syndrome* (New York: Springer, 2000).

Chapter Nine

Intervention Strategies and
Policy Implications

> Treat people as if they were what they
> ought to be, and you help them to become
> what they are capable of being.
> —Goethe

Individuals are responsible for the choices they make, the behaviors in which they willingly participate, and the consequences of their actions. The participants of this investigation would be the first to agree with this statement. In fact, several of the women explicitly admitted personal responsibility for their entry into and continued involvement within the street-level sex-industry. However, the most vulnerable populations of our society, as is frequently recognized, often lack basic avenues for self-advocacy and thus, also lack *viable* choices for promoting optimal health and well-being. They are frequently indigent, suffer various forms of discrimination, lack political power, and in many cases have experienced lives dominated by exploitation and abuse that, whether directly or indirectly, convince them that they are of little consequence and "deserve" what they get.

With this in mind, this chapter is intended to present strategies for intervention aimed at street-level prostituted women who desire to exit the sex industry. It is important to note at the outset that few programs or intervention services are uniquely designed to address the multifaceted needs of this very unique, very vulnerable population. Among those which do exist, including the nationally-recognized WellSpring program, evaluation data are scarce. This is unfortunate because evaluation data provide critical information for the creation and on-going development of successful programmatic services. Evaluation allows for the identification of effective services– information that is necessary for strengthening and building upon "what works." Evaluation data also provides a means for delineating ineffective and inadequate tools and strategies, thereby imparting knowledge necessary to modify or eliminate program components that do not work, or do not work as well as intended. Programmatic streamlining allows for the most efficient use of limited resources in order to "do the greatest good for the greatest number," an adage popularized by John Stuart Mills[1] that would be difficult *not* to defend.

In this chapter, a variety of intervention suggestions and policy implications are presented. These ideas are a direct result of my research with prostituted women, in conjunction with insight obtained from other scholars working with similar populations. Ecological systems theory (EST) provides the theoretical framework around which this chapter is organized and comprehensive intervention envisioned. Based on EST, individual-level issues are presented first, followed by exploration of community- and societal-level suggestions for education and advocacy.

Personal Motivation & Formal Support

As documented in the long-term developmental trajectories of Kiley, Amy, Yolanda, Rachel, and Marlee, new behavioral patterns can be created and maintained. Exiting the street-level sex industry is possible. However, personal desire and motivation are necessary preconditions for the development of new lifestyles to be created and permanent change achieved. Comprehensive formal assistance is also critical in assisting women maintain their exit commitments.

I readily admit that "personal desire and motivation" are *internal traits* over which formal support services exert little influence. However, ecological systems theory, with its systemic, contextual, and holistic vision of human development, provides a realistic framework for envisioning and designing the second half of the equation: that involving formal, comprehensive intervention. Certainly, not all women attempting to exit the sex industry will require assistance with each of the components I describe below. Heterogeneity is assumed, and service delivery must be geared to the unique personal needs, characteristics, and life-circumstances of each individual. This chapter provides a rather exhaustive discussion of potential services designed to mitigate "risk" of re-entry into street-level prostitution once the exit process has been initiated. The strategies and ideas presented are intentionally broad and extensive in order to capture a spectrum of *potential* needs for a particular population.

Individual-Level Issues

According to ecological systems theory[2], human development unfolds as a joint, mutually engaging and interactive process of adaptation between person and environment. That said, recognition of individual-level attributes and characteristics is obvious; no two people are exactly alike. Individual differences *do matter* and should be recognized as vitally important for understanding unique, person-specific responses to environmental contexts.

The women who participated in this investigation comprise a heterogenous group, with unique personalities, dispositions, senses of humor, physical characteristics, intellects, values, and belief systems. Nonetheless, they also share several commonalities–commonalities which have formed the basis of this research and about which this book is written. When examined in tandem, these commonalities provide clues that inform intervention services and about which such services should be fully prepared to address if the exit-process is to be optimally successful. Specifically, diminished *physical, emotional*, and *psychological* health were frequently described by the women who participated in this investigation. Others working in the field, including Williamson[3] and Farley[4], have reported similar information. Intervention at the individual level then, must be cognizant of these critical components comprising personal health and wellness; intervention aimed at harm-reduction within the physical, emotional and psychological dimensions of well-being are delineated below.

Physical Well-Being

Residential Housing
Safe housing is one of the most immediate, basic needs of street-level prostituted women. Assuming motivation to exit, a safe and secure residential setting for extended retreat is necessary. Unfortunately, the demand for residential treatment facilities is great and the supply scarce; residential facilities tend to be overcrowded with long waiting lists[5]. Further, many such facilities are co-ed, attempting to address the housing needs of homeless men and women alike. Co-ed facilities are not likely to offer residence to prostituted women, believing they will continue to trade sex with other residents for money or drugs. Importantly also, women *with dependents* who enter, or hope to enter, residential treatment must find appropriate care for their children, as many residential programs are not equipped with child care facilities to serve the needs of families.

For those with dense support networks comprised of trustworthy and reliable members, securing child care for an extended period of time may prove slightly problematic, but would *not likely present* an insurmountable problem. However, and as demonstrated repeatedly in this investigation, the social support networks of street-level prostituted women are grossly diminished. Child care for prostituted women seeking residential treatment presents a very salient challenge. Residential treatment for this population of women must address their unique needs and allow extended residence for them and their children. This is not to say that many of those seeking assistance in their attempts to exit would actually have children with them. As also learned from this investigation, physical disruption in the mother-child bond is a regular occurrence among prostituted women. Still, if family-friendly, extended-stay *residential programs were* available, perhaps more street-level prostituted women would seek refuge and assistance *prior* to experiencing child removal or state-based (i.e., CPS) intervention. Residential programs offering a spectrum of short-term, transitional, and long-term housing services that are accepting of women with children would be ideal.

Geographic location of the housing units (i.e., short-, transitional, and long-term) will play a key role in the exit process, as chemical dependence poses a significant risk for re-entry into sex-work. If a woman's initial place of refuge from the prostitution sub-culture is located in a drug infested neighborhood, temptation abounds. The situation is analogous to holding AA meetings in a local tavern. Yet, it is not uncommon for treatment facilities for homeless and vulnerable populations to be located in neighborhoods where access to drugs and prostitution is unobstructed.

Medical Care

A key factor contributing to the diminished physical health of street-level prostituted women is lack of medical attention and treatment[6]. Medical conditions frequently documented among prostitution-involved women include HIV, gonorrhea, syphilis, hepatitis, venereal warts, tuberculosis and herpes[7]. Provision of medical services to inform, treat, and prevent STD/STIs (sexually transmitted diseases/infections) and related health complications must be a primary focus of intervention efforts. Medical assessment should occur *early* in the exit process to alleviate prolonged health complications. Certainly, appropriate assessment of medical conditions, combined with provision and proper monitoring of medication, is a critical component of comprehensive service delivery to this population.

Significantly also, prostituted women are notoriously negligent in obtaining prenatal care[8-9]. Infants whose mothers fail to receive prenatal care are more likely to be born premature or with low birth weights[10-11] with greater incidence of nutritional deficiencies[12]. Teratogenic agents, such as alcohol, tobacco, and drugs, threaten optimal fetal development[13]. Numerous participants admitted that their children had been born with Fetal Alcohol Syndrome (FAS), addicted to crack cocaine, or with other health complications that might have been prevented had medical treatment been utilized. Pregnant, prostitution-involved women are reluctant to seek medical attention because they lack information on its benefits, transportation, finances, and because they fear that their children will be removed[14].

For those unwilling to commit to residential care, or who lack access to services, community outreach efforts offering education and direct care are paramount. Roaming medical units, staffed by licensed medical professionals, could most readily contact and treat prostituted women in need, or transport individuals to clinics specializing in the physical health needs of vulnerable, indigent, female populations. St. James Infirmary, a model clinic in San Francisco, provides medical and social services for female, transgendered, and male prostituted individuals[15] (www.stjamesinfirmary.org). St. James Clinic offers free services and is run by and for sex workers which mitigates feelings of stigma and fear of arrest or of having one's children removed.

Chemical Dependence

Weiner[16] and others[17] contend that addressing both physical and psychological chemical dependence is a priority among women entrapped within the "game" of street-level sex work. Information obtained in this investigation strongly supports their conclusions. Forty-one participants (95%) admitted drug dependence. Drug dependence and street-level prostitution comprise a vicious, difficult-to-break cycle. Addressing addiction is a critical first step. Among those women interviewed in 2001, chemical addiction was the *primary* factor precipitating a return to sex-work. All nine women who returned to both prostitution and drugs reported that drug use *preceded* prostitution re-entry.

Whether or not *initial entry* into prostitution is addiction-motivated or not, the data clearly indicate that chemical dependence and street-level sex work are intricately connected. And further, once addicted, long-term, extended exit success from the street-level prostitution sub-culture depends largely on overcoming drug-addiction. Sam's words "Once you get started on the drugs I think *it's impossible* to go back to just prostituting" serve as a powerful reminder of the entangled union between drug abuse and prostitution.

Chemical addiction would be ideally addressed within extended residential treatment facilities. Unfortunately, funding to support such programs are not typically a priority at the local, state or national levels. Economic fluctuations and cyclic downturns almost certainly impact programmatic quality as well as availability, given that social programs are frequently viewed as dispensable. Overcoming chemical dependence is nonetheless a cornerstone to successfully exiting the "game."

Outreach efforts targeting drug addicts are needed on a broad scale. Such programs would ideally provide street based education on HIV and AIDS, supplies (e.g., condoms) to prevent the spread of sexually transmitted diseases and bleach for disinfecting needles, risk-reduction counseling, and referrals to additional community resources including drug treatment and health centers. Reports from a multi-state, ethnographic study of the sex-for-crack culture, suggests that these outreach programs have proven records of success[18]. Harm-reduction outreach may be further conceptualized as treatment recruitment programs. In his book *Crack Pipe as Pimp*, Ratner[19] notes,

> One key finding of this study concerns the social isolation of chronic crack users. Their meaningful interactions are often only with other chronic crack users. Health programs are an effective way to provide bridges back to mainstream institutions, such as schools, social service agencies, and drug-abuse treatment programs.

Emotional and Psychological Well-Being

Plummer and colleagues[20] argue for a paradigm shift; research emphases on external circumstances, such as housing needs and employability, have left pervasive gaps in our understanding of internal mechanisms and psychological factors which influence, to an as yet unknown extent, female entry and continued involvement in the sex industry. I agree. Too narrow a focus on structural aspects of prostituted women's lives is but *one* of many multiple and complex challenges facing prostituted women. By the time women get to the streets, their lives are in shambles–physically, emotionally, and psychologically. Tunnel vision, or addressing only one need (e.g., housing) while neglecting others (e.g., mental health) may assist short-term recovery efforts, but likely sabotage long-term exit success.

Efforts geared at improving emotional and psychological well-being have been inadequately assessed among prostituted women. Still, the need for mental health services is undeniable. As evident in this investigation, mental health treatment and on-going monitoring of various psychological illnesses was rare, despite the overwhelming need.

Familial Abuse and Victimization

Childhood victims of physical and sexual abuse exhibit an increased prevalence of anxiety, depression, and symptoms of post-traumatic stress disorder (PTSD)[21-22]. PTSD and depression are frequently reported among street-level prostituted women[23-25]. Abused children also show higher rates of psychological distress in adulthood[26-27], and antisocial behavior including drug and alcohol abuse[28-30].

Further, symptoms of emotional distress (i.e., depression, poor self-esteem, sexual dysfunction) are consistently identified among adult survivors of childhood sexual abuse[31-32]. Unless addressed directly and early-on, emotional scars from years of abuse and exploitation among this population of women will likely challenge and disrupt programmatic efforts aimed at self-sufficiency and optimal well-being. Counseling and therapy are frequently utilized strategies in assisting individuals understand, cope with, and overcome traumatic life-experiences.

The women who participated in this investigation are, from my observation, strong and resilient. If they were not, they would not be alive to tell their stories. However, there is a monumental difference between *surviving* and *thriving*. These women were not thriving. Emotional and psychological bankruptcy contributes to sex-work entry and continued involvement.

Evidence further suggests that inter-generational patterns of abandonment, both literal and symbolic, are common occurrences in the familial relationships between street-level prostituted women and their parents and children. Addressing dysfunctional patterns of abuse, through education and mental-health counseling, should be a critical component of comprehensive intervention. Therapeutic approaches integrating concepts from family systems theory (FST)[33-34] might prove exceedingly useful in working with this unique population. In particular, education on transitional characters[35]– those heros who liberate future generations from destructive familial patterns–could easily be integrated into mental health treatment and provide a sense of agency and empowerment to target individuals. Applying such knowledge to one's own life is the difficult piece. Becoming a transitional character requires not only a desire to do so, but also the ability to develop new familial patterns and ways of relating and is contingent upon personal insight and self-efficacy. With regard to self-efficacy specifically, one cannot advocate on her own behalf or demand to be treated with dignity and respect, if she does not believe in herself or that she deserves to be treated with dignity and respect. Re-creating new family patterns would obviously be a long-term goal of mental health treatment. Short-term efforts focused on depression, post traumatic stress disorder, issues of self-esteem and confidence, chemical dependence, and inter-generational familial patterns of abuse are first priorities.

Unfortunately, provision of mental health care for street-level prostituted women presents numerous challenges. Most notable is that this is a highly mobile, difficult-to-access population. Mental health treatment, even with brief, solution-focused therapies[36], typically requires several sequential treatment sessions which may not be feasible among homeless, transient women. Needless to say, mental health assessment and treatment, provided as part of comprehensive care within a residential setting would be most effective. Such treatment would address *life-span* exposure to abuse and exploitation. Certainly, not all street-level prostituted women have experienced childhood sexual abuse, not all have directly experienced or indirectly witnessed familial physical violence, and not all have been the recipients of verbal degradation. However, *many have*; and some have experienced *multiple forms* of abuse throughout their entire lives—as evidenced by Char, Sam, Tami, and numerous others. Moreover, it would be difficult to find a woman prostituted on the streets *who had not been* the recipient of violence, including rape and physical assault, from clients, pimps, or partners. Victimization of women engaged in street-level sex work is all-too-common. Plummer and colleagues[37] contend that actively addressing affective and psychological issues plaguing prostituted women is, without question, a key component for intervention.

Parenting-Skills Training

Family dynamics, including patterns of interaction, ways of relating, and expectations for self and family members, are often transmitted from generation to generation. Family patterns are transmitted inter-generationally through (1) *modeling*, or repeating in future generations what has been observed in the family of origin, and (2) *direct instruction*, or explicit demands, discipline, and training.

The participants in this investigation were not, admittedly, ideal parents. Indeed, the majority has lost, or were at risk of losing, child custody. Foster-care is certainly a child-rearing alternative, as women prostituted on the streets are largely ill-equipped to provide adequate care to dependents. Still, despite it's clear benefits, out-of-home placement is *not a long-term solution*. Out-of-home placement provides a temporary, short-term reprieve only. Unless the patterns which *create* the need for out-of-home placement can be addressed and modified, the pattern itself will continue indefinitely. By and large, women attempting to exit the sex-industry have not been exposed to models of good, or even adequate, parenting.

Still, developing effective parenting skills founded on the principle of respect for self and one's children will not likely be possible until emotional, psychological, and chemical dependence issues have been addressed. For long-term well-being, and the well-being of future generations, parenting skills training is a necessity.

Interpersonal Relationships with Intimate Partners

One of the greatest challenges to promoting personal efficacy, confidence, and well-being among street-level prostituted women involves addressing their patterned relationships with abusive, exploitative male partners. The majority of participants characterized their relationships with men as emotionally, physically, sexually, and psychologically damaging. These data are not unique, as the academic literature is replete with similar reports[38-39]. Several of the women exhibited characteristic symptoms of "battered woman syndrome"[40]. These women described feeling personally responsible for their victimization, believing that they deserved to be beaten. For some, their support systems consisted *only* of their abusive male partners–men with a vested interest in keeping them chemically addicted and actively involved in the sub-culture of street-level prostitution. Thus, efforts to exit the sex industry, for many women, is thwarted by those in which the women feel dependent upon. The cycle of violence, male domination, and the central issues concerning power and control in abusive relationships *must* be addressed in counseling services provided to women attempting to leave the streets.

Spirituality

The five participants who had remained free of prostitution and drugs attributed much of their success to spirituality, organized religion, and/or faith in a "higher power." Because no former investigation of street-level prostituted women had mentioned religion as a central topic, I did not recognize it's significance, and therefore, did not purposefully question the women about their religious beliefs or involvement. I am now much more informed. Concepts of spirituality and religiosity prominently and spontaneously emerged in interviews with these women at both the original and follow-up interviews. I believe this is neither a fluke nor an anomaly.

With this in mind, intervention programs with prostituted women would be well-advised to incorporate spirituality, however broadly defined, into an overall programmatic structure. Exploration of personal feelings of connectivity to the larger world– and the world beyond– may provide, if nothing else, hope for a brighter future and a sense of belongingness. One would be hard-pressed to argue *against* the healing power of hope or the security engendered by knowing that one really does have a place in the larger scheme of life.

Economic Viability

Street-level prostitution and drug addiction represent *symptoms* of larger, systematically related issues. O'Neill[41] writes, "Issues of sexual politics are entwined with economic and political issues... to create a catch-22 situation for women who may not have freely chosen to work as prostitutes but nevertheless pragmatically have decided that it is the best option available to them." O'Connell Davidson[42] similarly reports, "We do not hear stories about [women] giving up their careers in order to become prostitutes."

One of the greatest challenges facing street-level prostitution-involved women includes economic viability and self-sufficiency. One must not automatically assume that prostituted women lack education or employability skills. (Keep in mind that the *range* of years of education and work experience varied tremendously among the women who participated in this study). Still, depending on length of time in the sex industry, skills and educational training that had been previously acquired may be obsolete. Thus, regardless of education level, job skills training or skill development may still be necessary to ensure a living wage for women transitioning into, or back into, legal employment venues.

All five women who had remained free of the "game" between 1998 and 2001, had secured work in entry-level positions earning minimum wage. After proving themselves capable and competent, they progressed into higher paying and prestigious positions. Service sector employment (e.g., food-service, maid work/janitorial) is most predictable for individuals lacking viable skills. Unfortunately, there is little room for advancement for unskilled, service-sector laborers.

Additional Employment Challenges. It is worth noting that tasks which may seem simple, such as developing a résumé, could prove daunting for someone who has never before created one. Relatedly, the very real issue of explaining to potential employers previous work experience, or length of absence from the job market, could not only be terrifying, but also cost someone transitioning out of prostitution a potential position. Moreover, adequate attire is an important component of obtaining, and then maintaining, stable employment. WellSpring as well as many other social service agencies offer "community clothes closets" where clients select professional clothing to assist them in making a positive impression during the employment search. Closet items are donated from local community members.

Employment skills training and education are critical; the creation of alternatives to prostitution is necessary for long-term exit success. Intervention programs would be ideally linked to community colleges and Job Corps programs in order to capitalize on pre-existing community offerings and the expertise of a vast array of service providers.

Figure 9.1 (see below) provides a summary of services a fully comprehensive program would ideally provide to address the physical, emotional, and psychological needs of prostituted women.

Figure 9.1: Individual-Level Intervention

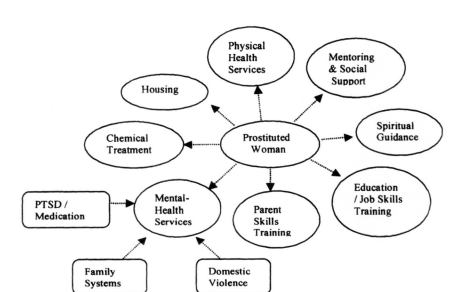

Comprehensive / Integrated Services

In an ideal world, resources to serve the most disenfranchised among us would be readily available; as would trained and committed professional staff. This however, is not an ideal world. Resources are limited for all human service programs, and especially for those serving marginalized populations. Street-level prostituted women survive on the periphery of society; they are unseen, unheard, and often go undetected. They are not a population likely to advocate on behalf of themselves; they are not "glamorous," nor are they viewed as deserving of assistance by the critical masses.

Moreover, the street-level prostituted population is a mobile group often leery and suspicious of formal agencies or professionals wielding power[43]. "Prostitutes are not easily served through normal agency service delivery. They are unlikely to approach agencies for help because of their lifestyles and fear of arrest," notes Weiner[44]. Thus, service providers are challenged to develop creative service access and provision.

Realistically, no one program can do it all. Planned collaboration and service integration must be a cornerstone of comprehensive intervention to prostituted women. Human service providers should be willing pool their resources, work together, and coordinate efforts through integrated in-house and out-reach efforts aimed at harm reduction and long-term optimal health. A panacea does not exist that will magically pave the way for a smooth and seamless transition out of the "game." The service needs of these women are great and resources few. However, the situation which seems complex and, perhaps overwhelming, from a service provider position, can be broken down into three ultimate issues.

✓ First and foremost is the desire and motivation, among street-level prostituted women themselves, to exit the "game" and live their lives differently.

✓ Second, the creation and provision of strategically planned, multi-pronged in-house and out-reach services that address the physical, emotional, and psychological needs of the target population, as described at length above, is undeniable.

✓ Third, at the local, state, and national level, education, support structures, and policy initiatives must be designed that will positively impact individuals, and the communities in which they reside, through both direct and indirect routes. These are described below.

Community and Societal-Level Issues:
Support Structures and Policy Initiatives

Informed by ecological systems theory[45], a contextual approach to programmatic intervention aimed at re-integrating prostituted women into the larger social fabric must, by necessity, address broader community and societal-level connections. Optimal long-term well-being is assumed dependent on societal integration. Intervention aimed at the physical, emotional, and psychological health of prostituted women is necessary, but insufficient; lacking broader societal support and advocacy, such efforts will ultimately fail. Bronfenbrenner's macro-system refers to cultural, economic and political forces that directly and indirectly influence and shape developmental trajectories. Macro-systemic issues of particular concern include: public education and innovation, service creation and delivery informed by research, and local, state, and national advocacy.

Public Education and Innovative Initiatives

Grass-Roots Efforts

In 2001, a Prostitution Task Force was created in Omaha, NE. The Task Force consisted of various entities representing a multitude of civic, non-profit, educational, and direct service organizations including police and probation officers, prosecutors and attorneys, counselors/mental health practitioners, researchers, and representatives from neighborhood organizations. The Task Force allowed for dialogue and discussion among a diverse group of individuals with a vested interest in reducing prostitution and advocating on behalf of people prostituted on the streets. The Task Force was headed by the Director of WellSpring and the Captain of the Northeast Police Precinct. The goals of the Task Force were to inform the public about prostitution (e.g., causes, consequences) and its prevalence within their communities, to serve as a resource for one another in a variety of venues and contexts, and to obtain additional resources to further advocate on behalf of prostituted individuals. Bringing together such a diverse group with unique agendas, stereotypes, and biases, was a monumental task; but proved quite successful on a number of fronts.

Most importantly, the issue of prostitution as a *local* phenomena received widespread attention and interest resulting in open dialogue, deeper understanding, and a multitude of new and expanded activities. The Dignity Coalition, aimed at assisting prostituted individuals specifically, and the Southeast Precinct Prostitution Task Force (SPPTF), aimed at community-level advocacy, are two sub-groups which emerged from the original Task Force efforts. Both groups have records of proven success in education and advocacy, some of which are outlined below.

Workshops and Symposia. The combined efforts of the Dignity Coalition (DC) and the Southeast Precinct Prostitution Task Force resulted in Nebraska's first all-day symposium focused on the street-level sex-industry: *Spotlight on Prostitution: Myths, Facts, and the Impact in Our Community.* The symposium was targeted at police, probation officers, direct service providers, and the general public. Public education and awareness were the primary goals. More than 200 individuals attended, with a waiting list of over 75. Evaluation of the Symposium indicated that the goals had been achieved and numerous attendees suggested that the event be held on an annual basis.

Similar efforts at the local, national and international levels also exist. For instance, the Social Work Department at the University of Toledo, in conjunction with the Second Chance Prostitution Program, recently sponsored the second annual *Prostitution, Sex Work, and the Commercial Sex Industry Conference.* The goals paralleled those of the *Spotlight* symposium in Omaha, and included the creation of collaborative research, advocacy and program development. The conference, chaired by well-known researchers and advocates in the prostitution field, targeted the academic community in addition to practitioners, criminal justice representatives, and those in the social service and health care fields[46]. Such efforts are extremely vital in awakening community leaders to the very real needs of prostituted persons within their geographic boundaries. Relatedly, collaborative networking engendered by such efforts is invaluable for creating and sustaining, advocacy and service delivery momentum. It is through such efforts that vulnerable female populations come to be viewed as populations *in need* and deserving of community and state funds largely because community members, not academics, comprise the target audience.

   Legal Maneuvering. Changes in the law have also resulted from grassroots efforts. Jan Quinley[47], Chairperson of The Southeast Precinct Prostitution Task Force, describes a recently-realized, hard fought victory. In Omaha, as in many cities, persons convicted of selling sex are treated noticeably different, and more harshly, than those convicted of purchasing sex. Jan witnessed a particularly infuriating incident in which a man arrested for buying sex plea bargained the charge to "lewd conduct" and received a $75.00 fine. The same man then took the witness stand, on behalf of the prosecution and against the woman from whom he had purchased sex. The woman was convicted of solicitation and received six months in jail (it was her fourth conviction). The penalty structure for solicitation at the time was as follows:

   ▸   First conviction: $75.00 fine;
   ▸   Second conviction: ten days jail-time and up to $500 fine;
   ▸   Third conviction: 30 days jail-time and up to $500 fine;
   ▸   Fourth conviction: six months jail-time and up to $500 fine.

   Conversely, there was no *minimum or maximum* penalty for charges of lewd conduct, regardless of the number of times convicted. Needless to say, johns who could afford attorneys would successfully plea bargain and receive a virtual slap on the wrist. The Southeast Precinct Prostitution Task Force worked diligently to amend the city statute. As a direct result of their efforts, lewd conduct and solicitation now fall under the *same penalty structure*. Additionally significant, for those convicted within a residential zone or city park, the punishment is automatically accelerated one penalty. Despite the victory, "Enforcement," Jan remarked, "is still a problem." The community building efforts of the SPPTF were recently highlighted in a January, 2005 CNN television special. Results such as these may seem minimal, given the scope and magnitude of issues needing to be addressed within the street-level sex industry, but the attempt at mitigating gender-based inequality in legal sanctions is noteworthy.

   Moving beyond education, drug court and family drug court, implemented through local and state tax dollars, could prove effective for addressing chemical dependence among prostituted individuals.

Drug Court and Family Drug Court

   Street-level prostitution and drug dependence create a vicious cycle that entraps women, ruins lives, and devastates families. Drug addiction, I believe, is the single most critical issue that must be addressed if real change is to occur in the lives of street-level prostituted women. Earlier, I discussed the need for quality, residential care for the treatment of drug-addicted women. Adequate funding for quality care presents a monumental barrier, as is typically the case. However, alternative approaches exist including the use of drug court and family drug court, which should be vigorously pursued.

Adult Drug Court. Adult Drug Court offers intense treatment to drug addicted offenders and may offer hope and necessary services to prostituted women. Dade Country, FL created the first Adult Drug Court program in the nation in 1989[48]. Currently, some 1600 specialized drug courts exist throughout the country. I focus here on Adult Drug Court in Douglas County, NE for two reasons. First, it exists in the state and county where the majority of women who participated in this research were interviewed. And second, it is one of the largest drug courts in the country with more than 350 participants.

Douglas County Adult Drug Court (DCADC) consists of two tracks: (1) the Diversion (or Pre-Plea) Tract, established in 1997; and (2) the Post-Plea Tract, established in 2003[49]. Eligibility criteria differ. Diversion participants must be first-time, non-violent offenders with a documented drug and alcohol abuse and/or dependent lifestyle. Eligibility in the Post Plea Tract requires admission of guilt to the current felony charge, no prior violent offense, no known gang involvement, and documented drug and alcohol abuse and/or dependence lifestyle.

The Diversion tract program runs 12-18 months, the Post-Plea Tract is an 18-24 month program. Both operate using graduated sanctions and rewards, with each program consisting of intense treatment divided into three phases. After in-take, participants are assigned a counselor who makes treatment recommendations. The program proceeds as follows:

Phase I consists of weekly one-on-one case management meetings with a licensed mental health practitioner who assesses progress on a number of fronts: attendance at AA/NA meetings, employment, education, and mental health assistance, as needed. Participants also attend a transition-to-treatment group, until in-house treatment services are available, and Drug Court on a weekly basis. Drug screening occurs three times per week.

In Phase II, case management sessions may be reduced to every other week and drug screening measures are reduced to twice weekly on a random basis. In addition, scheduled court visits in front of the Drug Court Judge may be reduced to every other week or even to every three weeks, depending on case-specific circumstances.

Phase III is the maintenance phase. Self-help recovery meetings are expected, and monitoring is reduced. At this phase, Drug Court participants have[50]:

- ► Completed primary treatment;
- ► Completed aftercare services;
- ► Maintained program fees;
- ► Integrated the information learned in treatment and in the Drug Court Program;

▸ Abstained from alcohol and other mind altering chemicals;
▸ Gained personal skills (e.g., tolerance, impulse control, delayed gratification, locus of control);
▸ Been stable in recovery;
▸ Completed GED or other assigned academic endeavors; and
▸ Completed all assigned community service hours.

Failure to comply to the provisions of the Diversion Tract results in the case being returned to the district court judge for plea, trial, and possible sentencing. However, because admittance of guilt is a requirement for acceptance into the Post-Plea Tract, program failure results in the case being automatically sentenced by a drug court judge.

The adult drug court is funded by county tax dollars. In March, 2004, the Criminal Justice Department at the University of Nebraska-Omaha completed a cost/savings analyses of the Douglas County Adult Drug Court program. According to the report, the cost savings is approximately $11,336 per participant, or $3,400,800 for 300 participants[51].

Family Drug Court. Nearly 80% of substantiated child abuse and neglect cases involve parents who regularly use or abuse alcohol or other substances[52]. Reunification depends on the ability of parents to remain drug-free. Moreover, with the 1997 passage of the Adoption and Safe Families ACT (ASFA), proceedings for the termination of parental rights begin anywhere from one year to eighteen months after children have been removed from the home. The time-frame presents an "insurmountable barrier for addicted parents unable to enter treatment due to waiting lists, or for parents in treatment who relapse"[53].

Family drug court offers "a comprehensive systemic approach to treating substance-abusing parents, while maintaining the goal of reunification and meeting the requirements of ASFA"[54]. According to a publication by the American Bar Association, "family drug courts offer intensive drug treatment intervention and supportive services within a structure of sanctions and incentives"[55]. There are approximately 20 family drug courts operational or in the planning phase across the United States.

I am not an advocate for the use of harsher treatment or penalties against drug-using prostituted women. I do however believe, should they choose participation, that drug court and family drug court may offer the much-needed intensive monitoring and structural supports necessary for actively and aggressively addressing chemical dependence among this population.

Education: The Buyers of Sexual Services
Discussion of prostitution with ordinary citizens, neighbors, and local community members will undoubtedly focus on the women who sell sex. Namely, the *supply side* of the equation. The men who buy sex are often an afterthought–if they are given any thought at all. The stigma associated with prostitution is felt, not by the buyers of sex, but by the suppliers. The sexual double-standard is alive and

well, indeed. The demand for commercial sex, one could reasonably argue, drives the industry; if the demand did not exist, there would be no need for suppliers.

Although academics are slowly turning attention to the buyers of commercial sex, public education on this front is minimal. Nonetheless, creative strategies aimed at public information and reform are beginning to emerge. For instance, the South East Precinct Prostitution Task Force of Omaha, Nebraska, was recently awarded two grants through community development organizations. The first grant funded the purchase of five billboards, strategically located throughout the city, which display the names, ages, and conviction dates of the purchasers of commercial sex. The second grant was used to purchase three additional billboards with the same purpose. The names of the convicted remain advertised for the period of one month and appear in both Spanish and English.

In other cities, the names and photographs of convicted customers appear on web sites or cable channels. "The idea behind such policies are to subject customers not only to the risk of legal sanctions, but also to the loss of reputation"[56]. However, it must be noted that these tactics often incur criticism and opposition as the unintended consequences of such maneuvers are shame and embarrassment to innocent family members.

Another relatively recent development is the advent of "johns schools" for men convicted of solicitation of prostitution. The schools' goals include: the provision of education about STDs and legal issues, to hold customers accountable for the perpetuation of prostitution, and to convey the notion that prostitution is harmful to women. The majority of johns schools located in the United States are modeled after the First Offender Prostitution Program, begun in 1995 in San Francisco[57]. There are many johns schools scattered in cities throughout the U.S. including: Buffalo, New York, Las Vegas, Nevada, Palm Beach County, Florida, Pittsburgh, Pennsylvania, and Washington, D.C. The johns school in Brooklyn, called Project Respect, has been in operation since 2002 and is considered enormously successful according to the Brooklyn District Attorney. In fact, of nearly 200 men who have gone through the classes since the program's inception, only two have been re-arrested for the same offense[58]. Still, some question whether the classes, lasting no more than a weekend in some cases, could really *change* long-established behavioral patterns. Moreover, according to Monto[59], the men typically arrested who participate in the classes are novices, inexperienced in the "game," and thus, less knowledgeable in strategies for avoiding arrest. The men with histories of purchasing commercial sex are the real predators with long-established behavioral patterns and most in need of reform. Yet, they are not likely to be the ones attending school.

State, National and International Advocacy

Policy and research implications of this work further suggest the need for advocacy efforts on behalf of prostituted women at the state, national and international levels. Advocacy for harm reduction entails a multitude of actions including: promoting a safer work environment, providing access to health care facilities, reducing the stigma associated with prostitution involvement, educating the public about prostituted women and challenges to exiting the sex-industry, and extending unbiased treatment by the police and other criminal justice organizations[60]. Although organizations exist to provide these services, their "resources are minimal and their presence is limited to but a few places in the United States"[61]. Most notable among these include COYOTE, PONY, the North America Task Force on Prostitution (NTFP), and the Sex Workers' Outreach Project (SWOP).

COYOTE (Call Off Your Old Tired Ethics)[62] was founded by Margo St. James (of St. James Infirmary noted earlier) in 1973. The purpose of this organization is to repeal prostitution laws, reduce stigma associated with sex work, and work for the rights of all sex workers (e.g., strippers, porn actresses, street-level prostitutes). COYOTE supports programs to assist sex workers in their right to change their occupation, works to prevent the scapegoating of sex workers for AIDS and other STDs, and to educate sex workers, their clients, and the general public about safe sex. COYOTE members have testified at government hearings, served as expert witnesses in trials, assisted police with investigations of crimes against prostitutes, and provided training to government and non-profit organizations serving sex workers. COYOTE chapters exist in San Francisco, Los Angeles, Seattle, and Boston.

PONY (Prostitutes of New York)[63] is a support and advocacy group for all involved in the sex industry. PONY works to decriminalize prostitution and end illegal police activity in the enforcement of existing laws. The organization provides legal and health referrals to sex workers.

NTFP was founded in 1979 in New York[64] to act as an umbrella organization for prostitutes and prostitutes' rights organizations in various North America localities. In 1994, its scope expanded to include other organizations and individuals who support the rights of prostitutes and sex workers.

SWOP[65] focuses on safety, dignity, and the changing needs of sex industry workers. This organization works to decriminalize prostitution and sex work through a variety of strategies including community and network development, initiating state legislation, creating positive media, and providing public education. Additional information on these and other prostitution and sex workers' advocacy groups can be found on-line (e.g., http://www.walnet.org/csis/groups/index.html).

Finally, numerous organizations with international scope also advocate on behalf of prostituted individuals. The Network of Sex Work Projects (NSWP)[66] consists of sex workers and organizations providing services to sex workers in over 40 countries. The Sex Workers' International Media Watch (SWIMW) was created for the purpose of observing and responding to the media on issues involving sex work[67].

The Future Agenda:
Where Do We Go From Here?

My suggestions for future research are many, with a diverse array of focal points spanning additional longitudinal work, theory development, and cross-generational studies. Research designed to critically examine the developmental trajectories of women (and men) involved in street-level prostitution would provide valuable information related to the sex industry entry-exit-re-entry cycle. Although the longitudinal research presented here is the first of its kind, the small sample size at the follow-up phase of data collection severely limits the transferability of results. More longitudinal research, involving larger participant samples and utilizing mixed-methods approaches, is clearly warranted.

Additionally, research aimed at theory development and testing is limited. Street-level prostitutes are embedded within unique social, historical, and political contexts. Application of pre-existing social theories is not a seamless process given the idiosyncratic issues which impact women prostituted on the streets. Phenomena-specific theoretical insights will open new doors for research, and by extension, practice and strategic efforts for direct care.

Moreover, few programs serving prostituted women incorporate an evaluation component. Program evaluation allows for critical monitoring of program effectiveness and efficiency. Too often, program evaluation is viewed as a "luxury" which many service agencies cannot afford. The result then, is that systematic monitoring of program strengths and weakness is not obtained and assessment of program effectiveness occurs anecdotally, if at all. Problems in service delivery may continue undetected and undeterred, and eventually compromise entire programs.

To illustrate, as a long-time WellSpring member, Chancey had weathered numerous director and staffing turn-overs. The result, in her opinion, was a diluted program that failed to meet the needs of its clientele. She explained,

> We [WellSpring clients] used to be a tight knit group. We gave each other a lot of support. We all knew what everybody else was going through and gave them support. And that was one of the main strengths of WellSpring. Now, everybody is isolated from everybody for [fear that] somebody is going to give somebody an idea of what they could do, or share information. Some counselors think that private things that are going on in people's lives should be dealt with in private therapy rather than in group. I don't agree. A lot of the people quit going to WellSpring because of the changes.

Change, in and of itself, is not necessarily problematic. In fact, change can result in better programs, better services, and greater client participation. Chancey statement illustrates the importance of on-going program evaluation. Lacking evaluation data, organizational staff are ill-equipped to provide the best services possible to their clients. As a results, program effectiveness and client success may be unintentionally compromised.

Finally, additional research is sorely needed to better understand johns/clients, pimps, and the developmental trajectories of the lives of children of street-level prostituted women. Their children, specifically, represent a "high risk" target population. The present research highlights the cross-generational nature of dysfunctional family dynamics which often results in out-of-home placement. The obvious problem is that all three groups (i.e., clients, pimps, and children) represent elusive populations that are not easily included in research. In fact, I had personally considered conducting research with the children of prostituted women, beginning with the children of those women who participated in this investigation. I gave up. The necessary work would require monumental effort, time, resources, and networking. For the right person however, who is willing to undertake such a massive endeavor, the research results would prove immensely valuable for academicians as well as practitioners and service providers. I applaud anyone who accepts the challenge.

Conclusion and Final Remarks

The life of the human soul is not a "being" but a "becoming."
–Alfred Adler[68]

When little girls are asked what they want to "be" when they grown up, "prostitute" is never, not ever, the response. Susan Cole[69] argues that women do not freely choose to become prostitutes. Rather, an accumulation of events and personal experiences, coupled with lack of viable alternatives and the oppressive influence of a male dominated society force the decision upon women. Developmental processes and the culmination of personal attributes, contextual forces, and interpersonal relationships, coupled with cognitive appraisal of life events and experiences through time, allow for the *option* of street-level prostitution to become a reality for some.

This investigation was designed to reveal "...personal attributes, contextual forces, interpersonal relationships, and cognitive appraisal of live events... through time" among a particularly unique population of women. Childhood familial environments were characterized as chaotic, affection as a rare commodity. Parental alcoholism and drug abuse, domestic violence, and various forms of brutality comprised the women's most significant childhood memories. Early abandonment, both literal and symbolic, was widely experienced. Emotional poverty resulted, as relationship dynamics learned in the early decades of life, became repeated throughout adulthood. Adult male/female relationships were largely devoid of support or emotional sustenance. Violence, in a variety of heinous forms, characterized those relationships.

This research provides further support that familial patterns established in the family of origin are frequently (and perhaps unwittingly) transmitted to future generations. Among those who participated in this research, the women's families of procreation mirrored those of origin. For many of the women, describing relationships with their own children was the most difficult part of the interview process. Most had lost their children, some permanently, because of their own actions and behaviors or for failing to protect their children from the actions of others. Some sank into an abyss of depression when their children were removed. Child removal became a critical turning point in the progression of addiction, marking the beginning of the most severe use for many.

The follow-up interviews documented risk for re-entry into the "game" following exit attempts. Exiting the street-level sex industry takes on new dimensions when viewed in cyclic fashion. Very few studies have examined the "entry-exit-re-entry" process and fewer still have focused exclusively on street-level prostituted women. More work here is clearly warranted.

Purpose Revisited

The purpose in writing this book was two-fold: (1) to explore developmental experiences which propel women into the streets and keep them there; and (2) to share the lives of these women with an audience that exists beyond the walls of academia. I was guided by the belief that, in providing a vehicle in which the lives and stories of these women could be told, that they would become "real" to the reader. My hope was that, through the power of pen to paper (or finger-tips to keyboard), affective responses and visual images would materialize– that feelings of empathy, rather than disgust or antipathy–would ensue.

Empathy is powerful and reflects an attitude of profound attunement to another's world of meanings and feelings[70]. It conveys appreciation, respect, and deep understanding. When we are able to empathize with another we implicitly share with them a sense of humanity and respect. We allow them dignity. Perhaps most importantly, empathy necessitates relatedness. It was my goal that by sharing the lives of these women–of Tami, Sam, Chancey and the many others–that this very population of women would no longer be "dismissible." For it is impossible to simultaneously *dismiss* another while *empathizing* with her.

Personalizing these women, as I have attempted to do here, renders them real. They can no longer be marginalized, stigmatized or berated if they come to be recognized as likenesses of ourselves. When our shared humanity is acknowledged and recognized, we are able to move beyond labels, and instead, see individuals. When speaking with my students about the women I have come to know through this research, I often begin by saying: "At our cores, you and I are no different from them. We share much more in common than you might imagine." I draw upon our *similarities* to counteract the power of labeling. Labels create psychological and emotional distance. Without labels these women are no longer "prostitutes," but rather, "prostituted *women.*"

When these women become real to us, when we understand developmental processes which created present circumstances, we as a society are forced to acknowledge and examine the entire phenomena of street-level prostitution in context. The issues are complex, with deeply embedded historical, cultural, personal and familial roots than *cannot* be over-looked or denied if real understanding is to occur.

In essence, what has been revealed in this investigation has been understood for many decades. Interpersonal relationships are vitally important for shaping who we are and what we become. This is not to say that social connections and interpersonal dynamics *dictate* human development or cause self-destructive developmental outcomes. As humans, we are uniquely equipped with the capacity for free choice and planned, purposeful behavior. It is to say, however, that social relationships, from birth onward, provide a framework which guides human destiny by impacting the psyche, including one's social and emotional functioning, personal goals, dreams, values and ambitions. It is through others that we come to see ourselves. Developmental processes are thus set in motion and unique life-styles created. On the door to Alfred Adler's guidance clinic in Vienna was the inscription "IT IS NEVER TOO LATE"[71]. I choose to believe this is so.

Notes

1. John Stuart Mills, internet citation, obtained February 26, 2005, from http://www.jsmill.com/

2. Urie Bronfenbrenner, "Ecological Systems Theory," in *Six Theories of Child Development: Revised Formulations and Current Issues*, edited by Ross Vasta (Philadelphia: Jessica Kingsley Publishers, 1989), 187-249.

3. Celia Williamson and Gail Folaron, "Understanding the Experiences of Street Level Prostitutes," *Qualitative Social Work 2*, no. 3 (2003): 271-87.

4. Melissa Farley and Howard Barkan. "Prostitution, Violence, and Posttraumatic Stress Disorder." *Women & Health* 27 (1998): 37-49.

5. Adele Weiner, "Understanding the Social Needs of Streetwalking Prostitutes," *Social Work 41* (1996): 97-105.

6. Weiner "Understanding," 97-105.

7. Williamson and Folaron, "Understanding Experiences," 271-87.

8. Adele Weiner "Understanding," 97-105.

9. Karen Hardman, "A Social Work Group for Prostituted Women with Children." *Social Work with Groups* 20, no.1 (1997): 19-31.

10. Greg R. Alexander and Carol C. Korenbrot, "The Role of Prenatal Care in Preventing Low Birthweight," *The Future of Children 5* (1995): 103-20.

11. Cynthia García Coll and K. Magnuson, "Cultural Differences as Sources of Developmental Vulnerabilities and Resources: A View from Developmental Research," in *Handbook of Early Childhood Intervention*, ed. Samuel J. Meisels and Jack P. Shonkoff (Cambridge University Press, 2000), 194-211.

12. Lawrence J. Aber and Neil G. Bennett, "The Effects of Poverty on Child Health and Development," *Annual Review of Public Health 18* (1997): 463-83.

13. Edward F. Zigler and Nancy W. Hall, *Child Development and Social Policy: Theory and Applications* (New York: McGraw Hill, 2000).

14. Weiner, "Understanding," 97-105.

15.St. James Infirmary. Retrieved October 13, 2003, from http://www. stjamesinfirmary.org/

16. Weiner, "Understanding," 97-105.

17. Lynanne Plummer, John J. Potterat, Stephen Q. Muth, and John B. Muth, "Providing Support and Assistance for Low-Income or Homeless Women," *Journal of the American Medical Association* 276, no. 23 (1996): 1874-75.

18. Mitchell S. Ratner, *Crack Pipe as Pimp: An Ethnographic Investigation of Sex-for-Crack Exchanges,* (New York: Lexington, 1993).

19. Ratner, *Crack Pipe as Pimp,* p. 29.

20. Plummer, Potterat, Muth, and Muth, "Providing Support and Assistance," 1874-75.

21. Christopher Bagley, and Richard Ramsey, "Sexual Abuse in Childhood: Psycho-Social Outcomes and Implications for Social Work Practice," *Journal of Social Work and Human Sexuality* 4 (1986): 33-47.

22. Patricia Cohen, Jocelyn Brown, and Elizabeth Smailes, "Child Abuse and Neglect and the Development of Mental Disorders in the General Population," *Development and Psychopathology 13* (2001): 981-99.

23. Scott Menard, "Short and Long Term Consequences of Criminal Victimization," in *Violent Behavior in the Life Course,* ed. Scott Menard, David. Huizinga, and Delbert S. Elliott (Thousand Oaks, CA: Sage, 2001), 16-32.

24. Roberto J. Valera, Robin G. Sawyer, and Glenn R. Schiraldi, "Perceived Health Needs of Inner-City Street Prostitutes: A Preliminary Study," *American Journal of Health Behavior 25,* no. 1 (Jan/Feb. 2001): 50-60.

25. Cohen, Brown, and Smailes, "Child Abuse and Neglect," 981-99.

26. Ronald C. Kessler and William J. Magee, "Childhood Family Violence and Adult Recurrent Depression," *Journal of Health and Sociological Behavior 35* (1994): 13-27.

27. James A. Chu and Diana L. Dill, "Dissociative Symptoms in Relation to Childhood Physical and Sexual Abuse," *American Journal of Psychiatry* 147 (1990): 887-92.

28. Christopher Bagley, Floyd Bolitho, and Lorne Bertrand, "Sexual Assault in School, Mental Health, and Suicidal Behaviors in Adolescent Women in Canada," *Adolescence 32* (1997): 341-66.

29. Bagley and Ramsey, "Sexual Abuse in Childhood," 33-47.

30. Jon R. Conte and John R. Schuerman, "Factors Associated with an Increased Impact of Child Sexual Abuse," *Child Abuse and Neglect* 11 (1987): 201-11.

31. Plummer, Potterat, Muth, and Muth, "Providing Support and Assistance," 1874-75.

32. Audrey M. Burnam, Judith A. Stein, Jacqueline Golding, Judith Siegel, Susan B. Sorenson, and others, "Sexual Assault and Mental Disorders in a Community Population," *Journal of Consulting and Clinical Psychology 56* (1988): 843-50.

33. Carlfred Broderick and Jeremy Smith, "The General Systems Approach to the Family," in *Contemporary Theories About the Family: Vol. II. General Theories/Theoretical Orientations,* ed. by Wesley R. Burr, Reuben Hill, Ivan Nye, and Ira L. Reiss (New York: Free Press, 1979), 112-29.

34. Carlfred Broderick, *Understanding Family Processes: Basics of Family Systems Theory* (Thousand Oaks, CA: Sage, 1993).

35. David M. Klein and James M. White, *Family Theories: An Introduction* (Thousand Oaks: Sage, 1996).

36. Steve De Shazer, Insoo Kim Berg, Eve Lipchik, Elam Nunnally, Alex Molnar, Wallace Gingerich, and Michele Weiner-Davis, "Brief Therapy," *Family Process 25* (1986): 207-21.

37. Plummer and others, "Providing Support and Assistance," 1874-1875

38. Celia Williamson and Terry Cluse-Tolar, "Pimp-Controlled Prostitution: Still an Integral Part of Street Life," *Violence Against Women* 8 (2002): 1074-92.

39. Jody Raphael, and Deborah L. Shapiro. *Sisters Speak Out: The Lives and Needs of Prostituted Women in Chicago* (Center for Impact Research, August 2002), 1-35.

40. Lenore E. Walker, *The Battered Woman Syndrome,* 2nd ed. (New York: Springer, 2000).

41. Maggie O'Neill, "Prostitute Women Now," in *Rethinking Prostitution: Purchasing Sex in the 1990s,* ed. Graham Scambler and Annette Scambler (London: Routledge, 1997), 3-28.

42. Julia O'Connell Davidson, *Prostitution, Power and Freedom* (Ann Arbor, MI: The University of Michigan Press, 1998).

43. Hilary L. Surratt, James A. Inciardi, Steven P. Kurtz, and Marion C. Kiley, "Sex Work and Drug Use in a Subculture of Violence," *Crime & Delinquency* 50 (2004): 43-59.

44. Weiner, "Understanding," 6.

45. Bronfenbrenner, "Ecological Systems Theory," 187-249.

46. Second National Conference on Prostitution, Sex Work, and the Commercial Sex Industry, retrieved June 28, 2005 from http://www.lisp.wayne.edu/baker/prostconf

47. Jan Quinley, Southeast Precinct Prostitution Task Force Chairperson, Omaha Nebraska, Personal Communication, June 26, 2005.

48. Florida State Courts: Court Programs and Initiatives. Retrieved June 28, 2005 from http://www.flcourts.org/genpublic/family/drugcourt/index.shtml

49. Paul Yakel, Drug Court Coordinator, Douglas Country Adult Drug Court, personal communication June 28, 2005.

50. Fourth Judicial District Court of Nebraska, Douglas County Adult Drug Court, retrieved June 28, 2005 from http://www.co.douglas.ne.us/dept/districtcourt

51. Douglas County Drug Court Program Evaluation. Retrieved June 28, 2005 from http://co.douglas.ne.us/dept/districtcourt/drugcourt/programevaluation.htm

52. National Drug Court Institute, Drug Court Practitioner Fact Sheet (1999), *"Family Drug Courts: An Alternative Approach to Processing Child Abuse & Neglect Cases,"* Available from National Drug Court Institute (703.706.0576).

53. *Family Drug Courts*, Fact Sheet, 1999.

54. *Family Drug Courts*, Fact Sheet, 1999.

55. *Family Drug Courts*, Fact Sheet, 1999.

56. Martin A. Monto, "Female Prostitution, Customers, and Violence," *Violence Against Women* 10 (2004): 182.

57. Martin A. Monto, "Female Prostitution, Customers, and Violence," *Violence Against Women* 10 (2004): 183.

58. The Village Voice. "School for Johns Arrested for Soliciting Sex," Retrieved June 25, 2005 from http://www.villagevoice.com/news/0519,hunter,63812,5.html

59. Martin A. Monto, *"Focusing on the Clients of Street Prostitutes: A Creative Approach to Reducing Violence Against Women,"* Washington, DC: National Institute of Justice (1999).

60. Surratt, Inciardi, Kurtz, and Kiley, "Sex Work and Drug Use," 55.

61. Surratt, Inciardi, Kurtz, and Kiley, "Sex Work and Drug Use," 55.

Chapter Nine

62. Call Off Your Old Tired Ethics (COYOTE). Retrieved June 25, 2005 from http://www.walnet.org/csis/grops/coyote.html.
63. Prostitutes of New York (PONY). Retrieved June 25, 2005 from http://www.walnet.org/csis/groups/pony.html.
64. Commercial Sex Information Service (CSIS). Retrieved June 25, 2005 from http://www.walnet.org/csis/groups/index.html.
65. Sex Workers' Outreach Project, USA (SWOP). Retrieved June 25, 2005 from http://swop-usa.org.
66. Network of Sex Work Projects (NSWP). Retrieved June 28, 2005 from http://www.nswp.org/home.html.
67. Sex Workers' International Media Watch, SWIMW Home. Retrieved June 28, 2005 from http://www.swimw.org/swimw.html.
68. Alfred Adler, "Contributions to the Theory of Hallucinations," in *The Practice and Theory of Individual Psychology*, ed. Alfred Adler (Paterson, NJ: Littlefield, Adams, 1963a), 51-58.
69. Susan G. Cole, "Sexual politics: Contradictions and explosions," in *Good Girls/Bad Girls: Sex Trade Workers and Feminists Face to Face*, ed. Laurie Bell (Toronto, Canada: Women's Press, 1987), 33-36.
70. Nathaniel J. Raskin and Carl R. Rogers, "Person-Centered Therapy," in *Current Psychotherapies*, ed. Raymond J. Corsini and Danny Wedding (Belmont, CA: Brooks/Cole, 2000), 133-67.
71. Harold H. Mosak, "Adlerian Psychotherapy," in *Current Psychotherapies,* 6th ed., ed. Raymond J. Corsini and Danny Wedding (Brooks/Cole, 2000), 54-98.

Appendices

Summary of Interview Questions

Original Interview Questions
(1998 - 1999)

History

Can you begin by telling me a little bit about the family you grew up in, for instance, how many siblings do you have and where you grew up? What were your parents like? Were both your mother and father in your home during your childhood? Can you describe your relationship with various members of your family (for instance, with your siblings and your parents)?

What are your most vivid memories about your childhood? Did your parents use drugs or drink alcohol? Was there physical violence in your family? Do you still have contact with your parents? Siblings? Grandparents, etc...? Why/why not? Tell me about school, for instance, did you like it? Did you do well in school? Did you graduate? What were your friendships like with school peers? Can you tell me about your first sexual experience– was this by choice or forced? How old were you?

Sexual Abuse

Were you ever sexually mistreated during your childhood? Are you comfortable talking about this? (If yes, move on...) Who was the perpetrator? How old were you when this began? How long did this last (e.g., months, number of years)? How did it end (e.g., what events led to the end)? Did anyone know about it / did you tell anyone? (If not, why not? / If yes, what was her/his response?) Do you feel that experience has had an impact on your development, such as the choices you've made or your feelings about sexual intimacy?

Entry Into the Sex Industry

How old were you the first time you traded sexual services for money, drugs, or anything else (e.g., housing, food)? Can you describe your very first prostitution experience for me? Why did you get involved? When your involvement first began, how long did you think it would last (e.g., number of months, years)? Why did you stay involved? What, if anything, would have made a difference in your life so that you would not have become involved in prostitution? Does/did your family know about your prostitution involvement?

Drugs

When did you first use drugs or alcohol? Can you describe those experiences for me? Were you ever addicted to any drugs? When did you know that you were "addicted"? How did your addiction progress?

Jail/Imprisonment

Why were you sent to jail/prison? Have you been here before? On what charges? When will you be released? What will you do when get out?

Social Aspects of "The Game"

Can you describe the range of money available for different types of sexual services? Were you ever involved with someone who could be considered a "pimp"? (If not, why not?) How did that relationship develop? How long did it last? Can you describe your experiences with your "pimp"? Can you describe some of your most vivid experiences with specific clients or dates? Did you have "regulars"? How did those relationships evolve? Do the women on the streets look out for one another or protect one another? Can you give me some examples? Did you have any female "friends" on the streets? Why/why not?

Violence

Were you ever afraid you would get hurt or maybe killed while working the streets? Can you describe some of your most frightening experiences on the streets? How were you able to go back to the streets after these incidents? What steps did you take to protect yourself on the streets, if any?

Family of Procreation

Do you have any children? How many? What are your children's ages? Do they currently live with you? (If not, where do they live? Please tell about how they ended up living there). Do/did they know about your involvement in the sex industry? Did you have children before or after you were involved in the sex industry? Did you work the streets while pregnant? How did children impact your involvement in the sex industry? What have been the impacts of your sex-industry involvement on your children, if any?

Can you tell me a little bit about your long-term intimate relationships (e.g., how did those evolve? Did they know about your prostitution? Did they encourage/discourage it? Were they also involved in the sex industry?)

Services

What types of services have you used (e.g., counnseling, Alcoholics Anonymous, etc...?) In what ways were these services helpful for you? In what ways were they not helpful or could they have been improved? What types of services do you think are *needed* for women involved in street-level sex work, but *not* available?

Future

What do you see yourself doing two years from now? What are your goals for the future? Where do you see your children in the future, for instance, two or five years from now? What are your goals for them? How are you working to reach your goals? What do you need to be successful? What are the biggest challenges you face over the next six months?

Follow-Up Interview Questions
(2001 - 2002)

Progress

Can you tell a little bit about the most significant developments in your life since we last talked together? (Have you maintained contact with WellSpring?) Do you currently work in the paid labor force or are you legally employed? Please tell me a little bit about the type of work you do. Did you receive job-training or educational services? How long have you been at this place of work and what are your plans for remaining employed here?

If She Returned to Prostitution

What were the biggest challenges you faced with regard to remaining out of prostitution? What services or programs would have helped you remain prostitution-free? Were these services available to you or not?

Please describe for me how, if at all, prostitution has changed over the last few years– for instance, do you have the same clients as before? Is it more dangerous Why/why not? Have you experienced any kind of threats or violence on the streets since the last time we met? Please describe the incident(s) to me and your reaction. Did you contact the police? Why/why not? Are there some of the same women working the streets that were there before? Do you look out for one another? Tell me how the threat of jail influences street-work?

Drugs

Have you remained drug-free since our last interview? What facilitated your ability to remain clean? What were the biggest challenges to remaining drug-free?

What types of services would have eased the challenge of drug-addiction that were not available to you? What advice would you give other women seeking to lead drug-free lives?

If She Relapsed into Drug Use. Why did you begin using drugs again? Can you share with me what was happening in your life at the time? What role, if any, did drug use play in your returning to prostitution? Can you describe for me the role of your friends, family, and partner(s) in your decision to use again?

Children

Please tell me a little bit about where your children are right now– for instance, do they live with you or someone else? Is this a permanent custody arrangement? How often do you see them? What types of activities do you share with them? Would you like to have more children? What are your fears for them and their futures? How has your recovery / return to prostitution impacted their lives?

Family

Can you tell me a bit about your relationship with your mother/father since the last time we spoke? How have those relationships changed, if at all? What about the relationship between yourself and your siblings and other significant family members? Who is your greatest source of support right now? How does this person provide support to you? How has your family challenged/facilitated your recovery process? What has been their reaction to your returning to prostitution/remaining off the streets?

Partners

Are you currently involved with a partner? Will you please tell me a little bit about that relationship. (*If it is a new relationship:* how did you meet? What attracted you to this person? Describe how the relationship has progressed?) (*If same partner as before*: what have been the challenges of this relationship over the past few years? How has the relationship changed/remained the same? Where do you see this relationship going?)

Services

What types of services are you currently receiving (e.g., AA, NA, counseling). What types of services to you feel you need but are not receiving or are not available to you? What are the biggest issues/challenges in your life right now?

Future

What do you envision your life to be like two years from now? What are your goals for the future? How are you working on reaching your goals? What are the biggest challenges you face in the next six months?

Selected Bibliography

Aber, Lawrence J., and Neil G. Bennett. "The Effects of Poverty on Child Health and Development." *Annual Review of Public Health* 18 (1997): 463-483.

Adler, Alfred. "*The Progress of Mankind.*" Pp. 3-8 in *Essays in individual psychology,* edited by Kurt A. Adler and Danica Deutsch. New York: Grove Press, 1959.

—. "Contributions to the Theory of Hallucinations." Pp. 51-58 in *The Practice and Theory of Individual Psychology,* edited by Alfred Adler. Paterson, NJ: Littlefield, Adams, 1963a.

Alexander, Greg R., and Carol C. Korenbrot. "The Role of Prenatal Care in Preventing Low Birthweight." *The Future of Children* 5 (1995): 103-20.

Aronson, Jodi. "A Pragmatic View of Thematic Analysis." *The Qualitative Report* 2, no. 1 (1994): 1-3.

Bagley, Christopher, and Richard Ramsey. "Sexual Abuse in Childhood: Psycho-Social Outcomes and Implications for Social Work Practice." *Journal of Social Work and Human Sexuality* 4, (1986): 33-47.

Bagley, Christopher, and Loretta Young. "Juvenile Prostitution and Child Sexual Abuse: A Controlled Study." *Canadian Journal of Community Mental Health* 6 (1987): 5-26.

Bagley, Christopher, Floyd Bolitho, and Lorne Bertrand. "Sexual Assault in School, Mental Health, and Suicidal Behaviors in Adolescent Women in Canada." *Adolescence* 32 (1997): 341-366.

Baltes, Paul B., and Jacqui Smith. "Lifespan Psychology: From Developmental Contextualism to Developmental Biocultural Co-Constructivism." *Research in Human Development* 1 (2004): 123-144.

Barry, Kathleen. *The Prostitution of Sexuality: The Global Exploitation of Women.* New York: New York University Press, 1995.

Broderick, Carlfred B. *Understanding Family Process: Basics of Family Systems Theory.* Thousand Oaks, CA: Sage, 1993.

—. "Family Process Theory." Pp. 171-206 in *Fashioning Family Theory*, edited by Jetse Sprey. Newbury Park, CA: Sage, 1990.

—. *Understanding Family Processes: Basic of Family Systems Theory.* Thousand Oaks, CA: Sage, 1993.

Broderick, Carlfred and Jeremy Smith. "The General Systems Approach to the Family." Pp. 112-129 in *Contemporary Theories About the Family: Vol. II. General Theories/Theoretical Orientations,* edited by Wesley R. Burr, Reuben Hill, Ivan Nye, and Ira L. Reiss. New York: Free Press, 1979.

Bronfenbrenner, Urie. "Ecological Systems Theory." Pp. 187-249 in *Six Theories of Child Development: Revised Formulations and Current Issues,* edited by Ross Vasta. Philadelphia: Jessica Kingsley Publishers, 1989.

Bronfenbrenner, Urie and Ann C. Crouter. " The Evolution of Environmental Models in Developmental Research." Pp. 357-414 in *Handbook of Child Psychology: Vol. I. History, Theory, and Methods,* edited by Paul H. Mussen. New York: Wiley, 1983.

Brown, B. Bradford. "You're Going Out With Who?": Peer Group Influences on Adolescent Romantic Relationships." Pp. 291-329 in *Contemporary Perspectives on Adolescent Romantic Relationships*, edited by Wyndol Furman, B. Bradford Brown, and Candace Feiring. New York: Cambridge University Press, 1999.

Bullough, Bonnie, and Vern L. Bullough. "Female Prostitution: Current Research and Changing Interpretations." *Annual Review of Sex Research* 7 (1996): 158-180.

Burnam, M. Audrey, Judith A. Stein, Jacqueline Golding, Judith Siegel, Susan B. Sorenson, et al. "Sexual Assault and Mental Disorders in a Community Population." *Journal of Consulting and Clinical Psychology* 56 (1988): 843-850.

Burr, Wesley R., Randal D. Day, and Kathleen S. Bahr. *Family Science.* Pacific Grove, CA: Brooks/Cole Publishing Company, 1993.

Burr, Wesley R., Reuben Hill, Ivan Nye, and Ira L. Reiss, eds. *Contemporary Theories About the Family: Vol. II. General Theories/Theoretical Orientations.* New York: Free Press, 1979.

Call Off Your Old Tired Ethics (COYOTE)Retrieved June 25, 2005 from http://www.walnet.org/csis/groups/coyote

Carr, Susan. "The Health of Women Working in the Sex Industry- A Moral and Ethical Perspective." *Sexual and Marital Therapy* 10 (1995): 201-213.

Chu, James A., and Diana L. Dill. "Dissociative Symptoms in Relation to Childhood Physical and Sexual Abuse." *American Journal of Psychiatry* 147 (1990): 887-892.

Church, Stephanie, Marion Henderson, Marina Barnard and Hart Graham. "Violence by Clients Towards Female Prostitutes in Different Work Settings." *British Medical Journal* 322 (2001): 524-527.

Cohen, Patricia, Jocelyn Brown, and Elizabeth Smailes. "Child Abuse and Neglect and the Development of Mental Disorders in the General Population." *Development and Psychopathology* 13 (2001): 981-999.

Cole, Susan G. "Sexual politics: Contradictions and explosions." Pp. 33-36 in *Good Girls/Bad Girls: Sex Trade Workers and Feminists Face to Face*, ed. Laurie Bell. Toronto, Canada: Women's Press, 1987, 33-36.

Commercial Sex Information Service (CSIS). Retrieved June 25, 2005 from http://www.walnet.org/csis/groups/index.html

Connolly, Jennifer, Wendy Craig, Adele Goldberg, and Debra Pepler. "Conceptions of Cross-Sex Friendships and Romantic Relationships in Early Adolescence." *Journal of Youth and Adolescence* 28 (1999): 481-494.

Conte, Jon R., and John R. Schuerman. "Factors Associated with an Increased Impact of Child Sexual Abuse." *Child Abuse and Neglect* 11 (1987): 201-211.

Corey, Gerald. *Theory and Practice of Counseling and Psychotherapy,* 6th edition. Pacific Grove, CA: Brooks/Cole, 2000.

Corey, Gerald, Marianne Schneider Corey, and Patrick Callanan. "Issues and Ethics in the Helping Professions" 6th edition. Pacific Grove, CA: Brooks/Cole, 2003.

Corsini, Raymond J., and Danny Wedding, eds., *Current Psychotherapies* (6th ed.). Thompson: Brooks/Cole, 2000.

Delacoste, Frederique, and Priscilla Alexander. *Sex Work: Writings by Women in the Sex Industry.* San Francisco: Cleis Press, 1998.

De Shazer, Steve, Insoo Kim Berg, Eve Lipchik, Elam Nunnally, Alex Molnar, Wallace Gingerich, and Michele Weiner-Davis. "Brief Therapy." *Family Process* 25 (1986): 207-221.

DiChiara, Gaetana, and Alan North. "Neurobiology of Opiate Abuse." *Trends in Pharmacological Sciences* 13 (1992): 185-193.

Doherty, William J., Pauline G. Boss, Ralph LaRossa, Walter R. Schumm, and Suzanne K. Steinmetz. "Family Theories and Methods: A Conceptual Approach." Pp. 3-30 in *Sourcebook of Family Theories and Methods: A Contextual Approach*, edited by Pauline G. Boss, William J. Doherty, Ralph LaRossa, Walter R. Schumm, and Suzanne K. Steinmetz. New York: Plentum, 1993.

Douglas County Drug Court Program Evaluation. Retrieved June 28, 2005 from http://co.douglas.ne.us/dept/districtcourt/drugcourt/program_evaluation.htm

DSM-IV-TR. "Substance-Related Disorders." In *Diagnostic and Statistical Manual of Mental Disorders*, 4th ed., Text Revision [DSM-IV-TR], 223-250. Washington, DC: American Psychiatric Association, 2000.

Dunlap, Eloise, Andrew Golub, Bruce D. Johnson, and Damaris Wesley. "Intergenerational Transmission of Conduct Norms for Drugs, Sexual Exploitation and Violence: A Case Study." *British Journal of Criminology* 42, (2002): 1-20.

Farley, Melissa, and Howard Barkan. "Prostitution, Violence, and Posttraumatic Stress Disorder." *Women & Health* 27 (1998): 37-49.

Faugier, Jean, and Malissa Sargeant. "Boyfriends, 'Pimps' and Clients." Pp 121-136 in *Rethinking prostitution: Purchasing sex in the 1990s*, edited by Graham Scambler and Annette Scambler. New York: Routledge, 1997.

Feucht, Thomas E. "Prostitutes on Crack Cocaine: Addiction, Utility and Marketplace Economics." *Deviant Behavior: An Interdisciplinary Journal* 14 (1993): 91-108.

Finkelhor, David. "The Trauma of Child Sexual Abuse: Two Models." *Journal of Interpersonal Violence* 2 (1987): 348-366.

Fischman, Marian, and Chris E. Johanson. "Cocaine." Pp. 159-195 in *Pharmacological Aspects of Drug Dependence: Towards and Integrated Neurobehavior Approach Handbook of Experimental Pharmacology*, edited by Charles R. Schuster and Mike Kuhar. New York: Wiley, 1992.

Fourth Judicial District Court of Nebraska, Douglas County Adult Drug Court, retrieved June 28, 2005 from http://www.co.douglas.ne.us/dept/districtcourt

Fullilove, Mindy T., Anne Lown, A., & Robert E. Fullilove. "Crack 'Hos and Skeezers: Traumatic Experiences of Women Crack Users." *The Journal of Sex Research* 29 (1992): 275-287.

García Coll, Cynthia, and K. Magnuson. "Cultural Differences as Sources of Developmental Vulnerabilities and Resources: A View from Developmental Research." Pp. 194-211 in *Handbook of Early Childhood Intervention*, edited by Samuel J. Meisels and Jack P. Shonkoff. Cambridge University Press, 2000.

Gladding, Samuel T. *The Counseling Dictionary: Concise Definitions of Frequently Used Terms*. Upper Saddle River, NJ: Prentice Hall, 2001.

Glenn, Evelyn N. "Social Constructions of Mothering: A Thematic Overview." Pp. 1-29 in *Mothering: Ideology, Experience, and Agency*, edited by Evelyn N. Glenn, Grace Chang, and Linda R. Forcey. New York: Routledge, 1994.

Goldstein, Paul J. *Prostitution and Drugs*. Lexington, MA: Lexington Books, 1979.

Goffman, Erving. *Stigma: Notes on the Management of Spoiled Identity*. New York: Simon & Shuster, Inc., 1963.

Graham, Nanette, and Eric D. Wish. "Drug Use Among Female Arrestees: Onset, Patterns, and Relationships to Prostitution." *Journal of Drug Issues* 24, no. 2 (1994): 315-329.

Groth, Nicholas A. "Guidelines for the Assessment and Management of the Offender." Pp 64-98 in *Sexual Assault of Children and Adolescents*, edited by Ann W. Burgess, A. Nicholas Groth, Lynda L. Holmstrom, and Suzanne M. Sgroi. Lexington, MA: Lexington, 1978.

Hagan, John. *Structural Criminology*. New Brunswick, New Jersey: Rutgers University Press, 1989.

Hammer, Allen L., and Susan M. Marting. *Coping Resources Inventory-Form D*. Palo Alto, CA: Consulting Psychologists Press, 1987.

Hanson, Glen R., Peter J. Venturelli, and Annette E. Fleckenstein. *Drugs and Society*, 8th edition. Ontario, Canada: Jones and Bartlett Publishers International, 2004.

Hardman, Karen. "A Social Work Group for Prostituted Women with Children." *Social Work with Groups* 20, no.1 (1997): 19-31.

Hatsukami, Dorothy, and Marian Fischman. "Crack Cocaine and Cocaine Hydrochloride." *Journal of the American Medical Association* 276 (1996): 1580-1588.

Hays, Sharon. *The Cultural Contradictions of Motherhood*. New Haven, CT: Yale University Press, 1996.

Hill, Reuben. "Modern Systems Theory and the Family: A Confrontation." *Social Science Information* 10 (1972): 7-26.

Hirschi, Travis. *Causes of Delinquency*. Berkeley, California: University of California Press, 1969.

Hood, Albert B., and Richard W. Johnson. *Assessment in Counseling: A Guide to the Use of Psychological Assessment Procedures*, 3rd edition. Alexandria, VA: American Counseling Association, 2002.

Inciardi, James A. "Crack, Crack House Sex, and HIV Risk." *Archives of Sexual Behavior* 24 (1995): 249-269.

Inciardi, James A., Dorthy Lockwood, and Anne E. Pottieger, *Women and Crack Cocaine*. New York: Macmillan, 1993.

James, Jennifer, and Jane Meyerding. "Early Sexual Experience and Prostitution." *American Journal of Psychiatry* 134 (1977): 1381-1385.

Kessler, Ronald C., and William Magee. "Childhood Family Violence and Adult Recurrent Depression." *Journal of Health and Sociological Behavior* 35 (1994): 13-27.

Klein, David M., and James M. White. *Family Theories: An Introduction*. Thousand Oaks, CA: Sage. 1996.

Kvale, Steinar. *Interviews: An Introduction to Qualitative Research Interviewing*. Thousand Oaks, CA: Sage, 1996.

Lazarus, Richard. *Psychological Stress and the Coping Process*. New York: MacGraw-Hill, 1966.

Lazarus, Richard S., and Susan Folkman. *Stress, Appraisal, and Coping*. New York: Springer, 1984.

Lazarus, Richard S., and Raymond Launier. "Stress-Related Transactions Between Person and Environment." Pp 287-327 in *Perspectives in Interactional Psychology*, edited by Lawrence A. Pervin and Michael Lewis. New York: Plenum Press, 1978.

Lerner, Richard M. "Theories of Human Development: Contemporary Perspectives." Pp. 1-24 in *Theoretical Models of Human Development*. Vol. 1, of the *Handbook of child psychology*, 5th ed., edited by Richard M. Lerner. New York: Wiley, 1998.

Lewin, Kurt. *Field Theory in Social Science*. New York, New York: Harper & Brothers, 1951.

Lincoln, Yvonna S., and Egon G. Guba. *Naturalistic Inquiry*. Beverly Hills, CA: Sage Publications, 1985.

MacMillan, Ross. "Violence and the Life Course: The Consequences of Victimization for Personal and Social Development." *Annual Reviews of Sociology* 27 (2001): 1-22.

Maher, Lisa. "Hidden in the light: Occupational Norms among Crack-Using Street-Level Sex Worker." *Journal of Drug Issues* 26,*(1996)*: 143-173.

Manopaiboon, Chomnad, Rebecca E. Bunnell, Peter H. Kilmarx, Supaport Chaikummao, Khanchit Limpakarnjanarat, Somsak Supawitkul, Michael E. St. Louis, and Timothy D. Mastro. "Leaving Sex Work: Barriers, Facilitating Factors and Consequences for Female Sex Workers in Northern Thailand." *AIDS Care* 15 (2003): 39-52.

Månsson, Sven-Axel, and Ulla-Carin Hedin. "Breaking the Matthew Effect- On Women Leaving Prostitution." *International Journal of Social Welfare* 8 (1999): 67-77.

Marshall, Catherine, and Gretchen B. Rossman. *Designing Qualitative Research,* rev. ed. Thousand Oaks, CA: Sage, 1995.

Matheny, Kenneth B., David W. Aycock, John L. Pugh, William L. Curlette, and Silva Cannella. "Stress and Coping: A Qualitative and Quantitative Synthesis and Implications for Treatment." *The Counseling Psychologist* 14 (1986): 499-549.

Menard, Scott. "Short and Long Term Consequences of Criminal Victimization." Pp. 16-32 in *Violent Behavior in the Life Course,* edited by Scott Menard, David Huizinga, and Delbert S. Elliott. Thousand Oaks, CA: Sage, 2001.

Miller, Eleanor M. *Street Women.* Philadelphia, Pennsylvania: Temple University Press, 1986.

Miller, Jody. "Gender and Power on the Streets: Street Prostitution in the Era of Crack Cocaine." *Journal of Contemporary Ethnography* 23 (1995): 427-452.

— .'"Your life is on the Line Every Night You're on the Streets': Victimization and the Resistance Among Street Prostitutes." *Humanity & Society* 17, no. 4 (1993): 422-445.

Miller, Patricia H. Miller. *Theories of Developmental Psychology,* 3rd ed. New York: W. H. Freeman and Co., 1993.

Montgomery, Marilyn J. and Gwendolyn T. Sorell. "Love and Dating Experiences in Early and Middle Adolescence: Grade and Gender Comparisons." *Journal of Adolescence* 21 (1998): 677-689.

Martin A. Monto. *Focusing on the Clients of Street Prostitutes: A Creative Approach to Reducing Violence Against Women.* Washington, DC: National Institute of Justice (1999).

Monto, Martin A. "Female Prostitution, Customers, and Violence." *Violence Against Women* 10 (2004): 160-188.

Mosak, Harold H. "Adlerian Psychotherapy." Pp. 54-98 in *Current Psychotherapies,* edited by Raymond J. Corsini and Danny Wedding. Belmont, CA: Brooks/Cole, 2000.

Nandon, Susan M., Catherine Koverola, and Eduard H. Schludermann. "Antecedents To Prostitution: Childhood Victimization."*Journal of Interpersonal Violence* 13 (1998): 206-221.

National Center for PTSD. *What is post traumatic stress disorder.* Retrieved February 11, 2005 from http://ncptsd.org/facts/general/fs_what_is_ptsd.html

National Drug Court Institute, Drug Court Practitioner Fact Sheet (1999). *Family Drug Courts: An Alternative Approach to Processing Child Abuse & Neglect Cases.* Available from National Drug Court Institute (703.706.0576).

Network of Sex Work Projects (NSWP). Retrieved June 28, 2005 from http://www.nswp.org/home.html

Neukrug, Ed. *The World of the Counselor* (2nd ed.). Brooks/Cole, 2003.

Norbeck, Jane S., Ana M. Lindsey, and Virginia L. Carrieri. "The Development of an Instrument to Measure Social Support." *Nursing Research* 30 (1981): 264-269.

Norbeck, Jane S., Ana M. Lindsey, and Virginia L. Carrieri. "Further Development of the Norbeck Social Support Questionnaire: Normative Data and Validity Testing." *Nursing Research* 32 (1982): 4-9.

Norris, Fran, Krzysztof Kaniasty, and Martie P. Thompson. "The Psychological Consequences of Crime: Findings from a Longitudinal Population-Based Study." Pp. 146-167 in *Victims of Crime,* 2nd ed., edited by Robert Davis, Arthur J. Lurigio and Wesley G. Skogan. Thousand Oaks, CA: Sage, 1997.

O'Connell Davidson, Julia. *Prostitution, Power and Freedom.* Ann Arbor, MI: The University of Michigan Press, 1998.

Oetting, Eugene R., and Joseph Donnermeyer. "Primary Socialization Theory: The Etiology of Drug Use and Deviance." *Substance Use Misuse* 33, (1998): 995-1026.

Olson, David H. "Family Systems: Understanding Your Roots." Pp. 131-153 in *Research and Theory in Family Science,* edited by Randal Day, K. Gilbert, B. Settles, and Wesley Burr. Pacific Grove, CA: Books/Cole, 1995.

Olson, David H., Hamilton I. McCubbin, Howard Barnes, Andrea Larsen, Marla L. Muxen, and Marc Wilson. *Family Inventories: Inventories Used in a National Survey of Families Across the Life Cycle,* 1982. Available from 290 McNeal Hall, University of Minnesota, St. Paul, MN, 55108.

O'Neill, Maggie. "Prostitute Women Now." Pp. 3-28 in *Rethinking Prostitution: Purchasing Sex in the 1990s,* edited by Graham Scambler and Annette Scambler. London: Routledge, 1997.

Overall, Christine. "What's Wrong with Prostitution?: Evaluating Sex Work." *Signs* 17, no. 4 (1992): 705-724.

Pareek, Udai, and Venkateswara T. Rao. "Cross-Cultural Surveys and Interviewing." Pp. 127-129 in *Handbook of Cross-Cultural Psychology.* Vol. 2, edited by Harry C. Triandis and John W. Berry. Boston, MA: Allyn and Bacon, Inc. 1980.

Pheterson, Gail. "The Category 'Prostitute' in Scientific Inquiry." *The Journal of Sex Research* 27, no. 3 (1990): 397-407.

Plummer, Lynanne, John J. Potterat, Stephen Q. Muth, and John B. Muth. "Providing Support and Assistance for Low-Income or Homeless Women." *Journal of the American Medical Association* 276, no. 23 (1996): 1874-1875.

Potter, Kathleen, Judy Martin, and Sarah Romans. "Early Developmental Experiences of Female Sex Workers." *Australian & New Zealand Journal of Psychiatry* 33 (1999): 935-940.

Potterat, John J., Lynanne Phillips, Richard B. Rothenberg, and William W. Darrow. "On Becoming a Prostitute: An Exploratory Case-Comparison Study." *Journal of Sex Research* 20 (1985): 329-336.

Potterat, John J., Richard B. Rothenberg, Stephen Q. Muth, William W. Darrow, and Lynanne Phillips-Plummer. "Pathways to Prostitution: The Chronology of Sexual and Drug Abuse Milestones." *The Journal of Sex Research* 35 (1998): 333-340.

Prochaska, James O., Carlo C. DiClemente, and John C. Norcross. "In Search of How People Change: Applications to Addictive Behaviors." *American Psychologist* 47 (1992): 1102-1114.

Prostitutes of New York (PONY). Retrieved June 25, 2005 from http://www.walnet.org/csis/groups/pony.html.

Quinley, Jan. Southeast Precinct Prostitution Task Force Chairperson. Omaha Nebraska, Personal Communication, June 26, 2005.

Raphael, Jody, and Deborah L. Shapiro. *Sisters Speak Out: The Lives and Needs of Prostituted Women in Chicago.* Center for Impact Research, August 2002, 1-35.

Raskin, Nathaniel J., and Carl R. Rogers. "Person-Centered Therapy." Pp. 133-167 in *Current Psychotherapies,* edited by Raymond J. Corsini and Danny Wedding. Belmont, CA: Brooks/Cole, 2000.

Ratner, Mitchell. *Crack Pipe as Pimp: An Ethnographic Investigation of Sex-for-Crack Exchanges.* New York: Lexington, 1993.

Reiss, David. *The Family's Construction of Reality.* Cambridge, MA: Harvard University Press, 1981.

Romero-Daza, Nancy, Margaret Weeks, and Merrill Singer. "Qualitative Analysis of Sex Workers in Hartford, CT." *International Quarterly of Community Health Education* 18 (1998): 107-119.

——. "'Nobody gives a Damn if I Live or Die': Experiences of Violence Among Drug-Using Sex Workers in Hartford, CT." *Medical Anthropology* 22, no. 3 (2003): 233-259.

Rook, Karen S. "The Functions of Social Bonds: Perspectives from Research on Social Support, Loneliness and Social Isolation." Pp. 253-267in *Social Support: Theory, Research and Applications*, edited by Irwin G. Sarason and Barbara R. Sarason. Boston: Dordrecht, 1983.

Russell, Diane E. H. "The Incidence and Prevalence of Intrafamilial and Extrafamilial Sexual Abuse on Female Children." Pp. 19-36 in *Handbook on Sexual Abuse of Children*, edited by Lenore E. Auerbach Walker. New York: Springer, 1988.

Rutter, Michael. "Protective Factors in Children's Responses to Stress and Disadvantage." Pp. 49-74 in *Primary Prevention of Psychopathology*, edited by Martha W. Kent and Jon E. Rolf. Hanover, NH: University Press of New England, 1979.

Sampson, Robert J., and Janet L. Lauritsen. "Violence Victimization and Offending: Individual-, Situational-, and Community-Level Risk Factors." Pp. 1-114 in *Understanding and Preventing Violence*. Vol. 3, edited by Albert J. Reiss Jr. and Jeffrey Roth. Washington, DC: National Academy Press, 1994.

Sauzier, Maria, Patricia Salt, and Roberta Calhoun. "The Effects of Child Sexual Abuse." Pp. 75-108 in *Child Sexual Abuse: The Initial Effects*, edited by Beverly Gomes-Schwartz, Jonathon M. Horowitz, and Albert P. Cardarelli. Newbury Park, CA: Sage, 1990.

Scanzoni, John, Karen Polonko, Jay Teachman, and Linda Thompson. *The Sexual Bond: Rethinking Families and Close Relationships*. Newbury Park, CA: Sage, 1989.

Schwartlander, Bernhard, Karen A. Stanecki, and Tim Brown. "Country-Specific Estimates and Models of HIV and AIDS: Methods and Limitations." *AIDS* 13 (1999): 2445-2458.

Second National Conference on Prostitution, Sex Work, and the Commercial Sex Industry. Retrieved June 28, 2005 from http://www.lisp.wayne.edu/baker/prostconf

Seng, Magnus J. "Child Sexual Abuse and Adolescent Prostitution: A Comparative Analysis." *Adolescence* 24 (1989): 665-675.

Sex Workers' International Media Watch. SWIMW Home. Retrieved June 28, 2005 from http://www.swimw.org/swimw.html

Sex Workers' Outreach Project, USA (SWOP). Retrieved June 25, 2005 from http://swop-usa.org

Silbert, Mimi H., and Ayala M. Pines. "Early Sexual Exploitation as an Influence in Prostitution." *Social Work* 28 (1983): 285-289.

——. "Victimization of Street Prostitutes." *Victimology: An International Journal* 7 (1982): 122-133.

Simons, Ronald L., and Les B. Whitbeck. "Sexual Abuse as a Precursor to Prostitution and Victimization." *Journal of Family Issues* 12 (1991): 361-379.

St. James Infirmary, retrieved February 22, 2005 from http://www.stjamesinfirmary.org/

Sterk, Claire, and Kirk W. Elifson. "Drug-Related Violence and Street Prostitution." Pp. 208-221 in *Drugs and Violence: Causes, Correlations, and Consequences*, edited by Mario De La Rosa, Elizabeth Lambert and Bernard Gropper. Rockville, MD: NIDA, 1990.

Summit on Spirituality, Counseling Today (1995), 30.

Surratt, Hilary L., James A. Inciardi, Steven P. Kurtz, and Marion C. Kiley. "Sex Work and Drug Use in a Subculture of Violence." *Crime & Delinquency* 50 (2004): 43-59.

Swan, Neil. "31% of New York Murder Victims Had Cocain in Their Bodies." *National Institutes of Drug Addiction [NIDA] Notes* 10 (March/April 1995): 4.

Taylor, Steven J., and Robert C. Bogdan. *Introduction to Qualitative Research: The Search for Meaning*, 3rd ed., New York: John Wiley & Sons, 1998.

Thoits, Peggy A. "Social Support and Psychological Well-Being: Theoretical Possibilities." Pp. 51-72 in *Social Support: Theory, Research and Applications*, edited by Irwin G. Sarason and Barbara R. Sarason. Boston: Dordrecht, 1983.

Valera, Roberto J., Robin G. Sawyer, and Glenn R. Schiraldi. "Perceived Health Needs of Inner-City Street Prostitutes: A Preliminary Study." *American Journal of Health Behavior 25*, no. 1 (Jan/Feb. 2001): 50-60.

Vanwesenbeeck, Ine. "Another Decade of Social Scientific Work on Sex Work: A Review of Research 1990-2000." *Annual Review of Sex Research* 12 (2001): 285.

The Village Voice. "School for Johns Arrested for Soliciting Sex," Retrieved June 25, 2005 from http://www.villagevoice.com/news/0519,hunter,63812,5.html

Vygotsky, Lev S. *Mind in Society*. Cambridge, MA: Harvard U. Press, 1978.

—. "The Problem of the Cultural Development of the Child." *Journal of Genetic Psychology* 36 (1929): 415-434.

Walker, Lenore E. *The Battered Woman Syndrome*, 2nd ed. New York: Springer, 2000.

Watts, Charlotte, and Cathy Zimmerman. "Violence Against Women: Global Scope and Magnitude." *Lancet* 359 (2002): 1232-1244.

Webster's Encyclopedic Unabridged Dictionary of the English Language, Deluxe Edition, New and Revised. New York: Gramercy Books, 1994.

Weeks, Margarat R., Maryland Grier, Nancy Romero-Daza, Mary Jo Puglisi-Vasquez, and Merrill Singer. "Streets, Drugs, and the Economy of Sex in the Age of AIDS." Pp. 205-229 in *Women, Drug Use, and HIV Infection*, edited by Sally .J. Stevens, Stephanie Tortu, and Susan L. Coyle. New York: Haworth Medical Press, 1998.

Weiner, Adele. "Understanding the Social Needs of Streetwalking Prostitutes." *Social Work* 41 (1996): 97-105.

Whitechurch, Gail G., and Larry L. Constantine. "Systems Theory." Pp. 325-352 in *Sourcebook of Family Theories and Methods: A Contextual Approach*, edited by Pauline G. Boss, William J. Doherty, Ralph LaRossa, Walter R. Schumm, and Suzanne K. Steinmetz. New York: Plenum Press, 1993.

Williamson, Celia. "Entrance, Maintenance, and Exit: The Socio-Economic Influences and Cumulative Burdens of Female Street Prostitution." *Dissertation Abstracts International, A: The Humanities and Social Sciences* 61 (2000): 773-A.

Williamson, Celia, and Terry Cluse-Tolar. "Pimp-Controlled Prostitution: Still an Integral Part of Street Life." *Violence Against Women* 8 (2002): 1074-1092.

Williamson, Celia, and Gail Folaron. "Violence, Risk, and Survival Strategies of Street Prostitution." *Western Journal.of Nursing Research* 23, no. 5, (2001): 463-475.

—. "Understanding the Experiences of Street Level Prostitutes." *Qualitative Social Work* 2 (2003): 271-287.

Yakel, Paul. Drug Court Coordinator, Douglas Country Adult Drug Court, personal communication June 28, 2005.

Yahen, Carolina E., William R. Miller, Lilly Irvin-Vitela, and J. Scott Tonigan. "Magdalena Pilot Project: Motivational Outreach to Substance Abusing Women and Street Sex Workers." *Journal of Substance Abuse Treatment* 23 (2002): 49-53.

Zigler, Edward F., and Nancy W. Hall. *Child Development and Social Policy: Theory and Applications*. New York: McGraw Hill, 2000.

Subject Index

victimization of prostituted women, 116-17;
    self-protection and, 117, 121-22; develop-
    mental consequences and, 116; rape, 118-19;
    bodily injury and, 120-21
violence from clients, 118-121; from pimps, 123-
    126; from partners, 123-126
voluntarily exiting prostitution, 144-47; hitting
    bottom and, 144; children and, 145; sub-culture
    changes and, 145-46; spirituality and, 146;
    life-threatening events and, 145

WellSpring, definition of, xix, 32-33
Williamson, Celia, 117-18, 121-122; and Stage
    Model of Prostitution Involvement, 143

Participant Index

About the Author

Rochelle L. Dalla is a fifth-generation native of Durango, Colorado. She received her bachelor's degree in 1991 from the University of Colorado-Boulder, where she studied psychology and cultural anthropology. She began graduate school in 1991 at the University of Arizona (UA). Her research interest with marginalized female populations began while a graduate student majoring in Family Studies and Human Development at UA. Using an ecological framework, her research focused on the developmental trajectories of adolescent parenting, Navajo Native American women. Interviews were conducted with adolescent Navajo mothers, their mothers, and a host of community members. Results of this work have been published in several academic journals, including: *Family Relations, Journal of Family Issues,* and the *American Indian Culture and Research Journal.* She earned her masters degree in 1993 and her doctoral degree in 1996 in Family Studies and Human Development at UA under the supervision of Dr. Wendy Gamble.

In 1996, she was hired as an Assistant Professor in the Department of Family and Consumer Sciences (FACS) at the University of Nebraska-Lincoln (UN-L). Although a UN-L faculty member, she is based on the University of Nebraska-Omaha campus where she teaches a variety of undergraduate and graduate courses including: Family Science, Adolescence and the Family, and Gender and the Family. She also supervises all Omaha-based FACS internships.

Her work with prostituted women began in 1998 and is on-going. She plans to expand this research internationally. Rochelle has received numerous teaching and research awards including: the *Charman Outstanding Professor Award* (2004), the *Award for Young Achievers* (2004), the *Distinguished Alumni Award* (2003), and the *Distinguished Teaching Award* (2003).

DATE DUE	RETURNED
10/26/15	JUN 07 2017

CPSIA information can be obtained at www.ICGtesting.com
Printed in the USA
LVOW10s2026190515

439070LV00001B/50/P

9 780739 123256